WHOLISTIC CHRISTIANITY

Amy Beth # 1124

WHOLISTIC CHRISTIANITY

DAVID O. MOBERG
Marquette University

Foreword by David Allan Hubbard, President
Fuller Theological Seminary

BRETHREN PRESS
Elgin, Illinois

Wholistic Christianity

Biblical quotations are from the King James Version (KJV), or New International Version (NIV), copyright © 1973, 1978, International Bible Society.

Brethren Press, 1451 Dundee Avenue, Elgin, IL 60120

Cover design by Kathy Kline

Edited by Leslie R. Keylock

Library of Congress Cataloging in Publication Data

Moberg, David O.
　　Wholistic Christianity.

　　　　Bibliography: p.
　　　　Includes index.
　　　　1. Theology—Addresses, essays, lectures.
　　2. Sociology, Christian—Addresses, essays, lectures.
　　3. Christianity—20th century—Addresses, essays, lectures.
　　I. Title.
　　BR50.M54　1985　　　　230　　　　84-29216
　　ISBN 0-87178-932-9

Printed in the United States of America

Contents

Relevance Versus Transcendence
Dilemmas of Institutionalization

FOREWORD

In a world of religious thought that is marked by increasing polarity, the center can be a dangerous place. It takes considerable courage to risk the cross-fire from opposing forces, each of which is fully persuaded of the rightness of its cause and the need to attack its perceived enemy. Yet that risky center is where David Moberg has tried to live and work for the thirty-five years of his professional career.

He is there again in this book, raising a gentle but persistent voice in the midst of the clamor that jars the Christian scene with tribal shouts and sectarian slogans. Moberg not only exposes and deplores the foolish divisions, the ill-chosen battles, the distorted perceptions that plague the churches, he grieves over them.

The wide-ranging reading on which he draws documents the thoroughness of his work. His close acquaintance as a participant in many facets of the evangelical movement sharpens the insight he shares. And the very tenacity with which he has argued against the foibles of our selectivity and, in hearing God's Word, our limited definitions of what discipleship means, and our cookie-cutter caricatures of Christian obedience evidences the passionate desire he has for us as believers, individually and as a community, to be what we were meant to be.

As a seasoned sociologist he has read the trends of our culture and senses how flat-sided we have become, whether in conforming compliantly to or reacting extravagantly against the lure and the threat of these trends. As a thoughtful Christian he has read the revelation with its breadth of promises and its wealth of demands and has discerned the difference between the wholeness of commitment that the kingdom of God calls for and the narrow causes that we rally to and live with.

My first meeting with Dr. Moberg I shall remember vividly. It was nearly twenty-five years ago. Love was the theme of a lecture I gave in his presence, and my concluding line was something like this: "Love is what we are called to give persons in Christ's name, and we can only do that loving for people one at a time." His rebuke when he tarried to speak

ix

to me was as measured and as forceful as is this book: "Isn't it possible for us to love people in *groups* as we see that justice and welfare are done for them in Christ's name?"

My flat-sideness he helped to round with that one question. We did not call it wholistic in those days. But what else was it?—an experience in seeing how much "both-ands" there are to Christian discipleship along with the "either-ors."

I was moved to reflection and prayer when I heard some of those chapters in an earlier setting. My hopes are high that many of God's people will have these same reactions as they ponder them here. There is much room in the middle—along with much risk—for those who want to hear the whole Word and begin to do it.

David Allan Hubbard, President
Fuller Theological Seminary
Pasadena, California

PREFACE

The essays in this book result from a lifetime of observation, reflection, and study of Christian values and practices.

My observations have been made in many contexts. My father was the pastor of small ethnic congregations, so my childhood homes were church parsonages. I have been a member of several churches and have visited countless others in the USA, Canada, and Europe. I have filled such roles in churches as janitor, construction carpenter, treasurer, deacon, trustee, moderator, adult Sunday school teacher, student pastor, committee member, and guest preacher. As a sociologist of religion I have had the opportunity to read widely, to engage in some original research, to evaluate research by others, to write extensively on relevant topics, to participate in national and international professional societies concerned with religion, to lecture on many campuses of colleges, universities, and seminaries, and to become acquainted with large numbers of stimulating lay and professional people who are sympathetically or critically interested in religion.

My comparisons of biblical ideals with the actual behavior of Christians as individuals and as members of various groups have often revealed discrepancies of varying breadth and significance. The gaps between the various parties or schools of Christian thought are often even greater. One of the most significant questions raised by my observations asks how followers of Jesus Christ can be at war with each other. If they claim to be disciples of the Prince of Peace, why should they fight? Even more important, what can be done about it?

Over the years I have been driven increasingly to one central conclusion: Much of the disagreement and conflict flows from a lopsided emphasis upon only portions of the riches that constitute the Christian gospel. A wholistic orientation must replace the incomplete and unbalanced versions that characterize so much of contemporary Christendom (Chapter 1).

This book examines selected aspects of that subject, including some evidences of the dualisms and divisions found among Christians and a series of issues that flow primarily out of the cultural setting of Western civilization (Chapters 2-4).

Paradoxes and dilemmas, some of which are found even in the Bible, help to explain why Christians waver between divergent opinions and are caught in perplexing dialectical problems of thought and conduct (Chapter 5). There are several specific areas within which the disagreements manifest themselves (Chapters 6-9). The book concludes with suggestions for implementing and practicing a truly wholistic Christianity (Chapters 10-12).

Although the chapters are organized around the central theme of wholistic Christianity in a logical sequence, they may be read in any order. Each is a relatively independent analysis of selected aspects of that fascinating and challenging subject.

References in the text are provided in contemporary social science style instead of in footnotes. An entry such as "Bayly, 1982:59" refers to page 59 of the work by Bayly that was published in 1982. For a periodical the numbers 12(3):469-483 mean volume 12, number 3, pages 469 to 483. If two or more works by the same author appear, they are listed in chronological order. If two were published in the same year, they are designated 1982a and 1982b, so that scholarly readers can find the precise source.

The references given in the text are documented in the bibliography at the end of the book. They are presented for two major reasons. One is to acknowledge the sources of ideas, information, or quotations that are incorporated into the text. The other is to suggest resources to which interested readers can go for additional information and perspectives on the respective topics mentioned here.

The Bible references included are not intended as prooftexts but only as summary statements that encapsulate significant truths of Scripture. They are beginning points for serious biblical study, not the only nor the final word of biblical truth. The letters KJV or NIV indicate that a quotation was taken from the King James or the New International Version.

To flesh out fully the many topics mentioned in these pages would take five or ten volumes. Readers will be glad that I have resisted my perfectionistic drive toward a wholism that makes me desire to examine and refer to "everything" on every subject on which there is even passing mention.

Undoubtedly, I have missed many significant resources on the respective topics. Yet, although the perspectives shared here are sketchy and incomplete, I hope they will prove stimulating and suggestive of the wide ranges of theoretical, empirical, philosophical, and pragmatic work that are needed for an exhaustive study. In other words, this is a series of essays, not a comprehensive encyclopedia, on the subject of wholistic Christianity.

The immediate impetus for writing this book was the invitation to give the lectures for the 1983 Finch Symposium on Psychology and Religion in the Graduate School of Psychology at Fuller Theological Seminary. The subject chosen was "Wholistic Christianity: A Sociologist's Interpretation." Three faculty members, one from each of the three schools at Fuller, were given advance copies of the lectures and responded publicly to one apiece. A wealth of insights and suggestions was incorporated into their comments, questions, and perspectives. I am grateful to Professors Charles Kraft, William Pannell, and Colleen Zabriskie for their stimulating commentaries. They have made a significant contribution to the improvement of this book as the lectures have been adapted and expanded, even though it has been impossible to follow up every clue that they gave because of my limitations of time and resources.

Responsive audiences to lectures on related topics that I have given in various places both before and since the Finch Lectures, as well as the students in classes on several campuses, also have helped me to sharpen and shape my thoughts about wholistic Christianity. They too deserve my thanks. Countless others have made indirect contributions by calling attention to the problems discussed, suggesting answers, or sharpening my awareness of the dialectical dualisms that pertain to the subject. Many of them are acknowledged through the references at the end of the book.

Last, but not least, I am grateful to our departmental secretary, Elizabeth Schuman, who supervised typing of the manuscript, and to Leslie R. Keylock, editor of Brethren Press, who has arranged for and supervised its publication.

David O. Moberg

PART I

DUALISMS AND DIVISIONS IN CHRISTENDOM

1

CONFLICTS AND POLARIZATION

When people talk casually with each other, it is not unusual for their conversation to turn to the human condition, the state of society and the world, and the question of whether things are getting better or worse. Disagreements and arguments about such topics are not rare. Some people optimistically see mainly the evidence of improvements and desirable conditions. Others give special attention to human problems and the signs of corruption and deterioration in society and the world.

Most Christians similarly tend to believe either that Christianity is advancing or that it is losing ground in its competitive struggle with secular humanism and non-Christian religions, both new and old.

In both instances the optimists and pessimists equally claim to have the correct appraisal of reality. They each think the others are wrong. Their actions are based upon beliefs about what is true, whether the beliefs are correct or mistaken.

Some of the optimists are imbued with the Idea of Progress (Nisbet, 1979) that dominated intellectual thought during the late nineteenth and early twentieth century. They believe that the quality of life is gradually improving, despite occasional minor setbacks. They assume that human beings are continually advancing and that society is evolving toward an ever higher level of existence. Stent (1983), for example, believes mankind is about to enter a new epoch in history, the Golden Age of a Polynesian future of leisure and abundance.

Their pessimistic friends admit that progress indeed is evident in the realm of science and technology, but they argue that it is accompanied by a wide range of significant problems on both the personal and social levels. "Just look," they say, "at conditions in society today. There are rising rates of crime and juvenile delinquency, divorce, illegitimacy, mental illness, alcoholism, drug abuse, suicide, abortion, and violence. These are accompanied by high levels of inflation, unemployment, and poverty, as well as by racism, sexism, and ageism. Whether one examines the sweeping international issues of terrorism, war, and

1

proliferation of nuclear weapons or the intensely personal problems of depression, alienation, worry, fears, and anxiety, it is obvious that things are getting worse."

Some of the pessimists add an anti-Christian bias. They argue that world affairs and the human condition are in a mess after Christianity has been tried for almost two thousand years and that this proves that Christianity does not work. Christians, however, are likely to respond that "true Christianity," meaning their own particular brand of faith or their own denomination or church, has never been universally accepted. If it had, they assume that the world would be in much better shape.

Some Christians refer instead to theological positions, holding that world conditions will continue to deteriorate despite the best of human efforts until Christ establishes the millennial kingdom. Still others assume that the Lord will work through the Christian church to accomplish that goal, returning only at the conclusion of the millennium.

Different perspectives on the nature of society and on the direction of its trends, as well as alternative biblical interpretations of them and divergent predictions of the future, hence arouse controversy among Christians. Yet these are but a few parts of the complex fabric of interwoven struggles that cut across contemporary Christianity.

DIVISIONS AMONG CHRISTIANS

Much of the history of Christianity can be summarized from the perspective of the conflicts and controversies that have divided groups of believers from each other. Sometimes they have taken the form of a struggle for leadership and power, as in the case of James and John (Matt. 20:20-28). Sometimes they have involved competition between the ideas set forth by false and true teachers (see 1 John 4:1-6). Sometimes they have involved questions of conduct (Gal. 2:11-14). Sometimes they have centered around personnel appointments, as in the dispute between the Apostle Paul and Barnabas over John Mark (Acts 15:36-39). Sometimes their focus has been scruples over convictions about diet or other details of personal morality (Rom. 14:1-15:6). Sometimes they have been linked with questions of which, if any, elements of other religious systems may be integrated into Christianity (Col. 2:16-23). Sometimes they have related to linkages of religious perspectives and groups with political leaders, as in many of the battles associated with the Protestant Reformation in Europe and the colonization of Asia, Africa, and the Americas. The specific details of every struggle vary widely, yet the broad outlines bear remarkable similarities.

Today as in the past Christianity is fragmented into countless factions. Some are openly at war with others, although most live in peaceful toleration. Not only are there hundreds of denominations and sects, but internally most of these are divided as well. The overarching perspectives of evangelicalism are in some ways like a great "golden mean" between the extremes of theological liberalism and militant fundamentalism. Yet even it is splintered by disagreements over a wide range of issues. This is evident from a mere mention of some divisions that are largely theological:

—Infant baptism versus believer's baptism
—Wine versus grape juice for communion
—Democratic versus autocratic structures of local and denominational church government
—Emphasis upon collective or individual forms of religious expression
—Premillennial, amillennial, or postmillennial views of Christ's second coming
—Arminian voluntarism versus Calvinistic predestination
—Ecumenical cooperation versus separation from all whose doctrines or practices are "defective"
—Social concern expressed through converting individuals or through action to change the institutional structures of society
—Helping the victims of sin and suffering, or changing the social systems that contribute to or cause human misery
—Charismatic versus noncharismatic views of how the Holy Spirit works
—Emphasis upon believing the gospel or upon living it.

Christians are also divided by their diverse views of which actions are proper in society and their contrasting opinions about "Christlike" relationships with outsiders. They have different patterns of relationships toward people who are not members of their own congregation or fellowship, toward other religious bodies, toward the communities of which they are a part, and toward national and world societies. They differ in their ideas of how members ought to live. For example, some consider a simple lifestyle to be a mark of true Christianity, while others assume that a lifestyle demonstrating material success brings glory to God as a reward for faithfulness.

Christian groups sometimes clash strongly with one another on pragmatic political, economic, and social issues. As a result, they often cancel out most of the expressly Christian influence they might otherwise have upon social policy. They are divided into numerous factions on their views about education (racial integration by busing, sex education, creationism, value clarification, school prayers, etc.); social welfare (work programs, AFDC, aid for unmarried mothers, family planning, tax funds used for abortions, and the like); government controls over business, industry, labor, commerce, zoning, banking, prices, the mass media, and the airways; federal taxation policies, military spending, and deficits;, moral issues (gay rights, abortion, alcohol controls, divorce legislation, pornography, censorship of the mass media, etc.); correctional philosophies (e.g., probation and parole, capital punishment, harsh or light sentences, maximum versus minimum security prisons, compensatory payments by offenders, increased or decreased police powers).

Orientations toward such issues sometimes result in labels like "conservative," "liberal," "radical," or "reactionary." Often, these are assigned so arbitrarily and used so loosely that one person's "conservative" is another's "liberal." The use of labels, in turn, hampers true communication and the dialogue by which Christians could discover the foundations for each other's positions. The internal differences among well-meaning members within a given congregation are sometimes so heavily laden with emotional commitments that none dares to open up the floor of church meetings to discuss such pragmatic issues as which of several alternative political positions ought to be supported by Christians. Many have a strong commitment to ancient precedents that makes them certain that there can be no other "Christian" position than the one hallowed by their tradition.

Tensions also arise in and among religious groups between those who wish to keep up with changes in the modern world and those who try to cling to traditional methods or goals. Whenever deviance from established norms, injustice, and hypocrisy are rife, the prevailing standards tend to weaken. The same results flow from rapidly changing circumstances that make the standards seem either unnecessarily constricting or irrelevant (Yinger, 1982:80).

Changes in values also tend to accompany major changes in the structure of power (Yinger, 1982:295). Factions within denominations and churches rightly perceive pending changes as either a threat or an opportunity. Which perspective is taken depends upon many things, including their ecclesiology (Does the Christian church consist of the local congregation, one's own denomination, or a broader collection of all genuine Christians?), their chronology (Is eternal life a present quality of the believer, or does it pertain only to a future beyond the grave?), and similar theological, ideological, and theoretical orientations.

Numerous difficulties have arisen in the life of religious bodies as well as of persons as a result of the choices that are essential in everyday living. These frequently are presented as dualisms from which one is expected to choose one or the other pole of opposite alternatives. That has led to a never-win dilemma, for in all too many instances the choices are not between two things that are good but between various versions of imperfect or even sinful alternatives. Yoder (1972:106-114), for example, has summarized five alternatives that are presented by "systematic tradition" in theology as a basis for moral choice: We must choose between the human context of the Jesus of history and the Jesus of dogma who is the divine Word incarnate; between the prophet who demands perfection and the institution that accepts evil and imperfection in order to diminish and destroy them; between the catastrophic kingdom of God and the inner kingdom; between the political and the allegedly "apolitical" personal-monastic-vocational or sectarian approach to government; between the restoration of individuals and the social call to integration into the healing community. Popular as these and other antinomies have been, all represent false choices when the complete teachings and example of Jesus Christ are taken seriously.

In addition to the other divisions found among them, theological schools have moved toward a schism between the formal theologians and practical people. Formalists emphasize the theological message and intention of their traditions and confessions. They get "better and better at their craft and further and further from the practice of ministry," while the "practical" people who emphasize clinical and pastoral "ministering" and caring have little that is distinctive to say (Marty, 1984). Marty hopes that the dangers of overspecialization and schism will be overcome through fusion of the "theological" and the "practical" in coherent, integrative educational programs for training the professional leadership of the church.

PROBLEMS OF SELECTIVITY

By their analyses of newspaper content in various parts of the world, the Naisbitt Group has discovered that societies, like individuals, can handle only so many concerns at any one time. The particular social issues that receive attention change as relentless restructuring occurs in movement from the old to the new. Issues popular in one decade give way to others in the next (Naisbitt, 1982).

Churches and other religious groups appear to be no different. Their major attention at any given time is devoted to but a few ministries, a few programs, a few social and political issues. These tend to vary from one period of time to another. While this reflects the finite human condition, it is not without danger. Samuel Wilson (1984:4), for example, has suggested that it seems "almost as if the Christian world must identify and respond to one and only one threat at a time."

For thirty or more years Christian missionaries have identified communism as the chief enemy of Christianity. Now their interest is beginning to shift toward Islam, seeing "the core of the conspiracy in terms of planned religious imperialism associated with Shiite Muslims" (S. Wilson, 1984:4). Yet there are dangers of misinterpreting that movement and oversimplifying conspiratorial thought by lumping all enemies together. Far more serious may be surprising attacks "from a new, unexpected quarter for which they might have been prepared" (p. 5). Among these is "the danger in the materialism spun out by our throwaway comsumerism." That enemy also is "at the heart of what is happening in many Muslim Nations" (p. 5), as are secularism, humanism, and others in "the pantheon of competitors" (p. 5).

> But perhaps balance is about to be lost once again in the Church's view of the world. Can it be that our focus and attention is in danger of being given more to Antichrist than to opportunity? The essence of the Christian message is hope and reconciliation, not attack and undermining (S. Wilson, 1984:5).

Lopsidedness and imbalance result from many of the choices made when Christians fail to recognize the wholeness of the world or of the gospel and are impaled on the horns of various dilemmas. The structural diversity from different forms of organization and the presence of hundreds of different denominations and sects may be less of a problem than the competing ideologies and theologies that profess to have "the truth" while others allegedly are in error.

A spirit of pride claims infallibility of biblical interpretation and of understanding world events. It attracts followers who seek a haven of security, but it alienates countless thinking people from the Christian faith. The great variation in what is alleged to be the social implications of the gospel tarnishes the reputation of biblical Christianity. Religious cults, pseudoreligious therapies, and new religious movements use the evidences of imperfection, conflict, and lack of balance as "hooks" to attract followers.

RESULTS OF IMBALANCE

When churches and other Christian groups allow themselves to be forced into a no-win position, many interpretations of the sickness of Christianity emerge. Harper (1980), for example, has identified six symptoms of disease in Western Christianity: Doctrinal standards have lost their functions as beliefs have been eroded by theologians and the clergy; moral standards have declined as Christians have succumbed to the new morality; the faith has been politicized by Christians with more concern for social morality here and now than with the ethereal qualities of immortality; spirituality has declined under the impact of institutionalism and the labeling of piety as a dirty word; Unitarianism, denial of the Resurrection, and other modern forms of iconoclasm are results of departure from the particularity of the Christian faith, and prophecy has been redefined in terms of social action alone without the stress of the Old Testament prophets upon both social justice and spiritual realities. He attributes all of these to a disease—the humanistic worship of man, accepting the human claim to sovereignty and lordship.

Bockmuehl (1980: 276) similarly observes:

> The kingdom of God stands for: God shall rule. In our historical setting, this means a constant conflict with "man shall rule," the philosophy of secularism. Shrewdly, Karl Marx observed: "Either God is sovereign, or man is sovereign: One of the two must be untrue." Christians, too, must become aware of this basic alternative that underlies all of today's public debates.

He bemoans the enormous subjectivism, a highly emotional preoccupation with the religious self, that is found among evangelicals, as well as other people. Seeing its error, we have a tendency to advocate a mechanistic collectivism that slips into the opposite mistake of making the individual nothing, instead of everything, with no right to a separate existence. "Christianity goes beyond the either-or of individualism and collectivism, and points as a third way to Christian *brotherhood*." The first concern of Christians therefore should be to move on from individualism to the cooperative brotherhood of people, comprising a team for the service of the Lord, not just for fellowship or celebrating togetherness (Bockmuehl, 1980: 274).

In like vein, Colson (1982: 20) has said,

> The fact is, we are a nation overrun by hordes of little tin gods all made in our own image, their charge led by the crown prince of self riding his shiny golden calf. Our various sins spring from one common cause: we do precisely what we want to do, answering only to the whims of our desires.

Even as our churches fill with people professing to be born again, conditions in society appear to be worsening. Perhaps God's judgment is already upon us. The destruction and enslavement of sin result as natural fruits of our disobedience:

> . . . perhaps God is simply allowing us to wallow helplessly in the mire of our sin. . . . Our passions and lusts are insatiable; the more we

continue to indulge them, the more they imprison us. Unrestrained license can only lead to bondage. . . . With God's hand removed from us, there is nothing to restrain our sin. It makes us hate ourselves. It impels us to pull down our leaders—yet it is never satisfied until it infects everything we touch. And so the cancer spreads. . . . Only by radical repentance, and the deepest hunger for God's justice and righteousness, can we be saved from our judgment (Colson, 1982: 21).

Richard Halverson (1982), chaplain of the United States Senate, believes that conservative evangelicals are badly infected with secularism, hedonism, and a "live for the now" materialism that denies in practice the eternal reference we profess in our theology. The criteria for the success of a church are those taken over from the surrounding culture. The values of Christians are shaped by the mass media and tradition more than by the Scriptures. Our evangelism fails to develop relationships, to build New Testament community, to mature believers, and to make disciples.

A self-seeking principle lies behind the new narcissism. Christians who "hear God's truth a little differently" about social issues and other matters must live in wholesome tension with one another. They must give allegiance to Jesus Christ himself, not to some interpretation or method of evolving doctrine (Halverson, 1982).

Whether in regard to the struggle for nuclear disarmament and peace or other issues, Christians easily slip into the rut of finding psychological defense mechanisms to protect whichever positions they have adopted. They use denial, refusing to see any danger or error in their present position. They indulge in transference, misplacing confidence in the authority of their leaders. They allow semantic exercises, using abstract verbal concepts that give the surface appearance of good, to divert their thoughts and lull their minds away from thoughtful responses. Their lack of initial success in efforts to produce desired change may result in the "learned helplessness" of apathy. Love of the familiar, ingrained through routine, habit, repetition, and inertia, enslaves them to a "law of repetition: whatever has been done tends to be done again." When there is awareness of errors among those who suffer, it is easy to blame the victim. Tensions are allayed, demands for corrective action forgotten, and guilt feelings alleviated through such actions (Callahan, 1982).

Other consequences of the imbalanced perspectives and actions of Christians are very evident. Conflicts among themselves and with people and groups in "the world" often can be traced to the demonic influence of either-or dualisms. Much energy is consumed in these battles, diverting Christians from opportunities for evangelistic reachout, compassionate service, social action, and educational ministries. Their struggles create and reinforce even more dualisms in an unending vicious cycle.

Choice of but one aspect of a biblical antinomy means that much of the wholistic perspective of the gospel is lost in "halfism." Compounded with other incomplete doctrines and practices, this often amounts to sharing or applying but fractions of fractions of the fullness of the Christian message and the life in Christ. Enemies and critics of the gospel are given fuel for their burning anti-Christian passions. People whose misery—whether it is physical, material, mental, spiritual, or some other type—could be alleviated continue to suffer. They are harmed personally and, as congregations and fellowships, collectively. All of Christendom is weaker as a result.

FULL OR SELECTIVE OBEDIENCE?

God required his people to obey his will in Old Testament times (see, for example, Deut. 26:16-17; 1 Sam. 15:22-23; Jer. 7:21-23). Much of the history of the ancient Hebrews pertains to the rise and fall of their circumstances as they conformed to or violated God's commandments. God has not changed. People who are wise today not only hear the Lord's words but also put them into practice (Matt. 7:21-27; John 14:23). They take the Bible seriously as the God-inspired guide to faith and conduct.

Certainly this is consistent with the teachings of Jesus. He emphasized that he came to fulfill the Law and the Prophets, not to abolish them. His followers should keep even the least of the commandments and teach others to do the same (Matt. 5:17-20). Furthermore, all of the commandments are summarized in the threefold decree to love the Lord our God with all our heart, soul, mind, and strength and to love our neighbor as we love ourselves (Mark 12:28-32; Matt. 22:37-40).

Complete obedience as the norm is not often mentioned directly in the New Testament; it is simply taken for granted. In his farewell to the elders of the church in Ephesus, the Apostle Paul declared that he had not hesitated to proclaim the whole purpose, will, or counsel of God. He warned them to be on guard against those who would distort the truth (Acts 20:25-31). Similar warnings in other biblical passages are oriented toward those who want to accept only portions of the gospel or of biblical moral and ethical standards.

Possibly the most forthright declaration of the need for complete obedience comes from James' Epistle. A person who keeps the entire law except for one single point is guilty of breaking the law (James 2:10). But it is not simply the acts we commit that make people sinners. We sin also by inaction, not doing the good we know we ought to do (James 4:17).

Yet even as we verbally and intellectually profess the ideal of doing the full counsel of God, it is easy to slip into a pattern of choosing to obey some parts of God's will while ignoring others. Wagner (1981:19), for example, raises "the warning flag of selective obedience." Some Christians notice the "social signs" of the kingdom of God that apply to a general class of people like the poor and oppressed, while others restrict their sight to certain "personal signs" that apply to healing, restoring sight or hearing, casting out evil spirits, or raising the dead. As Wagner reads the Scriptures with "church growth eyes," he sees things others do not, but he also filters out some things that they believe to be important. "In a sense, are we not all selective in our obedience at times, though we don't want to be?" (Wagner, 1981:19).

Polarization is one of the forms that selective obedience takes. As Stott (1975:9) puts it,

> . . . one of the greatest weaknesses which we Christians . . . display is our tendency to extremism or imbalance. It seems that there is almost no pastime the devil enjoys more than tipping Christians off balance. . . . we should love balance as much as the devil hates it and seek to promote it as vigorously as he seeks to destroy it.
>
> By our "imbalance" I mean that we seem to enjoy inhabiting one or other of the polar regions of truth. If we could straddle both poles simultaneously, we would exhibit a healthy biblical balance. Instead, we . . . push other people over to one pole while keeping the opposite pole as our preserve.

Stott discusses four examples of "the folly of unnecessary polarization": intellect and emotion, conservative and radical, form and freedom, evangelism and social action. He emphasizes that the truth, biblically speaking, does not lie in either a golden mean somewhere in the middle between them or in one of the extremes. Rather it is in both extremes. Hence "we have good biblical warrant to replace a rather naive *either-or* with a mature *both-and*. Let us place our feet confidently and simultaneously on both poles" (p. 43).

Polarization generally is accompanied by selective church membership as people gravitate toward the religious groups that stress whatever they believe to be the "correct" position on issues that they believe are crucial. Within a congregation or denomination, taking sides typically involves arguments and church fights. Refusal to "compromise" and the goal of total victory have split many a church. Some pastors and congregations "are never so happy as when they are locked in combat, preferably with enemies without, but otherwise with each other" (Bayly, 1984).

Internal strife delights the enemies of the gospel. It separates Christians from each other, dilutes their influence on the world, drives many of their own youth away from the church and, all too often, away from the faith as well.

Some conflict may be inevitable or unavoidable. Some may be desirable. Yet much is created by an inadequate understanding of the Scriptures, of people, of social relationships, or of the world. Rather than fight each other, "If you're determined to fight the Holy War, make sure you have the right enemy" (Bayly, 1984).

Much of the difficulty comes from failure to discuss our various views with each other.

> There is too little interaction of thought on most issues confronting Christians today. We tend to be more insular, content with playing one note. . . . Each of us has limited information; each of us with our finite minds lacks the ability to think holistically. . . . We are emotional people with mindsets, and these mindsets can make us rigid or at least selective in our gathering of information (Palms, 1983).

The prevention and cure for such "intoxication" with any one segment of truth, thinking we have the whole truth, is to drink deeply of God's truth. "Always give time to God's Word, give time to careful thought, give time to listening, take care in speaking, and you will more likely be a sober Christian, not an intoxicated one" (Palms, 1983).

When we limit God by our own restricted "understanding," we often are conformed to this world. We are trying to force the Lord into the mold of our limited knowledge, whether it is based upon our education and science or our interpretations of the Scriptures. As we remember that "God has ways and means and methods and knowledge far beyond our power to comprehend," we will not restrict the Lord by our limited understanding (Elliott, 1983:1). Neither will we assume that we possess all truth. We will be open to the possibility that other Christians who differ from us may be as much correct as or more correct than we are.

THE PURPOSE AND PLAN OF THIS BOOK

The disagreements and conflicts among Christians reflect many things. They have different outlooks upon the past, present, and future world. They have divergent ideas about priorities for mission in the world today. They have contrasting interpretations of biblical paradoxes and antinomies. And they have diverse views on appropriate means for doing the work of Christ. They also have come from a broad variety of social backgrounds and religious traditions, and there are variations in the organizational structures and operational functions of the religious groups to which they belong.

As a result, many, if not most, Christians fail to develop and maintain a truly wholistic perspective on their faith. They snatch only the "choicest" fragments of the gospel and the more palatable morsels of its social ethics, so they tend to develop lopsidedly into unbalanced, incomplete, unfulfilled, hypocritical, and pharisaical Christians. They then are often viewed by cynics as compelling arguments against the Christian faith. The solution to this set of problems is the development of a truly wholistic Christianity, one that holds all of its rich dimensions in wholesomely balanced relationships with all the others.

Many aspects of these problems will be examined in the chapters that follow. Some that are deeply rooted in conditions of contemporary society will be presented first (Chapters 2-4). These include issues related to liberty, pluralism, relativism, secular humanism, values in conflict, sin and evil. All of these have contributed to polarization and strife among Christians.

These will be followed by a theoretical discussion of paradoxes that call for a dialectical response (Chapter 5.) The next four chapters (Chapters 6-9) present major examples of the need for dynamic Christian dialectics in several domains in which the views of Christians clash. These include issues that center around the styles and dimensions of personal religious commitment, the best way to deal with the problems of society, dilemmas of religious institutions, and the challenges posed by social change. Chapters 10 through 12 summarize practical principles and recommendations on how to cope with the dilemmas, polarities, and paradoxes in order to move toward a truly wholistic Christianity.

The background or "platform" from which I write is that of an evangelical Christian who is a sociologist specializing in the sociology of religion. As an evangelical, I assume that God instructs and guides people primarily through the Bible. It is illuminated by the Holy Spirit, who guides Christians into truth. In fellowship with each other, they hence can discern how they ought to act, think, and believe in their specific social and cultural contexts. In community with each other and in communion with their triune God, they can experience the wholistic well-being of the "abundant life" that Jesus Christ provides.

Together with most of my sociological colleagues, I believe that ultimate values cannot come from our discipline. Yet the description of human values, analysis of their social sources, explanations of their direct and indirect effects, and suggestions of how to move toward desired goals can legitimately flow from sociological methods, insights, and resources (see Lyon, 1983).

Wholistic Christianity centers around biblical values, the ultimate transcultural basis for evaluative judgments. It is best discerned sociologically by the approach that Max Weber termed *Verstehen*. Using sympathetic insight, intuition, and introspection, this method draws heavily upon the imagination as well as upon analytical and interpretative work done by others. That kind of imagination is not the exclusive property of sociologists alone; it is widely disseminated among perceptive people in numerous walks of life, so I shall not limit my resources to my own discipline. To do so would be folly, for explicitly Christian appraisals are not often found within sociology.

> The sociological imagination . . . consists of the capacity to shift from one perspective to another; and in the process to build up an adequate view of a total society and of its components. . . . [It] is the capacity to shift . . . from the political to the psychological; from examination of a single family to comparative assessment of the national budgets of the world. . . . It is the capacity to range from the most impersonal and remote transformations to the most intimate features of the human self—and to see the relations between the two (Mills, 1959:211,7).

The perspectives of a Christian sociologist upon the contemporary scene can help to clarify the background against which all the work of churches, parachurch organizations, pastors, religious educators, clinical and counseling psychologists, and members of other helping professions is done. They can help to clarify and resolve puzzling paradoxes related to Christian commitment that all too often consume Christians in conflict or despair. In the context of biblical values, they enable us to change destructive polarizations into the dynamic dualisms that are at the core of wholistic Christianity.

PART II

THE CULTURAL CONTEXT:
SQUEEZED BY THE WORLD'S MOLD

2

THE LAND OF THE FREE

Many of the problems of lopsided Christianity can be traced to its social context. This holds true worldwide, no matter how great the differences among human cultures.

The imbalance in the religious scene is connected with the emphasis upon freedom that has characterized American life from its earliest beginnings. This imbalance contributes to additional problems of philosophical and ideological orientations that reflect still further the pressures of society upon all its members (see chapters 3 and 4). All of these issues reflect the tendency of Christians to allow themselves to be squeezed into the world's mold when they are not on guard against that temptation (see Rom. 12:1-2).

THE LAISSEZ-FAIRE SOCIAL SYSTEM

In eighteenth-century France arose a doctrine that government should not interfere in the economic affairs of individuals and society. This was a foundation for what came to be called "classical economics." It emphasizes free trade and a "hands-off" orientation toward government controls of any kind. Unregulated individual activity presumably will bring the greatest social benefits to society. "The belief stems from an optimistic view of the nature of man and the universe and a natural order or system of economic harmonies that will assure mankind the greatest advantage if permitted to work unhampered" (Bell, 1969:605).

This laissez-faire doctrine was also evident in philosophy. It was based upon the hedonistic assumptions that every person will seek pleasure and avoid pain and that people are their own best judges of happiness, so no barriers should block their objective. Theorists like Adam Smith, Thomas R. Malthus, John Stuart Mill, Richard Cobden, Jeremy Bentham, Herbert Spencer, and William Graham Sumner contributed to its development. Under its impact many laws were enacted in nineteenth-century political democracy.

Among them were the extension of the right to vote, changes in judicial procedure and in the laws of contract, and abolition of religious inequality. The pervading theory of this period was that the individual, pursuing his own desired ends, would thereby achieve the best results for the society of which he was a part. The function of the state was to maintain order and security, and to avoid interference with the initiative of the individual in pursuit of his own desired goals (Bell, 1969:605-606).

The laissez-faire concept of individual liberty has been a major theme of the history of the United States of America. It was prominent in American life even before the Declaration of Independence. It is evident in the division of powers within government, the Bill of Rights in the Constitution, and the political parties competing for power. Its influence is apparent in many decisions of the Supreme Court and other branches of the judicial system down to the present day. It is obviously a major component in our economic system, even though it has been compromised by governmental regulations in support of competing values. Popular views still hold that whichever government governs the least is the best government.

Freedom of choice extends much further, however. It is evident in our educational system as public and private institutions coexist, competing with each other for students at all levels. It dominates our legal system, which is rapidly making ours an excessively litigious society. It is present in our religious system, in which over 1,200 denominations, sects, and analogous organizations (Melton, 1978) and their local congregations and branches compete with each other and with independent churches for the attendance, beliefs, loyalty, and contributions of the population. It spills over into the domain of voluntary associations, in which recreational, youth-related, social service, fraternal, charitable, political, and advocacy groups compete for participation, funds, and political support. Even in the realm of the family it is present as members are bombarded with invitations and requests from numerous groups and young people are thrust upon an open, competitive market in the mate selection process. Parents are bombarded with countless competing theories of successful child rearing. Little guidance is given for job selection and many other areas of choice throughout the life cycle. The ideal of "free enterprise" still dominates much of American life.

Behind this laissez-faire system lies a set of values. Central is the idea that as each person and group seeks its own best interest, the greatest good for the greatest number will be attained. Self-interest hence is the foundation of both capitalism and democracy, and it lies behind much of the motivation to gain a higher education. The "greed syndrome" by which students are concerned first and foremost about themselves as opposed to society at large is increasingly evident in Alexander Astin's surveys for the American Council on Education. More concern for making money and being well-off financially and less concern for helping others, developing a meaningful philosophy of life, and cleaning up the environment is evident in the early 1980s (Browne, 1983). In most domains of human activity, self-seeking and greed are elevated to the position of dominant moral values.

Similarly, it is assumed that whatever political and ideological perspectives win out in the competitive democratic struggle will be the best ones to guide the nation. Standards of right and wrong are decided by majority opinion in the context of a free discussion of competing perspectives.

Envy is thus elevated to a virtue. It is one of the motivating forces impelling people to try to obtain what others possess (see Schoeck, 1970, Silver and Sabini, 1982). Even in international affairs we are tempted to believe that might makes right—except when the winners of power struggles and wars are the enemies of our own ideologies.

Few have gone further than Karl Marx to "to examine the impact of what Christians regard as sinful responses to God in the development of class conflict," although "he had little to say about wrong motivations and attitudes" (Lyon, 1981:84-85). Because much of the social ethics of Marxism has been derived from Christianity, many are tempted to opt for it in the contemporary struggle of ideas. Yet its system of dialectical materialism is pervaded by motivations of selfishness and greed just as much as that of capitalism, its chief political and economic competitor. In both capitalism and Marxism the creation of the "new man" liberated from the bonds of egotism cannot occur through sanctification of selfish pursuits (Bockmuehl, 1980).

To those who are well grounded in Scripture, I need not point out the ways in which selfishness, egotism, and greed are treated in the Bible. They are clearly designated as base and sinful motivations. (See, for examples, Prov. 15:27; Isa. 5:8; Amos 5:7-12; 1 Tim. 6:9-10; James 5:1-6.)

If the dominant values of society are condemned as sinful, can we also conclude that the system itself is wholly sinful? The problem is that of available alternatives for people who are sinful. None is likely to function better or be less sinful on the level of basic motivational foundations. It seems as if ever more social control mechanisms, including government regulations, are necessary to control the sinfulness that universally characterizes human nature and would be even more destructive to the human race if untrammeled competitiveness were allowed. Society attempts to control the most harmful excesses that flow from avarice and egotistic self-seeking, yet at the same time it subtly cultivates them as guiding virtues for social life.

Christians are caught in a double dilemma. We in everyday life see many alternative, competing positions from which we are forced to choose. We recognize clearly or faintly that many of our choices are made for impure reasons. Few can be fully sanctioned by the ideals of our faith.

INDIVIDUALISM, PRIVATISM, AND NARCISSISM

Strong emphasis upon "rugged individualism" has characterized most of the history of American society. Each person presumably had the opportunity to succeed in the competitive struggles of life. Rural and urban frontiers were opened and settled under its impulse. Industries and businesses were established and family dynasties founded under its incentives. It gave independence from the shackles of ascribed status, under which social position was assigned solely by chance of birth. Success was attained in the New World solely by personal achievement, according to this myth.

Long observed and both praised and condemned, individualism has had many spin-offs. One of these is a distinctive pattern of "privatism" by which people plead for personal freedom and withdraw from social institutions into their own selves. At its logical extreme of complete self-indulgence this "cult of personalism" rejects all meaning and authority outside the individual's own self. It "seems unbridled by any social norm or tradition and almost void of notions for exercise of responsibility toward others," and its ethic "turns into a kind of romantic withdrawal. . . . retreat into the totally personal world can be an escape from responsibility to others and to the society" (Hadden, 1969:33, 69).

Separation of the private spheres of life from the public sphere in modernizing societies has relieved the family of many former roles. Most obvious are those of education and economic production, which now occur almost entirely outside the home. This gives people a domain of privacy that enables many to escape from the pressures of the workplace and public life to "be themselves" and "enjoy life." Many labor diligently for five days of the week in order to have the means to indulge in private hedonistic pleasures during the weekend's leisure time. Among them are Christians who escape into inspirational weekend religious activities.

Many Christian activities are largely irrelevant to most of the surrounding world because they are oriented in a purely private person-plus-family direction. Personal convictions related to the politics of the marketplace force labor, government, international relations, and civic affairs to be left behind when one enters the place of Bible instruction and worship in the context of "spiritual narcissism." Such religion has been caged in to amount to

> little more than a private preference, a spare-time hobby, a leisure pursuit . . . [by] the private-zoo factor, so called because it domesticates the hitherto untamable world of the spirit and fences in the once unbounded provinces of [God] (Guinness, 1983:72).

One of the clearest evidences of privatism is the insistence in many circles that one's politics, like religion, is one's own business. You must not talk about it with strangers, new acquaintances, persons met at business or political receptions, nor even fellow workers and members of your own church. This is changing in evangelicalism, partly under the influence of the Moral Majority, television evangelists, reactions against various negative moral influences, and secular humanism. The political arena has become a religious arena. Unfortunately, the change often is centered around single issues, each of which is lifted up as if it is the only important consideration in the democratic political process. This implies that all others are the private business of each voter. For example, in supporting parties and candidates for office because they are prolife, a group may indirectly and unwittingly also give its support to several other perspectives that are just as evil as abortion on demand.

Religion is often made into something that is considered to be primarily or uniquely personal. This privatization process often results in a high level of subjectivism. The preoccupation with the self often focuses religious life around personal problems of illness, physical suffering, grief, death and bereavement, psychological states, feelings of inadequacy, disappointments, difficulties at work, predicaments in social relationships, family problems, and the like. This emphasis among evangelicals has made them seem to be much more "relevant" to people's needs, but it also has led to "the domestication of conservative Protestant belief" (Hunter, 1983:100), limiting it largely to the private domain of personal and family life.

Many prominent leaders in televangelism appeal to this orientation. A hedonistic view infuses much of evangelicalism: ". . . if one is spiritual, one is happy and contented. Life is full and rich. Conversely, the routine mediocrity of everyday life . . . is often considered a measure of the lack of spirituality" (Hunter, 1983:98).

Even though a reaction against unbridled privatism may have

begun, its subjectivistic ethical and religious values are still widely accepted among people in general and even among Christians. Charles Colson of Watergate infamy and Prison Fellowship fame has astutely observed that many American religious leaders are "successful because they give people what they want":

> Much of the Christianity we slickly market today is nothing but a religious adaptation of the self-seeking values of secular culture. . . . That is heresy, at the very root of the "What's-in-it-for-me gospel" so prevalent in America. Loving God calls for more than gushing sentimentalities or pious mouthings: *loving God demands obedience* (Colson, 1984a:40, italics in the original).

The strong emphasis upon self-love in current society is closely linked to the sin of pride. Psychologist Myers (1980) has clearly indicated that its self-serving bias, not low self-esteem, is the most common defect in people's self images. Accepting oneself, foibles and all, and confessing one's sinful vanity is a major step toward the security and acceptance that accompany wholeness (Myers, 1982:1229-1230; see also Thorn and Kilpatrick, 1984).

Individualism shows its face also in the "new narcissism." Through it, the search of anxiety-ridden people for meaning is disguised in "the pursuit of happiness to the dead end of a preoccupation with the self" (Lasch, 1979). They hunger for "the feeling, the momentary illusion of personal well-being, health, and psychic security" rather than for salvation. Their "ideology of personal growth" typifies our "therapeutic age," according to Lasch. People always have been egocentric, but basic changes in society, especially in politics, advertising, education, and economics have deprived them of much moral responsibility, initiative, and confidence, thus stimulating the inward orientation of a narcissistic search for gratification.

The hedonistic pursuit of pleasure through drug abuse, alcohol, erotic stimulation, sexual promiscuity, self-actualization techniques, and the search for ecstatic experiences is another outgrowth of narcissistic individualism. So, too, is the subjectivistic spirit that establishes all values in terms of their immediate benefits to the individual rather than concern for other persons or society at large. For all too many people the ultimate criterion of morality is expressed by the phrase, "If it feels good, do it."

In his 1984 commencement address at Westmont College, Charles Colson spoke about the subtle seduction of American society by which many of the fears induced by Orwell's novel *1984* have materialized. Stimulated by the mass media and advertising, ours has become a self-indulgent society relentlessly pursuing pleasure and uncritically accepting declining moral values.

> We have yielded to the insidious enslavement of self-gratification. The villain, my friends, is us! . . . What kind of a tyranny does that create? It creates the tyranny of egocentricity—obsessive egocentricity—narcissism, if you will. Scott Peck, the psychiatrist . . . , says "Narcissism is the root of evil in our society." Consider the kind of tyranny it creates. . . . we have literally become enslaved to self-gratification in our own society (Colson, 1984b:6,7,8).

Possibly the most extreme exemplars of individualism are the "survivalists" who are preparing to meet the collapse of society by building huge stores of dried foods, canned water, and ammunition. In her comments upon them, Goodman (1980) suggests that the 1980s constitute "the decade of the paranoid 'haves'" in which "the me people of the 80s are learning to defend themselves," even as the me people of the 70s were learning to actualize themselves. These are but symptoms of the national cult of self-defense. "Individualism gone hostile" is acting out the widespread feelings of impotence and anxiety.

> In the new me decade, sharing your feelings is out; hiding your assets is in. The people who were once into personal growth are being replaced by the people who are into personal hoarding. . . . They bet that it won't be the righteous but the selfish who inherit the earth.
> I find nothing new in this message. It's the oldest cult on earth: every man for himself (Goodman, 1980).

The widespread myth that personal independence is the route to happiness has contributed to much loss of self-esteem, depression, and other sociopsychological problems in contemporary society. An individualistic frame of mind is not only common but is even encouraged in America today, although God "knows that aloneness can be destructive" (Wulff, 1982:1, citing Genesis 2:18). Wulff quotes psychologist James J. Lynch as stating that

> There is almost an unconscious cultural conspiracy to fool people into thinking that to be alone is a virtue. . . . We are told almost daily that the bad old days were when you were stuck in a relationship. Today's liberated, individualistic, free person is portrayed as a single and very self-sufficient person. This doesn't allow us to recognize loneliness. In fact, it forces us to deny it altogether.
> This myth of independence, which one sees every day in advertising and other media, makes it appear that to admit that we need each other is a sign of weakness. No one has trouble understanding why Adam couldn't live alone in paradise, but we somehow tell ourselves we can make it alone in today's world (p. 1).

The human sciences in general and, even more, psychology in particular are in danger of becoming part of an anarchistic "cult of the individual self" (Van Leeuwen, 1982:136). Many psychologists, pastors, and other professional helpers have been swayed by the importance of a humanized psychology. It is easy for them to slip from the tendency of the natural sciences to neglect the individual to "the opposite abuse of absolutizing individual autonomy and denying any communal norms and obligations . . . which do not happen to suit one's own immediate tastes" (pp. 136-137; see also Vitz, 1977). Sociologists, on the contrary, are prone to observing a concern for people in the mass and ignoring them as individuals. Both forms of collective neglect represent dangerous reductionisms.

The American emphasis upon individualism is clearly evident in religion. People seem less interested now than in the past in many of the rituals that take place in group settings, but more interested in personal religious experiences, prayer, and meditation. As Wuthnow (1980) points out, they increasingly make up their own minds on theological issues. They are thus contributing significantly to an erosion of the authority of their church. At best, their antielitism vis-à-vis institutions may have the effect of trying to live holy lives all week long, not just on Sundays, but it can also result in greater susceptibility to religious fads.

Evangelical and fundamentalist Christians are especially prone to accept an unbridled individualism because it is very close to central tenets of their belief system. Emphasis upon the importance of making a personal faith commitment to Jesus Christ as the means of receiving God's free and unmerited gift of salvation contributes to person-oriented forms of evangelism, Christian education, and church life. This easily spills over into individualistic interpretations of moral and ethical issues. It nourishes the perspective that all social issues, national problems, and international relationships are at root simply matters of personal decision or individual action. A logical inference is that if we merely get individual persons straightened out spiritually, then their groups, institutions, and society—hence eventually the nation and the world itself—will be straightened out as well.

Unfortunately, social issues are not that simple. The morality of moral individuals actually can help to sustain an immoral society's sinful practices and institutions (Niebuhr, 1932). Yet the opposite abuse is also possible. To deal with only the collective, structural, and societal aspects of human problems can easily result in the neglect of many individual needs. Both at home and in missionary ventures abroad (see Cook, 1984; McLean, 1984:111) the cause of Christ has suffered whenever radical individualism has reigned supreme.

Whenever any virtue is practiced to excess, a reaction sets in. There are many indications today of a rising revolt against unbridled individualism. Actress Liv Ullman, for example, tells of her personal response:

> Today. . . . We're told so much to be free. It's pushed upon us. We have so much choice that in the end it's no choice. We are losing our sense of belonging. People don't believe in family. They don't believe in God. They don't believe in the future. That kind of freedom is also a ghost. It is making us inhuman (Richards, 1982).

Yankelovich (1981) likewise has indicated that new moral rules are emerging. People seem to be swinging away from extreme individualism and an inner-oriented search for self-fulfillment toward a search for fulfillment through commitment to something outside themselves.

RELIGIOUS PLURALISM

A major characteristic of society in the United States is an exceptionally wide range of associations and institutions coexisting and competing with one another. This is both a consequence and a cause of the high value placed on freedom, competition, and individualism. In the religious sector it is very evident on several levels. All of the major world religions have been imported to our nation and compete with one another here. More than 1,200 denominations, sects, and cults have been identified in the United States (Melton, 1978), but some scholars say the number of religious bodies is closer to five thousand.

The fragmentation of American Christendom is legendary. Within each of the major branches—Protestant, Catholic, Orthodox, Mormon, and other—are numerous subdivisions. Within many of those denominations and sects, in turn, there are significant variations from one congregation, parish, chapel, assembly, stake, or other local subdivision to another. Even within each of those local branches there are diversities of language, theological understandings, and ideas about the purpose and goals of the church. These sometimes cause conflict, and they often create subtle tensions that make people feel uneasy or disturbed.

The coexistence of over two hundred widely recognized Christian denominations (Jacquet, 1982), in addition to hundreds of additional smaller Christian and pseudo-Christian bodies (Melton, 1978), has been viewed as a "scandal." This attitude contributed to the rise and growth of the ecumenical movement and, within it, to efforts by several major mainline Protestant denominations to work toward union through COCU, the Consultation on Church Union, also known as the Church of Christ Uniting.

Others, however, view the diversity of American Christianity as a sign of strength. It cannot be coopted by any single religious or political hierarchy into actions that later historical and theological perspectives may prove to have been unwise. It makes available to persons of widely divergent needs a great variety of orientations from which to choose. It thus provides a wider range of viable religious options and contributes significantly to the relative high levels of religious participation that characterize American society. Everyone can find a religious group that fits his or her own interests, beliefs, and needs. The religious scene is like a great supermarket in which people pick and choose.

In addition to the denominational and ecumenical structure of Christianity in the USA, there are thousands of parachurch associations. Some are tiny one-person ministries, others are huge television and radio networks ("the electronic church"), old and venerated service programs like the American Bible Society, and the large and increasingly diversified ministries of agencies like World Vision and the Billy Graham Evangelistic Association. These often were established to do what could not be done, or at least could not be done easily, through bureaucratic denominational and ecumenical agencies. Many of them represent efforts to move quickly into areas of need and opportunity at times when the harvest seemed ripe and laborers were available. Some were attempts to implement the vision of a charismatic leader who harnessed the financial support necessary to make the dream come true.

Pastors of churches have a tendency to feel that these parachurch agencies are stealing both energy and finances away from the local church. Denominational leaders are tempted to blame declining support of their ventures on the competition from parachurch ministries. North (1982) believes that the established churches lost out in the competitive struggle because they failed to contribute to independent charities that are beyond the abilities of church leaders to operate directly. As a result, the churches are not represented on the boards of directors, and there is no accountability back to the churches. When churches fail to meet cultural, educational, social, and health needs that must be met somehow, other agencies do so. Since

> . . . meeting basic human needs is an important aspect of gaining authority and influence, . . . power flows to those who are willing to exercise responsibility. . . . The churches, by abandoning their financial responsibilities, have steadily transferred authority to independent ministries, especially authority in social and economic matters (North, 1982:2).

Parachurch organizations are much like the substructures of tribal systems and the orders of the Roman Catholic Church. They are sodalities—voluntary, contractual, purposive, and decentralized agencies that are not biologically sustained. Usually they emerge out of an indigenous setting to meet some particular need. Historically they provide much of the background of the modern missionary movement. Many of them have been taken over by denominational or ecumenical agencies, while hundreds of others remain independent "faith missions." Much new missionary work has been begun by these independent voluntary societies. Instead of continuing the current tensions between them and the denominations, there ought to be cooperation for the mutual benefit of both (Winter, 1980; Dugan, 1980).

New religious movements, mystical and occult sects, pseudo-religious human potential groups, and esoteric cults emerge every year. Some are clearly Christian, others marginally so, and still others of non-Christian origins. Some quickly die. Others survive until the death of their charismatic founders, while still others grow in strength and respectability to become fully recognized "denominations" coexisting peacefully alongside the older groups.

Many of their leaders use concepts and phrases from the Bible in an effort to demonstrate their respectability and win new converts. They often tear these out of the original biblical context as they imply that their faith and praxis are newly revealed biblical teachings. For example, the Maharishi Mahesh Yogi who founded Transcendental Meditation has incorrectly quoted Psalm 46:10 as the words of Christ, "Be still and know that I am God." He then commented, "Be still and know that you are God and when you know that you are God you will begin to live Godhood, and living Godhood there is no reason to suffer" (Sire, 1980). Naive persons who know neither the Scriptures nor the proper way to interpret them are sometimes led astray by such distortions. Sometimes they are swayed as well by the argument that one can belong simultaneously to both the new religion and the Christian faith.

Abuse of the Scriptures is not a monopoly of new religious movements. It is common also within the internal factions and sectarian movements of many established Christian bodies. All too often lay members, and sometimes even the clergy, of conventional Christian groups distort biblical teachings. It is wise to remember that the Rev. Jim Jones, the founder of Jonestown, Guyana, which ended in the tragedy of mass suicides, was an ordained minister in a mainline Protestant denomination and had won considerable favor and support in ecumenical and governmental agencies for his ministries to the poor in San Francisco.

"Power abusers" often lead sectarian movements. Authoritarian leaders provide satisfactions that followers desire. They give their members clear-cut answers for personal and social problems, convey a sense of security in a troubled world, impart a distinct personal identity, provide a feeling of solidarity with a group, guide people in making troublesome decisions, and satisfy the cravings of spiritual hunger. Similar forms of authoritarianism call for blind loyalty to religious leaders and unquestioning obedience to their directions. They claim to have a purely correct position in contrast to the allegedly wholly wrong alternatives presented for action on complex issues by others. Their claims and tactics are not unknown within major Christian denominations.

Pluralism is evident not only within the various denominational bodies; it is present within every congregation and parish. The members have come out of different religious backgrounds; about two of every five Protestants in the USA are in a denomination that is not the same as their previous membership (Roof and Hadaway, 1979). Even the most faithful members of a church have different internalized definitions of God, Jesus, the church, faith, salvation, and other religious concepts. They hold diverse theological perspectives on a wide range of issues related to salvation, prophecy, Bible interpretation, Christian lifestyles, and other subjects. They have divergent expectations of what their local church and its denomination can and ought to offer. They hold dissimilar levels of faith commitment. They demonstrate different patterns and levels of personal involvement in religious activities. The local church is a pluralistic social structure.

Religious pluralism is both a cause and a consequence of the religious liberty and separation of church and state that have characterized American society since shortly after the end of the colonial period. Nine of the thirteen colonies had officially established churches. When they formed the United States, no established church could gain preeminence. Their power struggle led to the disestablishment of all churches. The liberty of each depended upon liberty for all. The principle of free and voluntary association became the foundation of religious life (Handy, 1966).

Religious pluralism has also made all Americans into "heretics" from the perspective of Berger's (1979) sociological definition. There is no one societally established correct way of thinking about, worshiping, and serving God. People therefore are compelled to choose from among competing dogmas, none of which is defined by society as firmly orthodox.

Religious certainty prevailed in many premodern situations as people took a particular world view for granted. This was only occasionally ruptured by heretical deviations. The modern world, however, is one of religious uncertainty. Picking and choosing is imperative, and, Berger (1979) alleges, every choice is fraught with the insecurity of feeling one may be in error. Even those who are "born into a religion" are confronted in their mature years with the possibility and opportunity of departing from it. "The truth or falseness of religion becomes a matter of individual choice" (Hunter, 1983:14).

In most modern communities there is a great smorgasbord of religious groups and perspectives from which to choose, like the opulent offerings of a lavish buffet lunch (Guinness, 1983: 91-106). Yet, surprisingly, the pick-and-choose mentality also is evident within religious bodies. Members often select whatever they want from the doctrines and traditions of their church and ignore the rest. Two-thirds of 1,017 respondents in the "Faith and Ferment" study in Minnesota saw no harm in not only ignoring but directly rejecting some of the doctrines of their church. Attitudes toward sin, prayer, divorce, abortion, contraception, social action, and other topics reflect these inconsistencies (Woodward, 1983; Bilheimer, 1983).

Some denominations take pride in their internal diversity. American Baptists, for example, have long lived with doctrinal differences, agreeing to disagree on many things. They emphasize soul freedom and have no official confession of faith. However, the work of their staff is governed by policy statements adopted by its General Board. Resolutions on a variety of social and political issues on the national and international scene have tended to take priority over basic theological aspects of the Christian faith. A prominent pastor asks editorially, "Is it all right to appeal to Baptist soul freedom to avoid theological positions but not all right when it comes to this new American Baptist doctrine?" (Swank, 1984).

Most political decisions are the results of compromises, so political action is at best mottled with mixtures of right and wrong; it is never purely right. The mixing of diverse biblical and ethical values helps to account for the fact that dedicated Christians often take opposite sides of major political, social, and economic issues. They assign different priorities to the ethical principles involved, and they pay attention to different details of political and social reality.

Local churches and other groups that cooperate for one cause may oppose each other on another. The same applies to the larger bodies to which congregations belong. When they are lobbying for tuition remission from taxation programs, the National Association of Evangelicals (NAE) and agencies of the Roman Catholic Church often work together, but they tend to be on opposite sides of political struggles pertinent to relationships between the United States and the Central

American countries of Guatemala, Nicaragua, and El Salvador. Statements on social ethics by agencies in the National Council of the Churches of Christ in the USA (NCC) are sometimes undermined by contrary statements from its member denominations. The NCC and Roman Catholic Church tend to agree on issues related to capital punishment and international affairs, but they oppose each other on questions related to abortion. The NAE and the Church of Jesus Christ of the Latter-day Saints tend to support each other on many issues of conservative politics, but they disagree sharply on many basic doctrines of the Christian faith.

Yet we must also recognize that the diverse religious groups that exist alongside each other do not necessarily believe that they alone are God's people. Many of the divisions reflect special interests and tastes of the past or present, such as ethnic languages, racial subcultures, social class differences, preferred worship styles, and loyalty to moral commitments made by an earlier generation. Basic issues, like interpretations of details of the gospel of salvation, cut across denominational lines.

A denomination gives its members an identity. It organizes many religious functions, labels a confessional tradition, and enables the attainment of many goals (Marty, 1981). Membership within it usually is not so "particularistic" that its people feel that only those who belong to it can be saved.

An in-depth analysis of the statistical findings of significant surveys of religious groups in US society shows that the differences between them have been magnified out of proportion in the reports. In addition, the differences within the respective groups are considerably larger than those between groups (Ploch, 1974). American pluralism is not a sectarian exclusivism that assumes all who are outside one's own religious body are also outside the kingdom of God.

Where there is a sectarian spirit, the battles often are harshest against others who carry the label of the same denominational family, whether Baptist, Lutheran, Presbyterian, or other. By misrepresenting what the sectarian party believes they ought to think or do, they are presumably undermining the foundations of the true faith represented by the label. As Robert D. Brinsmead indicates, the sectarian spirit often emphasizes minor "truth," which "too easily becomes the thing which justifies the group's existence" ("The 'Sectarian Spirit,'" 1981). Subordinating the gospel to that distinctive detail becomes the heresy of elevating a good thing in place of the best.

Pluralism has eliminated many of the harmful linkages between church and state, but it also has eroded the idea that the United States is a Christian nation. That myth is based upon the mistaken belief that

Christian commitment can be made by the body politic for its members, as well as upon distorted ideas of specifically what is Christian.

Religious pluralism is supported for pragmatic reasons, but it also has a biblical foundation. Pluralism grows out of the limitations of God's power self-imposed by divine respect for human freedom of choice. It acknowledges that any of us may ultimately prove to be wrong in some of our decisions about what is good and true. It reflects the finite nature of all human knowledge and wisdom. Pluralism affirms respect for what others who acknowledge the one God have concluded to be authentic, recognizing that there is but one ultimate Judge. It maintains the God-given uniqueness of every person, hence the diversity that is found within the human community. "Though one body, we are many members, each responsible for our own choices, each of infinite value in our uniqueness" (Mollenkott, 1982:5).

Pluralism has contributed to the erosion of loyalty to specific religious bodies. When people see friendly relationships among the various churches and sects, they rightly or wrongly decide that there are no important differences among them. That being the case, what difference does it make whether one joins a Presbyterian, Methodist, Lutheran, Episcopal, or even Baptist church?

The "free enterprise" pluralism of the political, economic, educational, and other domains is thus accompanied by a parallel system in the religious realm. This accentuates the confusion and uncertainty of Christians, and it bewilders non-Christians who observe the consequences of the dilemmas it poses. The implications of pluralism in the domain of ethics and morals are evident most of all in the widespread dogma of relativism, to which we shall turn in the next chapter.

LONE RANGER CHRISTIANITY

We have seen that Christians often allow themselves to be shaped by the mold of the world around them. The free enterprise system based on a laissez-faire philosophy has been a major influence upon religious as well as economic and political life in the USA. That philosophy reached its peak shortly after the Civil War. By then modern society had become far more complex than that which prevailed when the philosophy was developed. New theories have developed, but "it still lives on and fights a vigorous rear-guard action" (Bell, 1969:606). It may be more alive and powerful in the domain of religion than in most other areas of human activity.

Under the influence of liberty it is easy for Christians to lose their perspective. The individualism it recommends tends to promote subjectivism and self-seeking narcissism. These, in turn, make Christians forget their dependence upon other members of the body of Christ, the need to respect their weaker brothers and sisters, and the necessity for cooperative efforts to influence society at large and its various institutional structures.

Individualistic emphases are a denial of wholistic Christianity, for they constitute but one part of the biblical mandate. If we are caught up in "a narcotic self-fulfillment gospel" that gives us excuses and a rationale for narcissistic behavior, we have succumbed to an old temptation, no matter how attractive the new wrappings may be (Woodbridge, 1983-1984). To use the words of Marvin R. Wilson (1983), Ockenga Professor of Biblical Studies at Gordon College:

> The current display of "rugged individualism" and private Christianity must give way to a greater emphasis on the corporate life of the community of faith. Unhappily, one of the characteristics of contemporary fundamentalism and evangelicalism is the emphasis upon what might be called "Lone Ranger" Christianity. That is, people seem to be losing their biblical sense of accountability to each other and think they can, for the most part, operate on their own. . . . Somehow the community-centeredness of the body of Christ is now in danger of being replaced by . . . a private kind of faith. . . . the church must be more than a group of independent individualists each going its own way. . . . In effect, the church is a community of faith, learning, and living, just as the synagogue serves as a house of worship, study and assembly. Thus a Christian's actions within that fellowship are not solely a private matter. . . . The lives of its members are intertwined and find their truest meaning in a network of relationships within this body (italics removed).

3

COMPANIONS OF LIBERTY

On the eve of entering the 1980s George W. Jones, director of religious affairs at Ball State University and editor of the newsletter of the Association for the Coordination of University Religious Affairs, wrote that pluralism is the most important social reality with which society, higher education, and churches must come to terms in this decade. When "a babel surrounds us about what is right or worthy, . . . the super challenge of the eighties will be how to deal with values" (Jones, 1979). Diverse views of reality, morality, and what constitutes the true, good, and beautiful are a root cause of much of our confusion about goals and standards. Among other responses, Jones said, we must train people to take advantage of the positive side of pluralism and counter its negative side.

The increased diversification of society in the modern world is a very significant change, not only a harbinger of other changes. It has produced a "consciousness reformation," according to Wuthnow (1976), who explains:

> Whereas there was once a normative standard that allowed only one or several kinds of family or economic or religious structures, the normative order appears to have become elastic to the point where a variety of diverse social forms can now be countenanced (p. 196).

Similarly, Rieff (1966:21) has commented that the current "cultural revolution does not aim, like its predecessors, at victory for some rival commitment, but rather at a way of using all commitments, which amounts to loyalty toward none." In this emerging therapeutic society anything that makes one feel good is considered equally valid, if only we "experience" it.

These and related changes in society have elevated several important perspectives that pose problems for committed Christians, especially those who live in "the free world," including those labeled relativism, reductionism, secularism, and humanism.

ETHICAL AND MORAL RELATIVISM

Throughout the history of the USA the diversity of society has been increasing. The Industrial Revolution, the growth of science and technology, the urbanization of the population, and the growing heterogeneity of people and their communities with immigrants from almost all parts of the world greatly magnified the complexity of society. That diversity has included the realm of moral and ethical values.

Tolerance for diverse viewpoints and novel ideas has brought many benefits, but it also has been accompanied by significant problems. Among them are increased difficulty in attaining consensus on community, state, and national policies; the necessity to expend tremendous effort to coordinate activities and programs to deal with social problems; the breakdown of moral standards for family life (Moberg, 1978b); the emergence of new religious and pseudoreligious groups, many of which profess to have *the* solution for personal and societal problems; and the widespread idea that all value systems are equally good, provided only that people have sincere commitments.

Along with tolerance and diversity comes the search for ever novel values and solutions instead of preserving past sanctions and time-tested norms. The search assumes that contemporary humanity is completely unique in history. "This attitude suggests that man has become a moral astronaut, weightless and no longer subject to the laws of this earth" (Houston, 1973).

The consequences of moral relativism permeate society. Choice itself—the act of making a decision—is elevated to the position of

> . . . a right, even one which has divine sanction. . . . the very fact that a choice can be made is seen as a thing to be celebrated. . . . The abortion ad and this belief in the right to suicide both assume that choice is not only morally important; choice in itself is made the highest morality. If it can be chosen, it should be permitted. What matters is not what is chosen, but the act of choosing itself. . . . Where choice. . . is the ultimate moral category, all of the ways which might be chosen are seen as equal—and equally unimportant (Garvey, 1982: 9-10).

The freedom, democracy, and pluralism of our society have contributed to a popular mentality that views whatever is legal—and much that is illegal but in essence "private"—as thereby ethically acceptable and moral. Anything not proscribed is permitted. Group pressures sometimes convert the permitted into the prescribed. This nearly antinomian perspective is closely linked with the concern of the "now generation" for only the immediate consequences of actions. It gives little or no thought to long-range effects in their own lives and much less to consequences to society as a whole.

People who are asked to write references for students or colleagues are sometimes caught up in a related moral dilemma. For example, the letters of reference for a teaching physician who had been convicted of raping a nurse and was charged also with attempted rape of patients won him a new job in another city. None of the letters mentioned the rape conviction. Upon investigation, the writers' response was that they were commenting only upon his professional skills, not upon character, personality, or past activities (Wermuth, 1982).

This shift to a very narrow view of professionalism is a result of several factors, including the radicalism of the past two decades that conceives all judgments to be "political," the narrowing of academic employment opportunity that makes referees help students or colleagues by writing "preposterously fulsome letters," and the willingness of employers to accept recommendations from anyone at all instead of insisting upon authoritative ones.

> Judgment lies at the heart of the recommendation problem. The ability to formulate a carefully considered, fair, and thoughtful assessment of a person's skills, character, and performance, combined with the honesty to state it clearly, is the heart of the matter. These processes have been corrupted by a flood of new values, many of them false, which have inundated intellectual life over the past fifteen years. These values assert that virtues like character, integrity, and responsibility must be redefined in various ways to suit the politics of the redefiner (Wermuth, 1982:28)

The corrosion of moral values pertinent to recommendations is not limited to medicine and academia. It is found in business and industry, psychological and social services, and even churches. For the sake of giving a fallen brother or sister "a second chance," gross sins and even criminal behavior are sometimes covered up. The erring person is "moved gracefully" in the hope of avoiding serious repercussions for the church or other agency of previous employment in which the deviant behavior occurred.

Similarily, Alan M. Dershowitz (1982), a civil-liberties lawyer who teaches at Harvard Law School, has discovered that students who graduate from any good law school with a high degree of idealism and strong commitment to truth soon learn from experience that "the system is based on a superstructure of distortion, of twisting, of turning. Some become cynics and, ultimately, liars. In the interests of a higher justice they, too, engage in distortion" (p. 63). They do so first as prosecutors, encouraging plaintiffs in civil suits to tell lies in the interest of having "justice" done. Then they do the same for corporation employers. "In every position they hold, some begin to believe the ethos of their client and are prepared to distort and twist and turn in order to achieve what they think is a just result" (p. 63). Even judges get caught up in the process of twisting the law in order to "do right." As a result, the entire judicial system suffers.

Cultural relativism is a fact. Divergent sets of moral and ethical values do prevail in the diverse societies of the world. Those differences are clearly reflected in the Bible (Moberg, 1962). To build these into a wholly subjectivistic system that allows every person to construct his or her own moral code with little or no consideration of social values or other goals is quite a different matter. To allow such to occur will mean that there is no set of ultimate social values by which the members of society can be judged and consensus for collective action achieved. There can be no progress without clear standards and ideals. Nothing can be "improved" when every position and action is equally valid. Nothing then can be labeled as crime, delinquency, evil, or sin. Every person considers his or her own ways to be right. Yet, no matter what one's personal and social standards may be, the Lord looks to the central issues of the matter and sees what is within the human heart (1 Sam. 16:7; Prov. 21:2).

Moral and ethical relativism as a creed or social policy is actually self-contradictory. It asserts the value of having no absolutes. It allows each subculture to develop its own values, attitudes, and prejudices. It claims that the values of no group can be taken as either better or worse than those of another. But the very act of viewing all value systems in their own terms—the value of relativism held by those who profess to be relativists—is itself the product of group values.

> In more precise logical terms, relativism is self-contradictory both in a general categorical sense and in a substantive, specific way. It postulates, on the most general level, a basic negative statement (there is no universal value) that is the implication of its own contradiction (there is at least one universal value, relativism). In more specific, substantive terms, it is also self-contradictory, since it asserts a general value (the values of all peoples are of equal worth), then contradicts it by implying the superiority of the values of the group consisting of relativists (it is good to see other peoples in their own terms), a value clearly not shared by most other peoples . . . (Patterson, 1980:150).

The relativistic mentality does not limit itself to cultural practices and moral principles; it extends to philosophical assumptions, basic perspectives on the universe, and ideological beliefs. For example, an advertisement for *Taking Leave of God* by Don Cupitt (1981), dean of Emmanuel College in Cambridge, indicates that he argues a stage has come in the spiritual and moral development of mankind

> . . . when we need to abandon theological realism, to part company with the thought of an objective God, . . . and struggle to realize religious values in this life. . . . The only God, he insists, is "the religious requirement"—our inner recognition of the call to self-appraisal, meditation, cosmic awe, unselfishness; and we ought to obey it for its own sake, not because anybody tells us to or in hope of reward. These key values can . . . best be learnt from Jesus, "the brilliant Jewish teacher of the religious requirement."

If all belief systems are equally valid, then every religion, every god, every other object of worship, every ritual, every creed, and every ecstatic experience is equally valid. Each coexists with the same validity as every atheistic pseudoreligion. This stands in rather stark contrast to the claims of Jesus Christ. He said that no one can come to God except by himself (John 8:24), and the early Christians preached that there is salvation in none other than him (Acts 4:12; see also 1 Cor. 3:11). It also is contrary to the claims of other people who believe that only their religion is correct.

Yet the opposition of Christians to cultural relativism usually derives mainly from their strong commitment to the culture of their own society. Idolizing it and seeking refuge in its security "is the very opposite of the transcendent security that true Christianity speaks of" (Walter, 1980:134). Their response is equivalent to the ethnocentric attempts of others to convince themselves that their own customs, norms, and values—and theirs alone—are absolutely and universally correct. They have absolutized a way of life that is a temporary product of a specific historical situation. They have failed to look beyond their own context to the transcendent values of the Bible that stand in judgment over all groups, including their own.

Thus we face a dilemma. We are caught between the evils of moral and ethical relativism, on the one hand, and a culturally based absolutism that imposes rigid standards and punishes all who deviate, on the other. Condemning past hypocrisy and the cruel treatment of deviants and moral minorities, we tend to accept all but the grossest of immoral acts. Even Christians are moved either to accept a full-blown, subjective, antinomian relativism that holds that whatever seems right for individuals or groups is right for them, or else they tend to sanctify cultural norms as if they are proper Christian values for all people everywhere. The impact of the modern sciences often seems to aggravate, rather than diminish, dilemmas such as these.

REDUCTIONISM

Contemporary society is so complicated that every effort to deal with all of its characteristics falls far short of being complete or fully "wholistic." What is more, that subject itself is abstracted analytically from a larger whole. All human efforts seem to fall short of the complete analysis of any phenomenon in the universe. For example, even if the study of a human enzyme were complete from the perspective of biochemistry, it would fail to cover the complex aspects of the human behavior associated with its secretion that are analyzed in such academic disciplines as sociology, psychology, history, anthropology, philosophy, theology, and literature.

In spite of the inherent impossibility of dealing with the complex wholeness of the universe from the viewpoint of any discipline or even from the combined perspectives of all of them together, there have been many significant attempts in the history of science to reduce reality to something simple. Reductionisms have taken many forms. Geographic determinism "explains" all social and cultural reality in terms of climatic and topographic features of the earth. Economic determinism reduces all social relationships to some form of materialistic exchange. Historical determinism dooms the future of humanity to the alleged stages of a cycle of patterned events. Sociological determinism interprets everything in terms of social constraints. Psychological determinism assumes that people are only the product of conditioning. And theological determinism removes human autonomy by insisting upon a rigid form of theistic predestination.

All of these have valid insights, but they err in elevating them to the position of some all-controlling influence that determines the nature or behavior of everything else. All are guilty of the fallacy of ontological reductionism, which MacKay (1974:36-47) has labeled "nothing buttery" for the tendency to say that X is *nothing but* Y.

Every scientific and scholarly discipline, as well as every type of professional practice, represents but a different limited perspective on the complex wholeness of the universe. All scientific disciplines operate primarily by reducing the phenomena with which they deal to ever-smaller component parts, only occasionally attempting to put them back together into the "whole." Yet every "whole" is part of a still larger whole. It is impossible for any human analysis to be fully "wholistic."

Sociobiology is one of the most significant current examples of reductionism. This is a modern version of the biological determinism that was used during the nineteenth and early twentieth centuries to support the evolutionary social Darwinist idea that the fittest survive. It helped to pass and sustain discriminatory immigration laws, to treat mentally ill people and criminals disrespectfully, and to uphold theories of racial superiority that contributed to the Holocaust and other acts of attempted genocide in many parts of the earth.

The leading sociobiologist is Edward O. Wilson of Harvard University, author of *Sociobiology: The New Synthesis* (1975) and *On Human Nature* (1979). He and his followers believe that all social behavior has a biological basis, that it is shaped by evolutionary processes that act upon the genes that determine human behavior, that the ultimate human goal is to perpetuate the species, and that this is accomplished as a result of inherently selfish genes that drive all human conduct.

> The neo-Darwinian assumption is that these genetically determined social traits are adaptive, providing their holders with greater reproductive success, and thus passing the trait on to future generations. Yet there is no indication that any of the complex human social behaviors discussed in *On Human Nature* are genetically specified (Weaver, 1980:31).

Sociobiology therefore is better described as an ideology than as an objective science:

> Sociobiology follows logically from the naturalism of an evolutionary world view. . . . The universe and all life found within it have evolved from random interaction of matter and energy over vast reaches of time. Consequently, in the human realm, no absolutes exist to guide moral decisions. Such a view denies our spiritual nature, and therefore reduces each of us to a meaningless blob in evolutionary time. Our only purpose, then, is to be an effective vehicle for the reproduction of a master molecule, DNA, by which we are enslaved (Bohlin, 1981: 87; see also Caplan, 1978).

Reductionism is not limited to sociobiology and other human sciences. We live in a society dominated by advertising and propaganda in much of the mass media and by appeals to the lowest common denominators of citizenship in political life. There are great pressures to simplify reality in communicated messages, reducing it to stereotyped themes and labels that can easily be understood and communicated. In the field of religion, for example, many simplified Christian creeds and "affirmations of faith" claim to summarize the essential beliefs of the faith. These often are very useful as mnemonic devices or shorthand summaries, but they can also contribute to ignorance by omitting attention to other important beliefs and doctrines.

> One of the lessons of Christian history is that a legitimate accent, a motif that is rightly bold while other themes are called to be bashful, often succumbs to megalomania. . . . An historically ripe, but nonetheless fragmentary, truth may develop imperialistic designs.

The part claims to be the whole, and in doing so censors out other vital dimensions of Christian testimony. Reductionism, the collapse of the total Christian message and style into a crucial but not exhaustive theme, is the root problem in the critical position, one that blurs both its sociological and theological vision (Fackre, 1966:286-287).

Various reductionisms in everyday life also diminish the rich realities of Christianity. Some see it as only Christian ancestry or heritage, citizenship in a "Christian nation," life-cycle rituals like baptism or weddings, membership in a Christian church, verbal consent to a statement of beliefs, or a declaration of allegiance to Christian ethical standards. Sectarian groups pick up one or another set of beliefs, practices, or experiences and claim that it is the essence of Christianity. Those fundamentalists who reduce Christian responsibility to only soul winning are just as reductionistic as theological liberals who declare that its essence lies only in efforts to promote social justice.

A lop-sided commitment to one or another of the numerous portions into which the gospel can be carved reduces its riches to an impoverished, incomplete, delimited fragment of its wholeness. To see but one perspective or part of the biblical message as if it represents the totality and to emphasize but one aspect of the Christian life as if it were the only important one are among the reductionisms that cry out for correction.

Even the distinction Protestants sometimes make between "saints" and "sinners" has had reductionistic effects. Non-Christians somehow pick up a message that the "saints" are proudly declaring superiority over them, the "sinners," not realizing that saints still sin in this life (1 John 1:8-9). Only Jesus Christ was perfect. Although fully justified in the eyes of God because of what Christ has done for us, we are hypocrites if we profess to have reached perfection in all our deeds, thoughts, and relationships. We are still in the process of growth, gradually developing toward "the measure of the stature of the fullness of Christ" (Eph. 4:13 KJV).

SECULARISM

At least until recently, most sociologists have assumed that secularization, the process of moving away from sacred religious orientations, is a characteristic of all modern industrial societies. The perspective of many of them is perhaps most starkly conveyed by the title of Barnes' book *The Twilight of Christianity* (1929). They believed that Christianity is gradually dying under the advance of modern science and education. There is no future in studying what soon will be gone.

Their predictions were in part a self-fulfilling prophecy. Because they did not "waste time" seeking objective evidence for the stability, decline, or growth of religion, their "general wisdom" was confirmed by the absence of the unsought evidence from most of their research. The "midcentury revival of religion" after World War II (Moberg, 1984a:40-43) caught them by surprise, yet many of them believed that it was only a temporary exception to the long-term trend of secularization.

Secularism, the condition of ignoring or even denying the reality of the spiritual and religious domain of life, indeed does characterize much of contemporary society.

Except when they are struck by some personal or family crisis or disaster, most people seem to give little attention to religious faith and values in daily life. Boyd (1980) quoted Alan Walker, world evangelism director for the World Methodist Council, as having stated that

> . . . there is more atheism and resistance to the Christian gospel in England, Europe, America and Australia than anywhere else on earth. . . . The practical rejection of God by the West now matches the theoretical atheism of the Communist states. There are probably as many people worshiping God in the Soviet Union as in England and in Europe.

One result is that people worship many "idols," including themselves and their automobiles, homes, artistic productions, jobs, games, comfort, and church. (Many of these are fluently described by David-man, 1978, and the problem is analyzed well by Hamilton, 1973.) Even persons who say they worship the Lord God Almighty may by their deeds and words betray a love for, service to, and worship of idols (see Walter, 1980; Redekop, 1970).

Secularism is both reflected in and promoted by the mass media. The appeals of advertising are directed toward hedonistic, narcissistic, and materialistic values. Except for some of the news that comes through explicitly Christian channels, most reports and interpretations of world events fail to convey the moral and religious values that infuse public issues (Pippert, 1978). The strongly secular orientations of "the media elite" make them "tone deaf" to moral and religious perspectives. Half of its members do not even profess to have a religion, and 86 percent seldom or never attend a house of worship. Despite the built-in system of checks in their profession, their world view strongly influences their reporting, for it

> . . . determines what they see, what they understand, what they think is important (or unimportant), how hard they work to check their sources, to what they choose to give prominence, the code words

employed (like fundamentalist, or extreme right), comparisons made, interpretations suggested, even when not stated, and value judgments of approval or disapproval (Editorial, 1982:3).

Similar bias appears in commercial movies. With but rare exceptions they sensationalize the aberrations of Christianity. They make sport of clergy and religious laity as if they are all hypocritical violators of their own moral creeds, and they contribute to the belief that traditional Christian values are a major source of personal depravity and social disintegration (see, e.g., Rifkin, 1981).

Interviews by Stanley Rothman and Linda and Robert Lichter with 104 top executives in the television industry found related evidence. Nearly all of them (96 percent) seldom or never attend religious services (Sobran, 1983). Their ideological commitments inevitably bias both news reporting and entertainment programs.

Secularism is very evident in education. Battles rage in many communities over the content of textbooks, prayer in the classrooms, religious clubs using school facilities, value clarification assignments, and many other issues in public schools. All of these relate to other changes occurring as society becomes increasingly pluralistic with fewer and fewer communities dominated by but one religious orientation.

National ideals of religious liberty and separation of church and state result in the removal of all activities that may be interpreted as "sectarian." In that process "nonreligious" philosophies become dominant. In avoiding the dogmatic positions of specific religious groups, or even of traditional Protestant or Catholic Christianity, another ideology is moved into the position of prominence. As George A. Petak Jr., a member of the Board of Education of the Racine, Wisconsin, Unified School District, expressed it during a textbook controversy in the community,

> Without clearly defined standards in all areas, the [educational] "system" in which we are raising our children makes no sense. Moral relativism and situational ethics leave these "clearly defined standards" totally out of the picture. The philosophy of "sometimes right, sometimes wrong" has become a part of our system in crucial areas. If children are allowed to believe that life has no rules, or if those rules have been eroded or neutralized by situational ethics, then the entire educational system will see its demise. . . . Values do exist! Values can and should be taught! (Petak, 1981).

Petak also affirmed that the Bible is the origin of most of the conventional values of society, but its values have been "eroded, compromised, and, in many cases, set aside."

Much of the thinking of key leaders in all areas of activity has been shaped directly or indirectly by higher education. Secular orientations dominate nearly all the academic disciplines, including professional studies. The natural sciences are based upon empirical observation—studying their subject matter through the use of the human senses. What is not observable occasionally enters their domain through influences and logical interpretations, but generally matters that pertain to the human spirit are ignored. It is easy to slip into the fallacies of logical positivism as a result—to believe that only those things that are empirically observable are "real."

Such modes of thought dominate the social sciences and often the humanities as well. A strongly secularistic emphasis prevails in the widespread orientations of determinism, behaviorism, and empiricism, as well as in the relativism and reductionism that are inevitable in dealing with the complexities of human life. These tend to treat human beings as mechanisms or other objects and to deny their capacity for self-determination (see Myers, 1978). Assumptions about human nature, the evolution and relativity of social values, the origin of world religions, and similar topics are often contrary to biblical views.

In the name of objectivity and neutrality textbook authors pass along many personal value judgments to students. Classroom instruction is strongly colored by the values of professors and other teachers, even when they are not aware of any biases. They often hold their values so unconsciously that they believe their hidden assumptions are "truth." (Many of these issues are dealt with in Armerding, 1968, and in Bube, 1068.) For example, a sociologist who has accepted metaphysical assumptions in the discipline that are antithetical to those of Christianity may erect sociology to the status of a world view.

> Once equipped with the "sociological imagination," it is extremely difficult to remember how one saw the world previous to sociological enlightenment. It is often presented very convincingly as a total explanation of the way society functions, and, moreover, why it functions in a particular way (Lyon, 1975:19-20).

This is one of the reasons why social and behavioral science research on the quality of life has almost completely ignored religion as a relevant variable (Moberg and Brusek, 1978). Similarly, the research literature and educational materials on relationships between religion and mental health sometimes refer to the role of Christianity as a source of guilt feelings, mental illness, and other problems. Outside of the domain of pastoral psychology and clinical pastoral education, they seldom even so much as mention that religious faith can be an element of therapy to help overcome depression, alleviate stress, promote mental health, prevent illness, and contribute to wholistic well-being.

Behind the optimism of secular humanism lies a failure to deal with the reality of death. Faith is placed in human powers for evolutionary self-development. There is an "expectation that men themselves are self-creative, and that God as the creator, the giver, the beginning and the end, as the Limit to human aspiration, has been replaced by man" (Smith, 1969:146). Along with other Scriptures, the book of Ecclesiastes in the Bible provides a corrective for such thinking. It deals with the "fatal weakness of secularist utopianism, . . . that it takes insufficient account of the twin facts of evil and death" (Hendry, 1954:538). The ultimate issue, however, resides in the denial of God, making people instead of God the absolute center of reality.

Most Christians in the human science disciplines have been trained under the impact of secular values. They may recognize that no school of thought is fully consistent with their faith commitment, yet they do not wish to be "excommunicated" by the academic community. As a result, they accept either an eclecticism that blends several views, or they align themselves with one of the prevailing traditions "with a postscript 'I'm a Christian too' attached. The next step is to reinterpret the Christian faith to provide a rationale for this situation. . . . One concession leads to another" (Russell, 1975:38).

Secularism has invaded many churches as well. Theological perspectives have been adjusted to fit the agnostic molds of rationalism and empiricism. Religion itself is treated by many as a human product that evolved without any ultimate authority out of the social experiences of people. Desacralized views also have emerged from an uncritical adoption of ideas from theorists like Freud and Marx. In both Catholicism and Protestantism theologies have been secularized to

> take the supernatural out of Christianity. These views eliminate redemption and need for a genuine conversion to the Lord and replace all this with a secular humanism. . . . One reason for the decline of the liberal churches is that secularist theology takes the heart out of Christianity, leaving nothing distinctive or compelling about it (Clark, 1982:27).

Religious education likewise

> has been heavily influenced by secular theories in education and psychology. The foundations of those theories leave no room for the supernatural, for the possibility of a genuine divine revelation. By their very nature they can have no other referents than secular ones. Thus to allow such theories to determine the nature of religious

education is automatically to rule out whatever cannot be fitted into the secular procrustean bed (Hitchcock, 1984:12).

Much pastoral work to counsel people and give them spiritual direction aims chiefly to make them feel good about themselves, come to terms with their feelings, and "live comfortable, essentially worldly lives, with no sense of guilt" (Hitchcock, 1984:12). This enhances their inclination to resist any supernatural religion that claims authority on the basis of divine revelation. It encourages them to resist every call to duty, self-discipline, repentance, and self-sacrifice. They prefer the idea that they can "find God in all sorts of worldly experiences, because it relieves them of the responsibility of really seeking him" (Hitchcock, 1984:13).

Under the impact of such thinking, Christianity is easily reduced to the level of an inward feeling. Its expression is seen as relevant to private conduct, not to the integration of society. People turn inwardly. In a culture dominated by a practical atheism that ignores God in everyday affairs, there may be nowhere else to turn. Yet even there the spiritual person can recognize a transcendent dimension, suspend assumptions that are not questioned in the larger society, and adopt a selfless approach of seeking the well-being of others (see Dupré, 1983).

Often secularization within religious groups comes by doing good. Convicted of the sinfulness of being unconcerned about those who are poor, widowed, mentally ill, in prison, victims of racism or ageism or sexism, suffering from institutionalized forms of injustice, lonely, or needy in other ways, they have established programs and projects to serve such needs. When all their efforts are thrown into such ministries, they may forget their responsibility to go beyond the material level, for "Man does not live on bread alone" (Deut. 8:3; Matt. 4:4; Luke 4:4). Christians must also meet other human needs, such as those for redemption and Christian education to nurture spiritual well-being.

> The Christian message is watered down into a concern about the injustices of the world, a commitment to peace, being at the service of others, and so on. With definitions like these, one does not really have to be a Christian in order to be Christian. Indeed, a pagan might be living a good Christian life (Clark, 1982:27).

The secular mentality has flowed, in large part, from the individualism, reductionism, and relativism that pervade modern pluralistic society. Harry Blamires (1981) discussed this in his lecture series on ten campuses of the Christian College Coalition:

> Our secular society has constructed . . . prescriptions for all branches of human behavior and enterprise which are rooted in naturalistic thinking in the assumption that cause and purpose, value and

meaning can all be exhaustively expressed in terms of humanistic and materialistic notions of well-being. This is the problem of our day, and acutely the problem of officially Christian institutions.

He indicated that it is impossible to carry over into the sphere of Christian thought and action the criteria, values, and verbal equipment that were

. . . specially devised to contain the facts of human destiny and the meaning of life within the framework of time-locked materialism. For there's no Christian statement about any fundamental issue of meaning or purpose that can be adequately articulated without explicit or implicit reference to a state of being beyond time which secularism ignores.

At the core of much secularism is an emphasis upon human reason as the ultimate criterion of truth, justice, morality, and other values. For over two centuries the autonomy of human reason has replaced earlier sacred bonds with empirical and matter-of-fact analyses of possibilities inherently present in the immediate situation. Traditional views have been cast off. Every doctrine has been subjected to rational criticism. When past perspectives, including those of the Scriptures, do not fit the level of present knowledge and understanding, they have been revised or thrown away (see, Smith, 1969:144-147). In effect, humanity has deified itself.

The ideology of rationalism holds that reason is a source of knowledge superior to revelation, tradition, and all other competitors. It inclines people toward quantifying human qualities. Rationalism produces a mind that is "intolerant of moral passion, of strong affective expression, or of spiritual vision" (Westerhof, 1980).

As long as pluralism prevails, there will be diverse perspectives on the findings and conclusions that result from the application of human reason. The question that arises among those who consider following that false god is who is correct. Past history is no comfort, for it demonstrates the falseness of many dogmas once held as firm, irrevocable truth. Victory in power struggles, whether fought with guns or educational propaganda, does not guarantee that ultimate truth has been attained. The relativity of every person's point of view, the inevitability of conflict and compromise, and the destructive misuse of human beings are among the legacies of secularization.

HUMANISM

Secularism is such a complex subject that a basic warning must be sounded: Those who discuss secularism and the secularization process do not always refer to the same thing. Not even the scholars agree on their definitions. "Historians and social scientists find it hard to agree on what secularization has been in the past and on what it is today—let alone on what its future course will be" (Berger, 1979:188; see also Fenn, 1978; Childress and Harned, 1970; Glasner, 1977; Robertson, 1974). One therefore must discern carefully which definitions are used. At the extreme, one person's definition of secularization may actually represent another's definition of increasing sacralization (Moberg, 1984a: 63-64).

One aspect of this is the tendency to forget that there are many varieties of humanism. Humanists like Thomas Jefferson played a significant role in founding the nation and establishing the religious liberty that is enjoyed in the USA. Earlier humanism was a major factor in the movement away from the "Dark Ages" of intellectual bondage to an autocratic ecclesiastical system through the Renaissance, Reformation, and Enlightenment. Even the King James Version of the Bible has a humanist heritage (Stagg, 1982).

Both the American Humanist Association on the left and fundamentalist Christians on the right tend to use the words *humanism* and *humanist* without any qualifiers when they refer to "naturalistic," "secular," or "atheistic" humanism. Lamont (1965) distinguishes between several types but ignores Christian humanism in his emphasis upon the naturalistic variety:

> . . . Humanism, in its most accurate philosophical sense, implies a world-view in which Nature is everything, in which there is no supernatural and in which man is an integral part of Nature and not separated from it by any sharp cleavage or discontinuity (p. 22).

His study of the philosophy of humanism reveals strong negative attitudes toward Christianity. He emphasizes "that in any case the supernatural, usually conceived of in the form of heavenly gods or immortal heavens, does not exist" (Lamont, 1965:14).

The first Humanist Manifesto issued in 1933 referred to its position as "Religious Humanism," but it also argued that "the time has passed for theism." It held that "the old attitudes involved in worship and prayer" should be replaced by "a heightened sense of personal life and . . . a cooperative effort to promote social well-being." Then "there will be no uniquely religious emotions and attitudes of the kind hitherto associated with belief in the supernatural" (Lamont, 1965:285-289).

Humanist Manifesto II, "A Secular Humanist Declaration" (Kurtz, 1980; "Philosophy," 1980), which has been signed by many educational, scientific, and social leaders, was even more blunt in its atheistic and antisupernatural statements. It is probably the best summary of the philosophy of secular humanism that pervades much of the public life of the USA. The Manifesto emphasizes a trust in human intelligence rather than divine guidance and rejects the divinity (to say nothing of the deity!) of Jesus Christ. It denies traditional concepts of God, warns that dogmatic religion is threatening intellectual freedom, declares that there are no moral absolutes, and suggests that people who are religious are deviants.

Affirmations like these have aroused the fears and rhetoric of many Christians, even though they may agree with some of the accompanying statements about the dignity and worth of individuals (Rouster, 1981; Schaeffer, 1981). Under the impact of the rank atheistic statements of secular humanists, Christians are tempted to overreact with negative caricatures and rhetoric. They too easily forget that concern for human dignity and well-being is part of their own scriptural mandate (Moberg, 1982; see Burton, 1982).

If such truly were the only humanist position, all Christians would oppose it. There is, however, a long and venerable history of Christian humanism dating back to biblical times. Based upon the gospel of Jesus Christ as its primary source, it has not been a separate, structured historical movement. Instead it has gently directed the light of Christ to the issues of what it means to be human.

Christian humanism is concerned with enhancing human existence, dignity, well-being, and fulfillment (Shaw et al., 1982; see West, 1970:123-128; Christian Life Commission, 1982). Although its concerns are "secular" in the sense of pertaining to life on earth in time, not just a future eternity, it can usually be distinguished sharply from the agnostic and atheistic varieties known as "secular humanism."

There is considerable agreement among Christian and secular humanists on many goals and objectives of enhancing the total well-being of humans, as long as these values are kept at a high level of abstraction. "The difficulties begin when we descend to earth and apply deductions from those values" (Hawton 1972:116). Concrete measures to fight injustice and decrease misery are often quite different when it comes to such means as abortions, divorce, euthanasia, artificial insemination, biological engineering, and, among Catholics, contraception.

Failure to recognize the distinctions between various kinds of humanism as well as to discern the long-range implications of some of their actions has led many on the "Religious Right" to sanction positions and perspectives that essentially are those of the atheistic secularists (Fackre, 1982).

Humanism has never been monolithic, always diverse. It includes atheists, agnostics, deists, theists, Jews, Christians, and others. All humanists are prohuman, affirming the worth, potential, responsibility, and freedom due every person. Where humanists most significantly differ is with respect to the transcendent. All humanists affirm the secular; some affirm the transcendent and some do not. All affirm responsibility; some see us as here alone and some see us as having help from God. For all humanists, freedom is nonnegotiable. . . .

It is an irony that the religious right which caricatures "secular humanism" as "the most dangerous religion in America" is itself a dangerous religion and is itself secular in trying to use political clout to impose religious dogma upon a pluralistic society. Not only is secular humanism caricatured and all humanism falsified, but such civil religion threatens both political and religious freedom. . . . freedom ends whenever any religion, philosophy, or ideology is permitted to become the custodian of knowledge (Stagg, 1982:4,5).

CHRISTIAN RESPONSES

A lack of wholistic balance lies behind the problems of relativism, reductionism, secularism, and humanism that pose problems for many Christians in the world today. In the case of relativism and reductionism, portions of the realities of the complex universe are taken as if they were the whole. Observed variations in the ethical and moral adjustments that people have made are interpreted as if they prove that anything whatever is right because some group somewhere has treated it as such. It must be remembered that

> while there is no question of relativity when individual traits are taken out of the cultural context and studied comparatively, these same traits do in actual fact generally have "absolutist" functions within the cultural whole from which they have been abstracted. Thus while, for example, the attitudes toward sex can vary greatly from society to society, each group nevertheless has a definition of what is immoral. In this way, undergirding the diversity there are in each culture some "absolutes" which are often readily translatable into Christian precepts (Loewen, 1972:138; see Moberg, 1962).

The fact of cultural relativism must not be confused with moral relativism as an ideal to guide human conduct. A biblical form of relativism is reflected in the divergent patterns of behavior that were allowed at various stages of the history recorded in the Bible. God gave many wives to King David (2 Sam. 12:8), implicitly permitted prostitution (Gen. 38:11-26; Hosea 1:2), and allowed for easy divorce in the

Mosaic code (Deut. 24:1-4). Henotheism, which acknowledges the existence of many gods, is a common perspective in the Old Testament (Exod. 12:12; 23:24,32; Deut. 10:17; 12:30-31; Psa. 95:3; 135:5; Zeph. 2:11; etc.). Slavery was not directly condemned and seems to be sustained by Paul's letter to Philemon. Variations in moral rules are reflected in the principle given in Romans 2:14-16 that those who lack the law will be judged by the rules and requirements written "by nature" into their own consciences. The Apostle Paul also adapted some of his own conduct to fit the social and cultural context of the people with whom he found himself (1 Cor. 9:19-23).

Instead of living by rigid, legalistic rules, Christians are under the flexible "royal law" of love (Matt. 22:35-40; Mark 12:28-31; James 2:8-13; 1 John 4:7-21; etc.). It is always practiced within a social context of relationships to God, self, and others.

Numerous recommendations and requirements for pleasing God are given in the Bible. It is easy to treat one's interpretations of some of these as if they were the norm itself (Prov. 21:2). Every group of people, including Christian churches and sects, tends to treat its own ways ethnocentrically as if they are the only ones that are normal and correct. All tend to judge others as peculiar, immoral, or sinful. That some people behave differently from us does not necessarily mean that they are wrong. Indeed, they may be right and we may be wrong.

Setting up absolute rules in domains of doubt is one form of idolatry. It displaces the one true Absolute, Almighty God, with one's own absolutes.

Reductionism is a form of the "beam in the eye" that is created when we focus so strongly upon some particular aspect of reality that we believe it constitutes or explains everything else. We must always remember that we now know only in part; we see but a poor reflection of total reality (1 Cor. 13:9, 12).

Secularism is a dominant theme of most public life in the USA, but it is tempered by humanistic values that, at least in outline form, owe their derivation to Christianity. Christian love for the neighbor, stewardship of all possessions, and other values overlap with the related goals of many secular humanists.

However much Christians and other humanists share, there is at least one major area of significant difference in their service to people. Both emphasize what "a good man or woman" should do in any given case, but Christians add the issue of what one ought to do as a Christian (Blamires, 1980: 33-67). They have the "double vision" of seeing human beings both in nature and under God. Christians are rooted in both the physical universe that will crumble and the kingdom that is not of this world. Therefore even when they use the same words as those of the secularists, there are often significant differences in meaning.

Important distinctions are also present in underlying ideologies and interpretations of reality. Even when engaging in similar behavior, Christians are different. In a secular society it is especially important to recall emphatically those aspects of faith that non-Christians do not share.

> And at the present time the Christian doctrine of man, the Christian view of his nature, his vocation, and his destiny, is so alien to prevalent thinking in the spheres of public affairs and educational pursuits that it is the last thing Christians can afford to be forgetful of in their confrontation with others. Ours is no longer a world where the supernatural basis of things natural is generally allowed for (Blamires, 1980: 65).

Aleksandr Solzhenitsyn's address upon receiving the Templeton Prize for Progress in Religion (1984) called attention to the trampling of spiritual and moral realities in the West. It is equivalent, though occurring in a different way, to the "leveling of mankind unto death" in the antireligious materialism of Eastern Europe. People and their material needs have been worshiped, while spiritual values are ignored as if human life had no higher meaning.

Outler (1981) similarly believes that radical secularism's rejection of the sacred and deification of the human has paradoxically resulted in the loss of the truly human. The upsurge of human self-sufficiency has been followed by many consequences. These include the separation of divine law from civil law, devastating effects in the realm of social control, broken families, unsatisfying marriages, and a plethora of self-centered substitutes for the sacred. Among those substitutes are the cult of positive thinking, reliance on psychological nostrums for "success," and secular supernaturalisms such as astrology, Eastern mysticism, new forms of sorcery, and parapsychology, all of which make false promises similar to those made to Adam and Eve in the Garden (Gen. 3:4). Only through recovery of the full richness of the sacred order as described in Romans 8 can we again truly live (Outler, 1981: 92-93). People liberated by the Holy Spirit will live "in the Spirit" because the Spirit dwells within them.

Christians therefore need to stand firm in their faith, putting on the armor of God and using the weapons of the Spirit in their struggle against rulers and authorities, powers of darkness, and spiritual forces of evil (Eph. 6:10-18). Otherwise they will be easily drawn into modes of thought and action that compromise their faith, or they will make only negative responses to the challenges of a secular society and thus miss many of the opportunities for effective service and witness in a society that is frustrated by the consequences of secularism.

There is, of course, evidence that society in our nation remains very religious. There are numerous indications that we have a civil folk religion: coins and currency that declare "In God we trust," place names that remind us of religious persons and events, life cycle rituals such as weddings and funerals that are usually celebrated in a religious context, the calendar years counted from the presumptive birth date of Jesus Christ, the words "one nation under God" in the Pledge of Allegiance to the Flag, and appeals to God and religion in presidential speeches and election campaigns. Public opinion polls reveal high levels of belief in God, the Bible, and Jesus Christ, confidence in religious leaders, the born-again experience, attendance at religious services, and other indications that ours is a very "religious" population (Gallup, 1981). Although the bestseller lists of the *New York Times* and similar literary publications ignore most religious books, sales for them have risen steadily for several years. Religious titles have outsold the highest of the alleged best sellers (Rifkin and Howard, 1979). Compared to most other nations by almost any measure of beliefs or practice, the United States is a highly religious nation (Gallup, 1976).

Fichter (1961) has warned against glib interpretations of our society as "secular." Its value system includes religious values with a genuine "trust in God." Materialism is offset by generosity, humanitarianism, sympathy for the underdog, and social movements that have improved the status and aspirations of all minority groups. Hence "while the American value-system is secular, it is by no means profane" (p. 141).

The facts lead to Greeley's (1979: 212) conclusion that there is no evidence of secularization, at least not in terms of the criteria of belief in survival, experience of the sacred, or praying to the Ultimate, in terms of any past that can be measured through survey data. Basic religious needs and functions have not changed significantly, Greeley (1972:1) believes, "since the late Ice Age; what changes have occurred make religious questions more critical rather than less critical in the contemporary world."

Orientations to Jesus Christ lie behind much of this issue. Whether we as believers affirm Christ at the expense of the world or as secularists affirm the world at the expense of Christ, we are equally in error.

> Christ was the truly secular man. . . . In his life there does not appear the theological abstraction of a double world, the world of nature and the world of supernature, or the appreciation of a sacred and a profane order of life. . . . the substance of Christian faith is its confidence in

the paradoxical unity of historical facts and eschatological reality. This message does not lead away from the world, but right into it (Smith, 1969:151,153).

Wholistic Christianity overcomes the temptation to slip into the fallacies of ethical, moral, and religious relativism. It recognizes the finite nature of the human condition and therefore does not fall prey to the pride of any reductionism that claims "all" knowledge. Rather than succumbing directly or indirectly to secular humanism, it sustains truly biblical and wholistic humanistic values. It is concerned with both the heavenly and the secular or earthly aspects of Christian beliefs and behavior. Centered upon Jesus Christ, it demonstrates the Christ-like virtues of love, humility, faith, and justice to all humanity, not only to those in the household of faith. It lives with the blessed hope that all creation eventually will be "liberated from its bondage to decay and brought into the glorious freedom of the children of God" (Rom. 8:21 NIV).

4

THE PRESSURES OF CULTURAL VALUES

We have already seen that several important social values press upon all who are a part of modern civilization. Individualism, freedom, religious pluralism, ethical and moral relativism, reductionism, secularism, and humanism belong to a complex network of values.

Several other elements also belong to it. For example, hedonism, the pursuit of pleasure, directs the lives and consumes the resources of a significant proportion of the population. Likewise widespread is chauvinism, the nationalistic spirit that views our nation as the military savior of the world and the exemplar of an ideal political and economic system that every nation on earth ought to adopt. (For elaboration of some of these and other core values of US society, see Williams, 1960.)

Many commentators on the current situation treat these as if they are new developments. Historical examination, however, reveals that they have appeared repeatedly in the history of the human race in various combinations, forms, and patterns. They constitute "the past writ large," not reversals of past history. They have many consequences. It is possible that they are now approaching full fruition.

Some argue that these values enhance human dignity, promote personal freedom, and produce an open society in which maximum self-actualization is possible. Others point to the widespread incidence of personal and social problems, attributing them to the very same value orientations and accompanying characteristics of society.

We can be sure of one thing: The results of social changes and trends are always mixed. Seldom, if ever, are all of the consequences of any major change beneficial and wholesome for all of the individuals, groups, and institutions within a society, as well as for society as a whole. What helps one person or group is often harmful to another.

We also know that it is impossible to determine exactly which sets of values and practices have produced a specific effect. All the elements are simultaneously a part of the causes and consequences of all the others. Whether we are concerned with positive contributions to the well-being of people and society or negative indications of the suffering and malaise that people experience, we cannot separate out exactly how much of each is a result of any specific one of the supposed causes. The causes and effects are part of an intricate whole. Even with the best of our research methods, we can grasp with reasonable certainty only a part of the total web of cause-effect relationships.

To be sure, the social values we have discussed seem to have gained considerable strength in our society during this century. During the same period of time, family breakdown and divorce rates have multiplied. Depression and other mental illnesses are widespread. Racism, sexism, and ageism are still rife despite official actions against them. Poverty, unemployment, drug abuse, abortion, marital infidelity, cohabitation, violence, and other social problems are at very high levels in many communities. Numerous professional people are experiencing burnout. There is much fear among people in many communities. This in turn leads to "what seems like a national obsession for more and more security" against violence and crime (Baker, 1982). Prisons are expanded but are still too small to handle all the adjudicated criminals and the suspects awaiting trial.

Yet the fact that such trends occur at the same time as the social values we have discussed does not necessarily prove that either one is the cause of the other. Correlation is not causation.

Each of those social values can be examined from the perspective of its contributions to both the well-being and the problems of society. Such work requires evaluative criteria as a basis for judgment. In our free and open society several sets of conflicting values that compete for dominance are implicated in any appraisal. Among these is the denial or acknowledgment of sin and evil. Another is the negative consequences of extreme forms of personal liberty.

COMPETING VALUES

In our society of extravagant expectations there is sometimes considerable tension between competing and often contradictory values:

> We expect anything and everything. We expect the contradictory and the impossible. We expect compact cars which are spacious, luxury cars which are economical. We expect to be rich and charitable, powerful and merciful, active and reflective, kind and competitive. We expect to be inspired by mediocre appeals for "excellence," to be made literate by illiterate appeals for literacy. We expect to eat and stay thin, to be constantly on the move and ever more neighborly, to

go to a "church of our choice" and yet feel its guiding power over us, to revere God and to be God (Boorstin, 1977:4).

Similarly, as McKenna (1980:5) points out, we live in a capitalistic system that is founded upon the puritan ethic of discipline and thrift. Yet, under the impact of modern advertising and "stimulating the economy," it encourages hedonism and extravagance (see Bell, 1976). There is a collision course between competing sets of values. The basic struggle "is not so much with external villains or forces as . . . with our own ambivalent values and commitments" (McKenna, 1980:5). We shift the blame at our own convenience. We point ever toward others as the alleged causes of our woes. We use them as scapegoats to project responsibility for misdeeds away from ourselves.

The dominant intellectual environment does not alleviate the situation. Its secular materialism, relativism, reductionism, syncretistic philosophy that eliminates the search for ultimate truth, and other features lead to "a confusion of twisted tensions." Individuals hence

. . . find themselves overcome by the meaninglessness of life. . . . The theological alienation of man from God is compounded by the ethical alienation of man from man, by the psychological alienation of man from himself and by the ecological alienation of man from nature (Brom, 1982:5).

Rapid change and mass communications produce a flood of imagery. These confuse so many people that Lifton (1970:319) has argued that modern man has adopted a "protean style of self-process." This is "characterized by an interminable series of experiments and explorations—some shallow, some profound—each of which may be readily abandoned in favor of still newer psychological quests." Many of our contemporaries are like Proteus, the Greek sea god who could change his shape at will in order to protect himself. They find it easy to change their principles and practices, yet difficult to cope with the dilemmas aroused by their own internalized but competing values. They also find it hard to deal with their relationships to other people whose views are similarly shifting and often internally inconsistent.

People continue to hunger for the satisfaction of their quest for meaning, which ultimately relates to their eternal destiny. They yearn for an identity that goes beyond a position and job title, as well as for a community that provides them with fellowship, social support, and security. When they fail to find "the answers" in more conventional channels, some overthrow old commitments. Their underlying "ideological hunger" may lead them into new religious movements (Balch and Taylor, 1978:52), or they may be enticed into pseudoreligious political, therapeutic, or action-oriented movements.

One of the most significant of these is Marxism. It appeals to many in all parts of the world. Ethically sensitive people who react against the individualism and ethical failures of the Christianity they observe are especially enticed to it. That undoubtedly is one reason for the deep penetration of Marxist perspectives into the various social sciences (Ollman and Vernoff, 1982). Seeing numerous evidences of alienation, oppression of minorities, suffering of the poor, and the idolatry of greed in capitalist society, they are attracted to the ideals of Marxist philosophy. Human beings are viewed as self-consciously and creatively expressing themselves in cooperation and community with others. They shape their own humanness through their work and social relations.

> What Marx wants is not simply political reform, but the fundamental transformation of human nature, the creation of the new man, a profoundly religious ideal. Marx's vision of the classless society is a secularized version of the coming of the kingdom of God on earth, or, we should say, the coming of the kingdom of man (Evans, 1984: 148).

This sustaining vision of Marx has inspired many of the competing camps in Marxism, which often functions psychologically as a religion. Much of its criticism of capitalism and many of its other elements have sprung from the roots of Christian values.

Liberation theologians especially have noted the ways in which they believe a rapprochement can be attained between Marxism and Christianity (Evans, 1984; see Lyon, 1981). Others, however, point to inherent contradictions and inconsistencies that make this impossible (see Bockmuehl, 1980: 109-167).

The wide range of therapies and "holistic health" cults that are parts of the human potential movement attract thousands of people who search for identity and meaning. Some searchers shift from one local church or denomination to another as they seek to satisfy cravings they themselves do not fully understand. Others drift into and out of various new religious movements and cults.

The range of available values to incorporate into one's world view and philosophy of life hence is very wide. It includes political, economic, nationalistic, psychological, sociological, and other options, in addition to countless possibilities in the area of religion. Modern society is clearly one with competing values. Among the clashing perspectives are diverse orientations toward sin.

THE DENIAL OF SIN

Sin is an important theological word. Yet it has gone out of favor in contemporary society, in part because of past overuse and abuse of the concept. Today people may slip, make a mistake, miscalculate, or be misled, but few acknowledge that they sin. In some churches the word sin is used only in creeds or liturgies that must be repeated to maintain the tradition. To use it in sermon or song might embarrass people who believe they are "enlightened" about the "true" nature of human frailties.

Much sociology "is an examination of the effects of sin on society" (Lyon, 1975: 65), but sociologists, like psychologists and others in the human sciences, avoid the use of the word sin. Only on rare occasions do they refer to the ideas people have about whatever they label as sin or to the guilt some feel as a result of it (see Menninger, 1973).

There are several reasons for this omission. The concept is ultimately theological, having to do with transgressions against God, who cannot be studied directly. It is grounded in religious dogma and documents like the Bible and is outside the domain of typical empirical observations. There are significant cultural variations in its definitions, so sin can be seen as a relative term that has little or no use in scientific research. The virtues of one group can be the vices or sins of another.

It is very difficult to designate precisely which sins and sinners are at fault in producing the complex problems of modern society. This is so because of the alienation that characterizes social relationships, the collective nature of guilt and pride, and the atomization of society that splinters it into minute competitive units and passes the blame to someone else.

The inherent selfishness of "natural man" is attested to by the Scriptures, but it also is demonstrated through psychological research (Myers, 1978: 47-50; 249-262). Immediate self-interest is pitted against the common good. Individuals pursue selfish behavior even when it is to their collective detriment.

Hardin's (1968) tragedy of the commons is enacted repeatedly in numerous domains of life: The meadow used by a hundred farmers to feed a hundred cows is used to capacity. But any one of the farmers may reason that he'll double his own production by adding one more cow. A mere one percent increase in the meadow is negligible and will do no harm. Applying his cost-benefit formula, he adds a second cow. But so also do the other farmers. The meadow then is tragically overcrowded, and all suffer.

Thus in environmental pollution, each polluter gains more from added "small" pollutions than he or she loses from pollution costs that are shared by the entire society. Exploiters deplete natural resources at great gain but to the collective detriment of society. In numerous other areas of life individuals and small groups selfishly gain much for themselves, while indirect costs and delayed detrimental consequences are distributed among all. Selfishness, which is a sin, rather than altruism, a virtue, characterizes the human race.

What is more, we deceive ourselves by hiding self-interest "behind our sense of superiority, or under the veneer of social graces, 'moral principles,' and religion" (Myers, 1978: 48). We also manage to cover personal greed by joining others and greedily but honorably striving for "the best interests" of our particular group. Democratic governments and capitalistic economies are based upon the principle that each person will seek his or her highest self-interest in a rational decision-making process. Marxist appeals similarly are to self-interest, even though many of the rewards promised are deferred to an indefinite time in the future.

Nevertheless, every society recognizes that controls are necessary. Self-seeking is limited to legal channels; burglary, theft, extortion, stuffing the ballot box, underhanded pressures on voting behavior, and violence are criminal behavior. In addition, our social policies insist that sharing is an essential aspect of the duties of citizens.

> Taxation and public welfare systems are rooted in a realistic distrust of the magnitude of voluntary generosity. No one who would completely do away with this system takes original sin seriously. The primacy of selfishness provides the driving force behind the great success of modern capitalism, but it also reminds us of the need for its control (Myers, 1978: 50).

It is much easier to see the sins of others than to notice one's own. Sin is not exclusively the acts of individuals. Self-deceit is itself a sin. It is especially difficult to discern our own sinfulness when it occurs in the context of honorable customs, institutional settings, and habits.

> There has been a division of labor in sin as well as in virtue, and each person can now point an accusatory finger toward others or toward a faceless massive monolith—the corporate structure of modern society. It is precisely in the recognition of division, corporatism, and neutrality that sin has reached its greatest heights. For modern sin is peculiarly nonhuman in its use of things and exploitative in its use of men (Lyman, 1978: 4).

It is true that great corporate automatons have become the masters of people. In effect, they have appropriated and neutralized the concept of sin and liberated people from their obligations to one another. Yet the seven deadly sins still are on a "soul-destroying journey" as each appears under many masks. The sociology of evil "ought to display it in terms of a great theater of human activities, a drama of social reality that is part of a sociology of the absurd" (Lyman, 1978: 4). Psychiatrist Peck (1983) believes that evil should be defined as a specific form of mental illness and dealt with like other psychiatric disorders. It seeks to kill life or liveliness. The word is itself "live" spelled backwards. Its existence is easier to explain, he believes, than that of goodness.

Myers (1982) sees numerous evidences that most people in the USA have been taking "an ego joy-ride" in recent years. We accept responsibility more readily for success than for failure. We attribute success to our own ability and effort but claim that failure is the result of bad luck or other external factors. We bias our self-ratings in an above-average direction and overestimate the rightness of how we would act under certain conditions, assuming only others could ever be cruel. We justify ourselves even when engaging in shady business dealings. Believing in our personal infallibility, we have an unrealistic optimism about future life events. We slip into the worst sin of all—playing God. Then when unemployment or other disappointment comes, we easily flip from the self-delusion of a superiority complex to that of self-disparagement and an inferiority complex.

To catalog the evidence of the numerous types of sinfulness that are found in modern society would be a huge task. Violations of all of the Ten Commandments would be included. So, too, would be a wide range of instances of the Seven Deadly Sins—anger, covetousness, envy, gluttony, lust, pride, and sloth. The summaries could include statistical data on crimes and delinquencies; survey research findings on various forms of sexual immorality; information about cheating in business, industry, schools, social agencies, and other contexts; indirect evidences of wrongdoing, like venereal disease and broken families; and numerous other categories.

A major category of modern sins would be the various forms of idolatry by which some ultimate concern other than God is made an object of worship. It may be worshiped privately, as by individuals who make sex, money, power, family, or some other goal their reason for living. It may be worshiped collectively, as in the nationalistic spirit that makes "the American way of life" the dominant value orientation and the nation infallible.

> When idolatry infects the people of God, it does so by denying its nature. An idol does not boldly present itself as an alternative to faithfulness towards God. Instead it sets itself up as *an aspect of faithfulness*. Loyalty to the idol is portrayed as a vital dimension of obedience to the Lord (Watts, 1984: 13).

The permanent source of temptation to idolatry is in what Hamilton (1973) has called "the idolatrous imagination." He bases this upon the phrase, "the imagination of men's hearts," which appears in many passages of the King James Version of the Bible (Gen. 6:21; Deut. 29:19;

1 Chr. 28:9; Prov. 6:18; Jer. 23:17; Luke 1:51). While it may take several forms,

> The modern idolatrous imagination still refuses to believe that the promises of the living God are sure and that his grace is sufficient for all our needs. It still looks to other powers and other authorities for support and guidance, transferring to them what belongs to the Creator alone (Hamilton, 1973: 41).

In numerous ways, ours is "a society that celebrates sin": The news media are quick to report the details of sensational instances of sex-related crimes and other events that deviate from conventional mores.

> . . . sins are often reported in full detail, then glamorized and finally made highly profitable. Our society continues to reject biblical virtues and to exalt, even reward, sin. Is it really so hard to understand, then, why crime, a most visible manifestation of sin, flourishes in our land? (Colson, 1981).

> Our society . . . possesses a legion of demons, which many of us fear. . . . Murders, family and sexual abuse, racism, political corruption, and war are only a small part of the legion. Demonic forces are real in our society, just as real as in the time of Jesus (Choy, 1981: 19).

This ought not to surprise us. Imperfection and sin characterize all humanity, even as the Bible declares (Psa. 53:2-3; Eccl. 7:20; Isa. 53:6; Rom. 3:23; Gal. 3:22; 1 John 1:8). Shortcomings, weaknesses, blunders, flaws, ruptured interpersonal relationships, goal displacement, conflict, disease, hypocrisy, and other consequences are a natural result of the human condition.

What is surprising, all too often, is that many Christians succumb to the same temptations as other people. They sometimes sugarcoat their rationalizations and excuses for sinfulness with biblical prooftexts and other justifications. They bless "the American way of life" as if it is ipso facto "*the* Christian way of life." In their pursuit of "success" evangelicals "do exegetical acrobatics to accommodate materialism into our theology of living. Will we ever fight this foe with the same fervor we use against evolution or immorality or abortion?" (Petersen, 1981: 5).

Richard Halverson (1982), chaplain of the U.S. Senate, has stated that conservative evangelicals are much more subtly infected with secularism and materialism than was true a quarter or half century ago. They tend to live for "the now" instead of maintaining an eternal frame of reference. They adopt the materialistic success orientation and criteria of society. They often allow tradition to become the basis for truth rather than the Bible. They accept pragmatic tests for the validity of their church work and give allegiance to an interpretation or a set of methods of evolving doctrine rather than to Jesus Christ. They are of the world, not simply in it.

THE TYRANNY OF LIBERTY

In these three chapters we have emphasized that liberty or freedom is a dominant theme in contemporary Western civilization. It is evident in the "free enterprise" or laissez faire philosophy that is the basis of the capitalistic economic system. It increasingly appears in the adjustments made in the economies of many socialistic societies such as China, Poland, Yugoslavia, and Hungary. It dominates the political life of democratic nations, at least as an ideal. It appears in the educational, welfare, mass communications, recreational, and entertainment institutions and wherever else competing alternative agencies to meet particular desires or needs are found. Laissez faire characterizes even the religious scene as churches, sects, cults, and parachurch organizations in every open society compete with each other for membership, financial support, attendance, and influence in society. People are free to go to the "religious marketplace" and choose whichever "product" or group seems most pleasing to them.

On the whole, the consequences of laissez-faire philosophy and practice are "the blessings of liberty." Opportunities for educational and occupational advancement are more open to people of all kinds than under any other major economic and political alternative devised to date. The relatively free flow of information stimulates invention, dissemination of new ideas and technology, and other innovative changes. Minority people and perspectives are protected. Religious bodies are autonomous and have equality under the law. There is freedom of worship and opportunity to share religious values and win converts. People are free to remain in the religious bodies of their parents or to change to any other religion or none. Personal choice is maximized in all domains of living.

People in the USA and other open societies rejoice in their freedom, for most of its results are what sociologists call manifest functional consequences. They are functional in the sense that they are beneficial to society as a whole, to its major social institutions, and to individual members. They are manifest in that they are deliberately planned, intentionally produced and sustained, and recognized by the participants.

Nevertheless, there also are latent dysfunctional consequences of almost every institutionalized practice, social structure, and activity.

These are latent in that they are unintended, unanticipated, concealed, or unrecognized. They are dysfunctional to whatever extent they are destructive, disintegrative, or harmful in some respect. They are the undesirable side effects of otherwise desirable practices. They are typically not anticipated when a change that is believed to be constructive is introduced. They are usually not noticed by the majority of the population. Their discovery is one of the goals of social science research and other critical analyses of society. Since they tend to be hidden, they will be the focus of attention in this section.

The latent dysfunctional consequences of liberty are evident on every hand. Moral and ethical relativism make it impossible for society at large to take firm positions on many current issues. There is freedom to indulge in the logical fallacies associated with reductionism, the tendency to treat some portion of reality as if it were the whole. Propaganda and publicity disseminate error as well as truth. No religious ideology can dominate society, so secularistic orientations take over in all public domains. Naturalistic secular humanism tends to become the operating religion of the body politic or society at large. Conflict prevails between competing sets of values in every area of public life.

Much of the drive for liberty has expressed itself in terms of desires to be free from various restraints rather than free for constructive action (Krass, 1973: 68). People have reacted against the prohibitions, limitations, and restrictions of society. In an ungrounded opinion stemming from relativism, narcissistic individualism, and privatism, they have thought that whatever feels good is good if it does no immediate, obvious harm to themselves or others. Offenses against the "public morality" that grew out of biblical values and centuries of human experiences were reclassified into "victimless crimes" and in many cases converted into legally protected behavior.

Substantial numbers of people are now raising questions about the indirect long-term consequences of some of those actions. They are beginning to realize that the wisdom gained through centuries of human experience with moral issues may still be valid in the modern world. Yet it may take decades of careful research in the human sciences to demonstrate which of the specific newly-established freedoms represent destructive behavior. Even then, those who make freedom a more important god than science in their idolatrous pantheon will find ways to qualify and negate the findings.

People in the USA pride themselves as citizens of "the land of the free and the home of the brave." Historically this has nurtured a "manifest destiny" philosophy that views the nation as a chosen people ordained by God to create a model society for the whole world to imitate. The nineteenth-century wars with Mexico and Spain were a part of the consequences. Periodic efforts have been made both directly and surreptitiously not only to protect democracy and the "American way of life," but also to export them to other nations.

Here in the United States, freedom has become an obsession. It's become not only our goal but our god. . . . The high value we put on individual freedom . . . has increasingly also been applied to the nation at large. We think it's our right to do what we want when we want—both individually and corporately. . . . In a strange twist of meanings, being "a free country" no longer means being a country of free people. It means being a country that's free to do what it wants in the world. And there's no greater freedom than the freedom to start a nuclear war. . . .

That kind of freedom is no virtue. . . . Far from being a Christian value—like freedom from oppression or freedom from economic exploitation—it's an anti-Christian one. It's grounded in arrogance, fertilized with greed, and bears only the empty fruit of self-idolatry (Olson, 1984: 13).

WORLDLY VALUES

Strong cultural pressures compel Christians to be conformed to worldly values. Sometimes they succumb to sinful practices and gloss them over with rationalizations to make them seem "Christ-like." More often, they are unaware of any sinfulness on their own part as they adhere to culturally approved behavior patterns. They need the revealing help of scholarly research that is joined with biblical values to discern unrighteousness and move toward more effective implementation of God's will.

Much of the difficulty and error associated with the issues we have discussed relates to our reaction only to parts of the total picture of social reality and our use of only selected portions of pertinent biblical values. A genuinely wholistic Christianity refuses to be conformed to worldly values. It emphasizes the importance of considering all biblical value orientations rather than lopsidedly choosing only abstracted portions of God's will. It aims to understand the entire context in which it works, not just the theological foundations.

In the following chapters we shall examine some of the ways in which Christians are torn between various dilemmas and paradoxes. Many legitimate alternatives divide their vision, deform their fellowships, detract from their witness, and dissipate their energies. They thus diminish the effectiveness of their service to God and humanity and demean their Lord.

PART III

THE CHRISTIAN RESPONSE

5

WAVERING BETWEEN OPINIONS

Christians are divided on almost every conceivable issue. Not only are there a variety of theological orientations cutting across hundreds of denominations and sects, but there are also diverse perspectives on the nature of the church and its rituals, organizational structures, and mission.

In addition, Christians sometimes assume that a specific issue, doctrinal emphasis, action program, or mission project for which they believe they have been given a "burden from the Lord" or the direction of Holy Spirit is the most important agenda item for all Christians. When others fail to share the same "vision," do not support it with finances or voluntary service, or even seem to oppose the efforts, they conclude that those brothers and sisters are sinning against Christ as traitors of the gospel or the kingdom of God.

There is a more rewarding and, I believe, a more biblical approach to the concerns that divide Christians. It is to focus upon those elements of truth that prevail on each side of their disagreements more than upon the errors.

There are, of course, some issues of basic commitment on which there absolutely can be only one truly Christian position. We are warned again and again in Scripture about the impossibility of worshiping both the Lord and idols, of serving two masters, of living for both God and money, of drinking the cup of the Lord and the cup of demons (for examples see 2 Kgs. 17:7-41; Matt. 6:24; Luke 16:13; 1 Cor. 10:21). We are cautioned about friendship with the world, which represents hatred toward God (Jas. 4:4). Even service of the right kind that is fainthearted or wavering displeases God; the doubleminded person is unstable and must purify both hands and heart (Jas. 1:6-8; 4:8). The indecisive or hesitant person who puts his hand to the plow but then looks back, still weighing the sacrifice it involves, is self-condemned (Luke 9:62).

Nevertheless, the choices that are available in most controversies among Christians are not simply and clearly between God and Satan nor between pure good and unmitigated evil. This is particularly true of the complex problems faced in everyday life. Whether the focus of attention is personal decisions, attempts to resolve social issues, political choices, or determining what action should be taken by a church, the alternatives usually are between a set of actions that can be viewed as a mixture of "good" and "bad" and one or more other sets that also can be viewed as "good" and "bad."

In personal life we may be attracted one day to the "good" of a particular choice and repulsed on the next by its "bad." In group decisions, some people give special attention to the "good" of one position and the "bad" of another, while others do the opposite. Often a position is chosen first and "reasons" for it only afterwards.

In other words, our choices usually are between varying mixtures of good and bad, seldom if ever between absolute purity and complete wickedness. The dilemmas associated with these problems have literally torn Christian groups apart. They have killed congregations and caused church splits and denominational schisms. Figuratively, they have torn individual persons apart as well, causing burnout, spiritual malaise, mental illness, psychosomatic ailments, dropping out of church, withdrawal from Christian service, and many other problems.

Some of the conflicts and differences of opinion among Christians are due to the different perspectives they have on the particular issues involved. Others reflect identification with a group that has taken a specific stand. Still others are an outgrowth of paradoxes that are found in the Christian Scriptures. Many reflect dilemmas imposed by living in the modern world that force most of us into dialectical modes of thought and action.

In this chapter we shall examine some of the issues related to the paradoxes that are found in the Bible as well as those that emerge from contemporary life. Use of a dialectical approach can help to resolve these problems, so several suggestions for action conclude the discussion.

A paradox basically involves the embracing of clashing ideas. Derived from the Greek *paradoxos*, it implies something that is unexpected, contrary to received opinion, or an apparent contradiction.

> . . . a paradox is an idea involving two opposing thoughts or propositions which, however contradictory, are equally necessary to convey a more imposing, illuminating, life-related or provocative insight into truth than either can muster in its own right. Now contradiction becomes articulate. What the mind seemingly cannot think it must think; what reason is reluctant to express it must express (Slaatte, 1982: 4, italics removed).

BIBLICAL PARADOXES

Many passages in the Bible seem to contradict each other or to be inconsistent with common sense. Yet orthodox Christian values see the Bible as the word of God, who knows all things and who cannot lie. Some of these are antinomies—principles that contradict each other directly or by inference, yet are equally true.

Some of the paradoxes pertain directly to Jesus Christ,

who, being in very nature God,
did not consider equality with God something to be grasped,
but made himself nothing,
taking the very nature of a servant,
being made in human likeness.
And being found in appearance as a man,
he humbled himself
and became obedient to death—
even death on a cross!
Therefore God exalted him to the highest place
and gave him the name that is above every name,
that at the name of Jesus every knee should bow,
in heaven and on earth and under the earth,
and every tongue confess that Jesus Christ is Lord,
to the glory of God the Father (Phil. 2:6-11 NIV).

Christ "was crucified in weakness, yet he lives by God's power." So too his followers "are weak in him, yet by God's power we will live with him to serve" others (2 Cor. 13.4 NIV). God helps us in our weakness, working in all things so that nothing can separate us from the love of Christ and making us more than conquerors through him who loved us (Rom. 8:26-39). "God chose the foolish things of the world to shame the wise; God chose the weak things of the world to shame the strong" (1 Cor. 1:27 NIV). Countless numbers of God's people found that their "weakness was turned to strength" (Heb. 11:34 NIV). God's power is made perfect in weakness (2 Cor. 12:7-10).

In describing himself and the others serving God with him, the Apostle Paul expressed a series of paradoxical contrasts. They were

genuine, yet regarded as impostors; known, yet regarded as unknown; dying, and yet we live on; beaten, and yet not killed; sorrowful, yet always rejoicing; poor, yet making many rich; having nothing, and yet possessing everything (2 Cor. 6:8-10 NIV).

Other paradoxical statements are found in Jesus' promise, "Whoever finds his life will lose it, and whoever loses his life for my sake will find it" (Matt. 10:39 NIV; see Matt. 16:25). While Christians are to "continue to work out [their] salvation with fear and trembling, . . . it is God who works in [them] to will and to act according to his good purpose" (Phil. 2:12-13 NIV). In Romans 10:14-21 and 11:25-32, as well as other passages, the interplay of God's work and ours is apparent. "Paul held fast at one and the same time to divine sovereignty and human responsibility. . . . first, everything is of God, and, second, everything is of human choice" (Barclay, 1957: 163, 153).

Christians are instructed to bear one another's burdens (Gal. 6:2), yet to carry their own load (Gal. 6:5) and to cast their care and anxieties on the Lord (Psa. 55:22; 1 Pet. 5:7). On the surface, the respective statements appear contradictory to each other. In fact, however, they complement each other and enrich the lives of all who heed their message.

Even some of the words of Jesus appear to contradict each other. On one occasion he said, "He who is not with me is against me, and he who does not gather with me scatters" (Matt. 12:30 NIV), but on another his words were that "whoever is not against us is for us" (Mark 9:40 NIV; see Luke 9:50). The social context determines whether inaction represents support for or opposition to Christ.

These samples of paradoxical passages help to make clear the fact that one can find different truths in Scripture, truths that may seem to conflict with others, through a selective process. Some "Bible-believing Christians" select and emphasize one part of biblical teaching, overlooking another that is equally valid, while other Christians select another part. While both positions seem biblically correct, both are incomplete as well.

Instead of selecting out only special passages for attention, we need to remember that "All Scripture is God-breathed and is useful for teaching, rebuking, correcting and training in righteousness, so that the man [and woman] of God may be thoroughly equipped for every good work" (2 Tim. 3:16-17 NIV).

By choosing only fragments of the Bible as our guide to twentieth-century living, we easily get sidetracked into secondary or tertiary issues and miss those that are the most important. A better alternative is to examine and apply biblical teachings in their totality, relating them to a realistic and accurate understanding of the concrete needs and specific contexts of people in contemporary society. This double-sided approach will greatly improve our efforts to serve them and thus enhance the kingdom of God.

PARADOXES IN MODERN LIFE

It is likely that the paradox has never before been used so widely and taken more seriously. It is not merely a clever scholar's invention. It is inherent in the problems of down-to-earth existence and perspectives, and it pertains to the basic problems and functions of human reason.

The tensions of both human thought and human action typically emerge in "either-or," "both-and," and "neither-nor" conclusions. The very fact that tensions exist implies something reciprocal about the contrasting positions. Hence

> . . . beneath most truth relevant to the individual of finite existence there is paradox, and that true paradox bespeaks a dialectical reciprocation of opposites without dissolving their polarity or distinctiveness. . . . Thus the paradox, like the tuning fork [of a musician], is more often than not a double-pronged idea, neither tine of which has the resolution, let alone description, of the tension, while both contribute to it (Slaatte, 1982:6).

Paradoxes, ambiguities, and dilemmas are evident in the oscillating pattern of much of Western society between passionate involvement in public issues and a preoccupation with private concerns. This in turn is related to questions about the relative stress upon collective and individual well-being and the associated hopes and disappointments that ebb and flow in the course of motivations and events (Hirschman, 1982).

Paradoxes are reflected in the psychological need to have the constraints of rules and guidelines in order to have personal freedom. They appear in the tensions between advocates of technological progress and champions of preindustrial smallness (see Florman, 1982, and Schumacher, 1973). They are demonstrated in the sophisticated knowledge of youth during the 1970s about computers, drugs, sex, and whoever were their current heroes while their educational test scores were falling to ever lower levels. They emerge from the unprecedented concurrence of inflation and economic stagnation. They are manifest in declining political allegiances even as key issues become ever more politicized. They are reflected in the increasing use of sophisticated models, scenarios, and computerized predictions of the future alongside of actual outcomes far removed from expectations.

> Our present is exploding with paradox. . . . Systematic research can teach us much. But in the end we must embrace—not dismiss— paradox and contradiction, hunch, imagination, and daring (though tentative) synthesis (Toffler, 1981: 128, 129).

In the tensions between alternative interpretations and actions there is a tendency to turn first one way and then, as disillusionment sets in, the other. Walter (1980: 179-184), for example, points out how the overconfident belief in the power of technology to bring universal prosperity led to counterattacks by the very ones whom one would expect to prosper most from technology, the affluent youth of the industrial world. They turned to nature, mysticism, and new religious movements to find the "salvation" that the old order had failed to deliver. Glorification of the individual led to power abuses by capitalists, who then had to be restrained by the state. Meanwhile in totalitarian countries the excessive power of the state provoked dissidents to praise the value of the individual.

In incident after incident the pattern is repeated. Idealized expectations are followed by disillusionment. New idols are set up which are

> believed to be the opposite of the discredited idol and therefore guaranteed to provide the salvation that the old one failed to deliver.
> . . .
> Thus the sacred comes in pairs, each component of a pair constantly firing salvoes at the other, and with dominance oscillating between them from one decade to another. The sacred always exists in conjunction with the profane (Walter, 1980: 179, 180).

THE DIALECTICAL APPROACH

The tensions between opposites that reflect the paradoxes of life and thought are the focus of dialectical analysis. Dialectic is "the art or practice of logical discussion as employed in investigating the truth of a theory or opinion" (Stein and Urdang, 1967:397). The concept is derived from Greek and Latin words that pertain to argumentation. It is related to *dialect*, a term that refers to the language, tongue, phraseology, jargon, or customary speech of an identifiable class or group of people. It therefore relates to conversing. Sometimes the dialectical discourse occurs within the mind of a person, sometimes between persons, and sometimes between groups such as ideological camps or political parties, to mention but a few possibilities. The process is at least as old as human history.

Every society has a variety of interests around which groups form. These groups compete with each other for resources and opportunities. The balance that results from their accommodation is threatened whenever new circumstances introduce strain.

Dialectical models of analysis of the interests, power struggles, and definitions of the situation, and other elements can help us to understand many aspects of social life. (For one example, see the dialectical model of deviance designation developed by Troyer and Markle, 1982). They make the contrasting positions of the persons and groups in conflict with each other stand out more clearly than otherwise would be the case. They enable us to recognize that some are more powerful and influential than others. Such participants in power struggles often play a greater role in creating the concepts, paradoxes, and issues of controversy than do the victims, for the latter have few resources of wealth, prestige, education, and authority (see Poppendieck, 1983, for one case). Yet coalitions are formed among those who have varying interests, knowledge, goals, and resources, so the resulting dialectical struggles involve more than a simple oppressor-victim relationship. Frequently the struggles are very complex, involving not merely two-sided skirmishes but numerous parties or camps opposing each other.

Contrasting paradoxical positions provide a basis for social science investigations of many issues. Thus a dialectical sociology assumes "that a tendency towards sameness and a tendency towards change counterbalance one another and determine where a society, a community, a family or an individual are in a given moment of time" (Mol, 1981:318).

The dialectic is not confined to the social class differences or modes of production that Marxists stress. It is defined more broadly "as a continual, inevitable, pull and counterpull between forces of integration and differentiation, needing and opposing one another, as order and progress both need and oppose one another" (Mol, 1981:318).

These tensions are obviously reflected in such dialectical struggles in Christian circles as that between homogeneity and heterogeneity in the controversies over church growth, between evangelizing individuals and evangelizing groups in world missions, between integration and differentiation in the tensions related to the ecumenical movement, between love and justice in social policy, and between emphases upon personal piety and social concern in Christian ethics. In the sociology of religion,

> The dialectic in question is not just simply between the synthetic (or more narrowly 'religious') and analytic proclivities of a person or between the integrative (or more narrowly 'religious') and differentiating tendencies of a society, it also operates between a large variety of nexuses in a complex field of open-ended and yet also boundary-maintaining systems (Mol, 1981: 319-320).

Much conventional dialectical thought has accentuated the negative; its stress is upon refutation of what exists. Each new position is typically presented as a corrective for the previous ignorance or errors of persons who supposedly lack the wisdom to truly comprehend reality.

Some of the advocates are like theological demythologizers who claim "to put naive and primitive statements into believable terms for sophisticated minds" (Hamilton, 1973:33). Such persons confirm their own wisdom as if it is final, unshakable knowledge

> by demonstrating continuously how it contrasts with previous ignorance. So long as attention is concentrated on his work of correcting the presuppositions of the unenlightened past, his own presuppositions will not be called into question.
>
> The demythologizing imagination, in short, feeds on beliefs that it rejects (Hamilton, 1973:34).

The classical thesis-antithesis-synthesis model of Hegel has also been an important influence in dialectical thought. The paired comparisons found in the work of Sigmund Freud, Max Weber, George Herbert Mead, Victor Turner, and other social and behavioral scientists typically present a "unity of opposites." That process is at the core of dialectical analysis. The paradoxical relationship causes tension and reinforces an ever-present potential for movement from one polar position toward the opposite. It contributes to the formation of countercultures that pose values and norms different from and often directly contrasting with those prevalent in the society (Yinger, 1982: 14-16). What is more, if any one theme is dominant above others for the study of the cultural-countercultural dialectic, it is religion. The entire history of Christianity can be examined from the perspective of its nature as a counterculture (Yinger, 1982: 225-230; see also Mott, 1982: 128-141).

It is therefore not surprising that religious groups can be classified by dialectically inspired typologies that focus on the conflicting polarities that are a natural part of human reality. Typological analysis leads to a series of hypotheses to explain the relationships of opposition and integration, rejection and acceptance, individualism and institutionalism, and similar processes and relationships within and among religious groups (Blasi, 1981). The dialectical approach aids in assessing the inherent inadequacy of any concept that arises in and from only any one perspective.

> Dialectics occur when paradoxically-related perspectives necessarily emerge from the same reality. . . . The paradoxical relationship within social realities need not be polarities, however; there are also cases of complementarity, mutual implication, ambiguity and reciprocity of perspectives (Blasi, 1981: 165).

DIALECTICS IN CHRISTIANITY

The integration of Christian faith with the insights, theories, and data of the various academic disciplines often involves an ongoing dialectical process of interaction. One's Christian world view can be used as a set of control beliefs over the academic knowledge; such knowledge in turn may bring about necessary changes in one's world view (Burwell, 1982: 394-395). Biblical truths emphasize the transcendence of God over his creation, but there are times, as in the pre-Copernican era, when Christians misinterpret biblical truths because of their limited knowledge. The dialectical process of the interpretation and application of transcendent values hence may be observed between the respective disciplines as well as among the scholars and scientists within them. It occurs even within the minds of individuals. Major problems of contextualizing the gospel—showing how it applies in a specific time and place—relate to these issues as well.

Many theological dichotomies have been the subject of dialectical battles in Christianity. These include controversies over predestination and free will, tradition and innovation, God's grace and God's judgment of sin, social control and personal autonomy, relevance and transcendence, internal and external evidence supporting the faith, cognitive and noncognitive data, revelation and observation, order and change, body and spirit, reason and emotions, ends and means, clergy and laity, cooperation and separation, justice and mercy, faith and works—to mention but a few.

Christian persons, congregations, and even denominations have a tendency to move toward one side or the other of the intermediate positions that are possible between the opposite poles of each set of ideological commitments or planned action. As they do so, they frequently are reacting to the real or alleged faults and fallacies of those who have chosen the opposite extreme. Not wishing either to commit those errors or to be identified with those who do, they move all the more strongly toward the opposite position. They then may become equally unbalanced, though in the antithetical direction. From the perspective of biblical values, they attempt to correct one error by committing another.

This helps to explain why many of the contradictions, disparities, inconsistencies, and discrepancies pertinent to the role and influence of religion in contemporary society can be traced to conditions within the churches. These can be studied from the perspective of "ideal types," a tool often used by sociologists to identify polar positions that are logically "pure." These types represent the extremes that presumably would prevail if each respective category were purified of extraneous conditions that modify the actual situations of people, groups, institutions, or societies. In this usage the word *ideal* refers to an *idea* drawn out to its logical extremity, not to moral perfection nor to a goal for which to strive.

Ideal types help to identify and call attention to ecclesiastical, theological, sociological, pragmatic, or other dimensions of the subject that is examined. Their characteristics typically are arrayed in a series of contrasting positions. Examples include church and sect, prophetic and priestly leaders, and autocratic, oligarchic, and bureaucratic organizations.

Ideal-type polarities appear in varying combinations, some of which seem at times to be inconsistent with each other. They overlap with each other as well. Combinations of some of them can be used to classify Christian groups into clusters of like-minded people who identify with each other on many issues, in contradistinction to other clusters that adopt opposing perspectives.

Even in regard to personal dimensions of the faith, there seems to be a developmental-dialectical process by which the person goes through periods of doubting and believing, not simply one act of weighing pros and cons and then choosing whatever seems the better (Slater, 1978: 162-163). The subject of uncertainty changes according to the attitudes and policies on which we act. Maturity comes from an initial trust that gives the background for later doubts. Mature persons can live with ambiguity and uncertainty, while the immature "rush into certitude on the basis of stereotyped thinking and insufficient evidence" (Slater, 1978: 163). Doubt becomes an instigator to personal growth in this dynamic dialectical process.

CONSEQUENCES OF DIALECTICS

The dilemmas associated with dialectics hence can be a source either of conflict and disintegration or of spiritual growth and constructive change. Poloma's study of a Christian covenant community (1980), for example, revealed several tensions and strains. Various dangers, but also a balancing process that permits and encourages growth and development for the community, were associated with the stress. The dilemmas grew out of the problems of dealing with several issues: personal freedom versus community structure, maintaining nuclear family ties while creating a larger community family, being in the world and yet not being of it, encouraging personal religious experience as a builder of community versus institutionalizing the religious experience.

Poloma (1980: 626) concluded that "a problem with rigidly organized groups is that they attempt to eliminate as many dilemmas or conflict situations as possible, rather than allowing them to be a source of life and growth." They are wiser when they live with the dilemmas than when they attempt to eliminate them.

The evidence of competing values is all around us. We see it in changing attitudes toward divorce and remarriage, in the factions and schisms within denominations and local churches, and in new orientations like liberation theology, feminist theology, black theology, and homosexual theology. Bayly (1982: 59) claims these new theologies "are alike in starting with a problem, a need, a desire, rather than with God; then building a construct that is unbalanced to support their teaching about that need. If Bible passages have to be explained away or even rejected to support their thesis, so be it."

But not all of them, nor only they, slip into error. Having adopted the "tolerant, caring, loving, 'who am I to judge?' attitude," the evangelical church has become "so sick that people are crowding in to join us. . . . We're no longer narrow; it's the wide road of popular acceptance for us" (Bayly, 1982: 48,59).

Whether we agree with Bayly or not, the warning is timely. Not all resolutions of dialectical problems are automatically wholesome for the church, its individual and family members, or the larger cause of Jesus Christ.

Pastors, denominational executives, parachurch directors, and influential lay leaders of churches are especially vulnerable to other dilemmas related to value conflicts.

The present-day religious leader is faced with somewhat of a dilemma, in that some trends which he may welcome will, with certain levels of probability, bring with them other trends which he may not welcome. If he works toward greater individualism, greater political participation, and more tolerance of cultural and religious diversity in American life, he will probably also be working toward reduced participation in the traditional church (Hoge, 1974: 191-192).

A dialectical approach to the complexities of competing values in both our external and internal world can improve our ability to grow in understanding, to cope effectively with current realities, and to become better servants of Jesus Christ. The dilemmas posed by destructive dualisms can be resolved through a consistently and thoroughly biblical approach. This will convert them into dynamic dialectics that have a constructive impact upon the lives, work, and witness of Christians.

LIVING WITH PARADOX AND DILEMMAS

We have seen that paradoxes and dilemmas are found throughout society, in Christian life and thought, and in the Bible itself. The complications connected with them are a part of the human condition. They cannot be avoided. To pretend that they do not exist is to deny reality and live in a dream world.

These problems of life and thought can be a means for growth and strengthening the kingdom of God. They provide opportunities to improve both theology and its applications in practical life. Hence dilemmas and paradoxes can become tools to stimulate spiritual maturity and enhance the mission of the body of Christ.

Edward Habert, a biology professor at Nassau Community College, has pointed out that

> ours is a religion of paradox. . . . Who but a Christian teacher would have the confident expectation of using the profane, the secular, and the temporal as tools to build the sacred, the holy, and the eternal? (American Scientific Affiliation, 1984).

Nevertheless, the very idea of paradox is revolting to people who expect everything to be either light or darkness with no shades of dawning or twilight nor cloudiness and gloom. Despite their feelings,

> . . . it may be that one of the highest forms of truth in the end proves paradoxical. It may be that those who embrace both sides of an apparent contradiction often will be nearer the full truth than those who surrender one or the other facet in favor of an artificial consistency. The mind seeking to be true to the *whole* man of concrete existence may welcome and defend a paradox, not because it is contrary to common or current opinion but in spite of it (Slaatte, 1982: 7).

Paradox cannot be escaped. Whether evidenced as the yes and no, the tit and tat, the pros and cons, the thesis and antithesis, it is always with us in some shape or form. It is an aspect of the one and the many, continuity and discontinuity (Slaatte, 1982: 245).

This inescapability of paradox is all the more evident when we realize that our scientific and rational interpretations cannot account for the wholeness of the one who does the knowing and the reasoning. The existential, knowing self who tries to account for the wholes of the natural order does so by trying to transcend itself and what is observed so as better to understand the whole of things. But this cannot be exhausted empirically or idealistically, so a higher transcendent view of the teleological process is in order. This is a clear existential reminder that the analytic and synthetic disciplines of reason are not the sole sources and media of truth (Slaatte, 1982: 243-244).

The dialectical approach to major orientations in a discipline such as sociology can help to produce a cease-fire in the battle among them

(Friedrichs, 1970: 290-291). So, too, the dialectical method can help to bring peace in the disagreements about various theological and practical issues facing Christians.

DYNAMIC DIALECTICS

Part of the process of constructive dialectics involves recognizing the scenarios in the minds of the advocates of alternative positions. Whether they pertain to deep theological subjects or to pragmatic details in the life of a Christian fellowship, images of the past, present, and especially the anticipated future have a strong bearing upon positions that the respective persons and groups take. Matters that seem to be mere petty details of no ultimate significance whatever may be life-and-death matters for others who see them as intricately connected with their ideas about serving God, Satan, or idols. Listening sympathetically to their positions, trying to draw out their viewpoints in order to clarify them, and engaging in honest dialogue are basic parts of the dialectical process.

When we learn about the "pictures in the mind" that people have built up for and against various alternatives, many positions that at first seemed ludicrous begin to make sense. When we honestly pay attention to others' reservations and criticisms of our own perspectives, we may identify flaws that need correction. Whether in scholarly or practical pursuits, groups in tension then may shift toward each other, experiencing "the power of synthesis and the energy of paradox" (Davids, 1982-83).

In dialogue with other Christians, we will find that many issues cannot be resolved unambiguously as either-or on the basis of biblical values. Some represent a both-and position, and others are neither-nor. Still others are in an adiaphorous category of indifference; for them the alternatives are neither right not wrong, neither beneficial nor harmful in themselves, so whatever position or action is chosen with reasonable Christian discretion is equally all right.

Paradoxes, dilemmas, antinomies, and dialectical problems are inescapable in our complex contemporary society, even as was often the case in biblical times. The open dialectical approach of wholistic Christianity offers the best possibility of constructive resolutions. Especially in the divisions and controversies that emerge among Christians, it is important to seek the elements of truth that are usually found on all sides of the issues.

Dialectical dynamics are facilitated by spiritual awakening, for it enables our senses

. . . to hear in more senses than one. . . . This fundamental change must alter the meaning of the basic words in ordinary natural language, like war and peace, kingship and lordship, power and service, brotherhood and fatherhood, eating and drinking, body and blood. Each will acquire new meaning inside old forms, and that meaning will reflect a new spirit. . . . All these images subvert or invert all the usual meanings. They invert and convert; turn upside down and change. Christian language is analogy, paradox, oxymoron, inversion, conversion. And it is set in the active-passive voice. Grace is the name of the altered load: it conveys the sense of the given. Grace is not an extra element or a coating of supernature but the old sense which has been made incarnate and embodied in the old form (Martin, 1979: 127-129; see also p. 26).

In the following chapters we shall examine some currently divisive issues that have paradoxical alternatives. Readers no doubt will recognize people and groups that take the respective extremist positions. They themselves may have moved too far toward one side or the other of the available alternatives. Our intent is not to attack any specific persons, organizations, or religious bodies but rather to help all of them and ourselves to move toward a wholesome and wholistic synthesis that is based upon biblical values.

PART IV

DOMAINS OF DISSENSION

6

STYLES OF PERSONAL COMMITMENT

Many disagreements and divisions in Christian history have resulted from differing opinions about lifestyle models and ideals. Examples include the apostolic dying into life, the masochism of the martyr, the outwardness of the monk, the inwardness of the mystic, Puritan asceticism, pietist mysticism, the classical American dream, and infinite resignation (Johnson, 1972). Sometimes such lifestyles coexist peacefully, but at other times they sharply clash as one or another is set up as a normative goal for all to attain. Ideas about the most important components of the Christian life are an important area for investigation when one is trying to diagnose and resolve controversies in Christian groups. They are useful for comparisons of groups with each other, and they can be used as evaluative criteria to chart the progress of a congregation or denomination.

Several components of religious commitment are used in social science research. They reflect the special emphases of many Christian persons and groups. We shall evaluate each of them by biblical criteria, survey tensions related to the dimensions of religiousness, and suggest ways to restore a wholistic balance.

DIMENSIONS OF RELIGIOSITY

Social scientists have often found it feasible to include only one question about religion in their research on family life, crime and delinquency, occupational adjustment of workers, population characteristics, and other subjects. The simplest of these is a self-classification under "What is your religion?" as Protestant, Catholic, Jewish, Other, or None. Other alternatives are whether the person is a church member or nonmember or has attended church or synagogue in the past seven days. The findings are then tallied, classified, and related to other variables as measures of "the religious factor."

Specialists in the study of religion have long been aware of the limitations of such simple categories, so they have used more than one bit of information about religion. (My doctoral dissertation, for example, incorporated questions about church membership and attendance, beliefs, church leadership positions, and religious attitudes [Moberg, 1951].) They recognize how reductionistic and misleading results are when, for example, all Protestants are lumped together as if they are a uniform category, or when it is assumed that mere membership adequately distinguishes religious people from the nonreligious. Confusion results from observing only a narrow aspect of religious identification, belief, or practice and failing to recognize its broader context of relationships to other expressions or evidences of religion.

The most significant solution to the research problems connected with the inconsistent and oversimplified "measures" of religion came from Glock (1962), who identified "five core dimensions of religiosity." He believed that the religiosity or religious commitment of any person may be manifested in one or more of these five ways:

1. The *ritualistic* dimension consists of religious practices, what people who are religious *do* in the external expression of their religion. Ritualistic deeds include such activities as attending church, praying, confessing sins, tithing, fasting and feasting for religious purposes, working on church boards and committees, genuflecting, and reading the Bible. These acts may or may not be labeled as "rituals" by those who practice them.

2. The *ideological* dimension deals with what religious people *believe*. Doctrines, dogma, creeds, statements in a catechism or church covenant, Bible promises, and theological views are among the kinds of items that might be included in research on this subject. Important, however, is the insistence on determining a person's own beliefs; those that are part of the church's official dogma may not be accepted by an individual member. The beliefs are of various kinds, and their negative, unbelief, also deserves investigation.

3. The *intellectual* or cognitive dimension pertains to what people know about their religion, sacred scriptures, church, and similar subjects.

4. The *experiential* dimension centers around what people *feel* when they practice their religion. It includes religious emotions and sensations, perceptions related to God and to ultimate reality, feelings when they participate in religious activities, and sentiments connected with personal or group religious experiences.

5. The *consequential* dimension has to do with the *effects* of one's religious rituals, beliefs, knowledge, and experiences upon everyday life. It therefore is on a different level of abstraction from the others. Researchers might observe people's honesty, kindness, life adjustment,

satisfaction, political behavior, diligence at work, family relationships, and numerous other attitudes, activities, and relationships to discover whether those who are high on the other religious dimensions differ from those who are low.

All of the five dimensions are interrelated, but not necessarily in the same way. Each can be studied with the methods and tools of the social and behavioral sciences.

Glock's schema of "five-dimension religiosity" was praised for its perceptiveness and conceptual clarity. It was quickly adopted by others and has been widely used in the scientific study of religion. (Cardwell, 1980, provides a summary and critique of many of the studies.)

One sweeping statement, however, brought on some negative criticism. Glock (1962: 98) said that "within one or another of these dimensions all of the many and diverse manifestations of religiosity prescribed by [all] the different religions of the world can be ordered." Because of the wide variability of human behavior and cultures, most social scientists respond negatively to any generalization that claims to cover "all" phenomena of any kind. Several noted gaps in Glock's typology.

One was the *communal* dimension—the association of people with one another in the context of a religious group that theologians label *koinonia* (Fichter, 1969). Other researchers listed as many as eleven dimensions discovered through advanced statistical techniques. Among the dimensions added were devotionalism, dogmatism, instrumentalism, intrinsic-extrinsic involvement, salience, and ultimate concern (Faulkner and DeJong, 1966; King and Hunt, 1969, 1972; Cardwell, 1980). Glock's reaction was that he would have placed each of the new dimensions under one or another of his five.

A CHRISTIAN APPRAISAL

The all-embracing statement of Glock that all of the manifestations of religiosity prescribed by all religions could be ordered by his dimensions aroused my special interest. If true, then the totality of the manifestations of Christianity, including any and all of its observable spiritual or supernatural elements, must eventually be subject to scientific analysis under the five dimensions. I used the subject as the focal point for my contributions and discussions in the International Conference on Science and Christian Faith in Oxford, England, July 17-25, 1965, and two subsequent papers (Moberg, 1967a, 1967b). A summary of a few of my findings is pertinent to our exploration of wholistic Christianity.

It became apparent that each of the dimensions is an inadequate means of satisfying the Christian ideal that is presented in the Bible:

1. Worship, giving cheerfully, studying the Scriptures, praying, and other ritualistic deeds are commended. Yet the testimony of Jesus and the Apostles is clear about the inadequacy of religious deeds, the ritualistic dimension. Jesus condemned the religious scribes and Pharisees for their failure to live up to their own teachings and for their close attention to minute details of religious rituals while they neglected the basic principles that lay behind the legal structure out of which the rituals evolved (Matt. 15:1-9; 23:1-39; etc.). He insisted that those who truly worship God "must worship in spirit and in truth" (John 4:24).

Scripture repeatedly reminds us that our religious "works" or deeds are insufficient to bring about salvation (Matt. 7:22-23; Rom. 3:1-5:21; Gal 2:14-21; 4:8-11; Eph. 2:8-9; Tit. 3:4-7; etc.). The prophets were likewise insistent that religious acts of sacrifice and worship displease God if they are not backed up by consistent attitudes and actions in daily life that implement righteousness, love, and justice (Isa. 1:10-20; Ezek. 33:30-32; Hos. 6:6; Mic. 6:6-8; etc.).

It is clear that one can engage in the outward forms of religious practices without truly worshiping God.

2. Several Bible passages suggest that mere beliefs are inadequate for a proper relationship with God. This is perhaps most clearly expressed in the statement that "faith by itself, if it is not accompanied by action, is dead" (James 2:17 NIV). Mere belief in God can be deceptive: "You believe that there is one God. Good! Even the demons believe that—and shudder" (James 2:19 NIV). This is contrary to the common Americanized viewpoint that any faith is all right, provided only that one be sincere. The object of one's faith ought to be Jesus Christ; that is just as important as believing, the act of faith (John 8:24; Acts 4:12; 1 Cor. 3:10-11; etc.).

True belief in the saving sense of the concept in John's Gospel (1:12; 3:16-18; etc.) involves more than mere intellectual assent. Francis Wheeler, a Greek scholar who was a colleague of mine at Bethel College, pointed out that a genuine saving faith involves the total commitment of oneself to the Lord Jesus Christ. Just as the planted seed in ancient Greece was "believed into" or fully committed to the soil, so the true believer dies to sin and is buried with Christ (Rom. 6:2-7).

3. In Jesus' day two groups of people knew more about their religion than any others—the scribes and the Pharisees. They ranked very high on the intellectual dimension. Yet Jesus called the scribes "blind guides" and blind leaders of the the blind (Matt. 15:14; Luke 6:39). He condemned them along with the hypocritical Pharisees (Matt. 23).

In addition, one of the chief lessons in the Apostle Paul's first letter to the Christians in Corinth is that human knowledge is imperfect, incomplete, and insufficient for salvation even at its very best (1 Cor. 1:17–2:16; 8:1-2; 13:8-10).

4. There is less explicit reference to the experiential dimension in the Bible, but the overall impact of the New Testament seems consistently to imply that it falls far short in itself. The Apostle Paul, for example, was "caught up to the third heaven, . . . caught up to Paradise" and had other mystical and ecstatic experiences (2 Cor. 12:1-12). Nevertheless he also said that he considered everything as rubbish or "a loss compared to the surpassing greatness of knowing Christ Jesus my Lord" (Phil. 3:8 NIV). Jesus' parable of the sower may be relevant as well; some people are like seed sown on rocky places; they hear the word and receive it with joy, but they are not rooted well, so when trouble or persecution comes, they quickly fall away (Mark 4:16-17). Emotions and feelings do not provide a solid foundation for the Christian life.

5. The biblical evaluation of the consequential dimension overlaps with the "works" referred to in connection with the ritualistic dimension. None can earn salvation through doing good deeds, although such behavior ought to result from and demonstrate the reality of genuine Christian commitment (Matt. 5:16; Eph. 2:10; Jas. 2:14-26; 1 Pet. 2:11-12; etc.). Many who perform good deeds will hear the Lord's words, "I never knew you" (Matt. 7:23). None can be justified in God's sight by observing the law (Rom. 3:30).

Salvation is a gift of God's grace, not a payment for good deeds (Rom. 11.6, Gal. 2.16; Eph. 2:8-9; etc.). In his great chapter on *agapé* love, the Apostle Paul emphasized that the very best of words and deeds are profitless for the speaker and donor unless they are accompanied by sincere and active love (1 Cor. 13). Such love is not simply an outward act. It flows from one's innermost being, the deepest existential springs of the person, in response to God's love.

6. The communal dimension is an important aspect of the Christian's life. We are admonished "not to give up meeting together, as some are in the habit of doing" (Heb. 10:25 NIV). As branches of a vine, Christians are to abide in Christ (John 15:1-8). As they do so, they will lay down their lives for one another, thus bearing fruit (John 15:9-17).

Yet since the very beginning of the Christian era there have been traitors, hypocrites, and trouble-makers who were members of Christian groups. Jesus was betrayed by one of his own disciples, and some of his followers deserted him (John 6:66). Others were defectors at a later date (see 1 Tim. 1:19-20; 2 Tim. 4:10; 1 John 2:18-19). Some teachers and leaders serve their own appetites rather than Jesus Christ. "By smooth talk and flattery they deceive the minds of naive people" (Rom. 16:18 NIV). We are warned against deceiving spirits, hypocritical liars, old wives' tales, and godless myths that creep into Christian fellowships (1 Tim. 4:1-7; see 2 Tim. 4:3-4 and 2 Pet. 3:17). Titus was told to rebuke the "rebellious people, mere talkers and deceivers" who spread prejudicial tales, teach things they ought not, "and that for the sake of dishonest gain" (Tit. 1:10-16 NIV). Those in the Christian fellowship who are idle, being busybodies instead of being busy, are told to settle down and earn their own food (2 Thes. 3:11-12).

These and other Scripture passages clearly indicate that not all who participate in Christian fellowship are loyal members. Deceivers and hypocrites mingle with the faithful. Communal participation provides no assurance of true Christian commitment.

SPIRITUAL COMMITMENT

We see, therefore, that all of Glock's five dimensions plus Fichter's communal one fall short as measures of Christian vitality. There seems to be a missing factor. Is it the combination of all six together? Perhaps. Yet it may be possible for a person to "fake" all six in the eyes of researchers and other people, although never in the eyes of God.

What is missing is not on the same level of abstraction as the other dimensions. It is the total person-with-God relationship that is referred to in the Bible as being "born again," "hid with Christ in God," and "written in the book of life."

All of the observable dimensions of religiosity, including those that go beyond the six we have discussed, are related to this central commitment. In order to have a "healthy" or "sound" relationship with God, there must be ritual (worshiping, praying, and other religious activities), beliefs (especially faith in Jesus Christ as Savior and commitment to him as Lord), knowledge (at least a minimal knowledge of human sinfulness and God's provision for salvation), feelings (emotions are involved in all human experience and are often intense at times of conversion, special revelations, developmental insights, and thrilling religious events), and consequences (the works without which faith is dead).

At the heart of all of these is a spiritual relationship with God that is the core of genuine Christian commitment. It is possible to measure indicators of each of the dimensions of religiosity and completely miss that foundation of religious faith, ultimate concern, or existential Christian commitment. Yet, even though the latter can be analyzed only indirectly through imperfect sets of indicators or reflectors, discovering ways of analyzing and reporting it is a significant challenge to social and behavioral scientists who study religion (see Moberg, 1979).

These six dimensions are not, of course, the entire range of possible emphases in the Christian life. Love, joy, peace, patience, kindness, goodness, faithfulness, gentleness, and self-control are Christian virtues that are the "fruit of the Spirit" (Gal. 5:22). They can provide a basis for evaluating one's level of spiritual maturity, even though there are no simple ways to quantify them for statistical measurement. It is possible to possess some of these and not others, or to possess some more fully than others:

> For this very reason, make every effort to add to your faith goodness; and to goodness, knowledge; and to knowledge, self-control; and to self-control, perseverance; and to perseverance, brotherly kindness; and to brotherly kindness, love. For if you possess these qualities in increasing measure, they will keep you from being ineffective and unproductive in your knowledge of our Lord Jesus Christ. But if anyone does not have them, he is nearsighted and blind, and has forgotten that he has been cleansed from his past sins (2 Pet. 1:5-9 NIV).

Another aspect of commitment is one's basic life orientation. For example, the difference between an intrinsic and an extrinsic faith style has received much attention from social psychologists (Paloutzian, 1983: 134-166). People who are intrinsically motivated *live* their faith; extrinsic persons *use* it. Intrinsic faith is internalized as part of the very fabric of one's personality. Faith is the master motive in life to which other needs are made subservient. If there is a conflict between one's faith and economic or sexual motives, the intrinsic person will uphold the faith rather than compromise it to other interests or desires.

Extrinsically oriented persons use religion for their own self-interest. They may participate in church activities primarily in order to make business contacts or to meet persons of the opposite sex. Theirs is likely to be a "Sunday only" or a "social club" type of religion that emphasizes the rewards and benefits they obtain from it. Besides the pure types, mixtures of intrinsic and extrinsic orientations are possible within a given person.

These differences have helped to explain why some church people (extrinsics) have high levels of prejudice and others (intrinsics) low. Intrinsics rank higher in levels of purpose in life and in profound religious experiences. Differences on several other variables also have been revealed through research (Paloutzian, 1983:134-166).

These two styles can easily be related to biblical teachings. Intrinsics worship God in spirit and in truth (John 4:24). Extrinsics are more apt to be like the hypocrites whose religious observance is designed to be seen and rewarded by other people (Matt. 6:5-6; Luke 18:9-14).

DIALECTICAL TENSIONS

The strain that arises from competing orientations, values, and dimensions of Christian faith has been evident in numerous controversies and schisms of Christian groups. Compromises are often essential. For example, in Benedictine monasteries "the establishment of routine is accomplished only at the expense of spontaneity" (Zerubavel, 1981:47). When the monastic life was entirely scheduled by the horarium (table of hours), it was in many ways reduced to the level of childhood (p. 49).

Personal piety has often stood in the way of theological education in sectarian groups. Their members would rather have an enthusiastic minister who has little learning but much zeal than a highly educated one who might have doubts or qualifications about some details of the Christian life or faith. For many pastors,

> The most difficult task may be how to combine piety and learning. It is not simply that many veer off in one direction or the other. We may affirm both piety and learning, but integration is the greater challenge. . . . The challenge of integration is before all of us. It confronts modern Seminaries where the specialization of the university has tended to dictate the patterns of theological education. It intersects the ministry where the ethos of professionalism can elevate product over process. In a world that . . . has tended more and more towards division and specialization, the vision of the integration of piety and learning offers more than ever a possibility of wholeness (White, 1983: viii)

Tensions between some of the dimensions of religious commitment are readily apparent in Scripture as well as in the lives and activities of Christian persons and groups. Romans 6:1-11, for example, emphasizes the mystical union of the Christian with Christ, but Romans 6:12-14 stresses the practical demand of Christianity as a way of life. To stop at the wave of feeling that comes from meditating upon Christ is to have a half-way Christianity.

> That emotion must be translated into action. Religious feeling can never be a substitute for religious doing. Christianity can never be only an experience of the secret place; it must be a life in the market place (Barclay, 1957:87).

Similarly, there is often tension between one's knowledge and one's deeds of both the ritualistic and the consequential types. Romans 7 reflects the tensions of being pulled in two directions. Paul had the ability to recognize the wrong and the inability to refrain from doing it.

> It is part of the human situation that we know the right and yet do the wrong, that we are never as good as we know we ought to be. It is part of the human situation that at one and the same time we are haunted by goodness and haunted by sin. . . . knowledge by itself does not make a man a good man. . . . To resolve to do a thing is very far from doing it (Barclay, 1957: 102,103)

Most of the dilemmas and paradoxes mentioned in this book can be related to the dimensions of religiosity. They all reflect the tensions that sometimes arise when two sets of seemingly opposed perspectives are both valued. In the practical affairs of the Christian life personal piety and social compassion, evangelism and societal reform, individual and institutional religion, relevance and transcendence, love and justice, and many other godly values are often in tension with each other.

> On the one side is the real life of mankind, dominated exclusively by material needs, instinctual reactions, intellect, by economics, science, and technology. And on the other side, ignored, kept under wraps, and ineffective, the world of the spirit—a tiny corner or sanctuary of the heart where one piously preserves the immortal spiritual values. . . . What characterizes our modern humanity, therefore, is not the absence of spiritual values—it possesses a spiritual elite, an abundance of faith and poetry—but rather the fact that these no longer have any decisive influence upon the destiny of culture (Tournier, 1977: 75, 76).

Bridging this rift in personal life is a step toward bridging it in the larger society. Rather than fearing such integration, Christians should recognize that God is concerned for all areas and domains of existence.

In the life of a given Christian there may be a dialectical relationship between different emphases and orientations. Father George A. Maloney, a Jesuit priest ordained in the Russian Byzantine Rite, emphasizes the need for contemplative prayer so that people can experience God personally (reported by Murphy, 1982). Through the Eastern experiential and mystical approach to spiritual life, people can feel God's presence *within* themselves. He believes that Western Catholics, Protestants, and Anglicans turn, in contrast, to God *outside* themselves. These divergent orientations indeed may dominate the respective groups, but it would be wiser to keep them in a constructive balance that blends objectivity about God and intimacy with God.

Sociologist Poloma (1984) has described her own personal struggle arising out of tensions between the intellect and the emotions. This was especially acute as she was engaged in research that examined her charismatic faith from a sociological perspective, but it relates to many other life experiences as well. Citing Matthew 22:37-38, which calls us to love God with all our heart, soul, and mind, she concluded,

> What I am coming to see is that the tension in us between intellect and emotions can be a healthy dialectical one that produces growth. It is when we battle to maintain the supremacy of the intellect (or toss aside the intellect for the reign of the emotions) that the struggle is dysfunctional. . . . As well-educated persons in a reason-worshiping society, most of us are not prone to allow the reign of emotions in our spirituality. We are more likely . . . to regard an intellectualized faith as the mark of a mature Christian. . . . Excluding the emotions through an overdependence on the intellect is not the balanced relationship God called for by Jesus (p. 7).

RESTORING BALANCE

The dimensions of religiosity were developed primarily for use in the study of the religious orientations of individual persons. Religious groups also reveal varying combinations and degrees of emphasis upon them. Some place heavy emphasis upon the ritualistic dimension, stressing the importance of baptism, church attendance, Bible reading, prayer, fasting, taking Communion, or other religious activities. Many fundamentalist groups place their heaviest emphasis upon holding correct beliefs. A few churches give priority to knowledge and religious education. Pentecostalists and charismatics tend to stress the experiential dimension. Some groups accentuate good deeds or social ethics as if that is the primary requirement of the Christian life. The communal dimension is most notable in groups that emphasize "the church family" and maintain strong ties of religious solidarity among the members.

All of the six dimensions are relevant and important for a well-balanced or wholistic Christianity. Any group that emphasizes one at the expense of the others is impoverishing itself. It is likely to shape its members lopsidedly, making them become unbalanced as well. Wholistic Christianity is possible only when all the dimensions are integrated with each other and centered around a solid spiritual commitment to God through Jesus Christ.

Perhaps it is essential for most Christians to be somewhat lopsided. Some have been given a gift of teaching that requires greater stress upon the intellectual dimension than upon others. Some have a spirit of wisdom that enables them to see more clearly and quickly than others whether or not new scholarly productions are favorable or opposed to God's kingdom. Some have a special gift of languages and the interpretation of tongues, which may include the ability to understand and empathize with the persons who communicate with them. Whatever the nature of their spiritual gifts and the context of roles and responsibilities in which they are exercised, there are variations in the demands, opportunities, and activities associated with them. Each one of us has only about a hundred hours a week after taking modest amount of time for sleep and eating. We are limited also by physical strength, so we cannot do all that we might like to do. These conditions make every Christian to some extent "unbalanced," especially when each stands all alone.

It is only through complementarity that a balanced or wholistic Christianity in terms of the various dimensions and orientations of the faith can be attained. My weakness, inability, or lack of time to serve a given need is compensated for by someone else who specializes in it. Alone we are weak; together we are strong.

Some dimensions of the Christian life and faith cut across the lives of everyone. The more specific we become in terms of our service to God through our specialized professional and volunteer activities, the more we are likely to be wholesomely lopsided. We compensate for the weaknesses of others and prop up those who are lopsided in a different way from our own.

When we individually think we are strong, we are weak. When we recognize that we are weak, then together with others in the Body of Christ we are strong. Wholistic Christianity is possible only through the cooperative effort of Christians associating and working with one another. Every solitary and individualistic Christian inevitably is unbalanced and incomplete.

7

SAVING PERSONS OR SERVING SOCIETY?

Controversies over the relationships of Christians to the surrounding society are often apparent. They emerge in almost every area of church life. For example, Silke Hansen, senior conciliation specialist for the Community Relations Service of the U.S. Department of Justice, has noted that many Christians take an either-or approach:

Either you're concerned with social issues or you're concerned with evangelism. Either you care about people's physical needs or you worry about whether they're going to be saved. . . . It's unfortunate there aren't more examples of combining those two stances because they are certainly both part of what Christ taught, preached and did while he was here (quoted by Dagley, 1982).

Hansen has observed that churches often fall into the same categories. Some center their activities around social issues. They provide social services and are well known for a foodline, daycare center, or low income housing, but they forget the gospel on which all of it is based. Others are so afraid of being part of the world that the church shuts itself off from it (Dagley, 1982).

Similarly, Raymond Fung (1982) of the Commission on World Mission and Evangelism of the World Council of Churches has noticed the "pseudodialectical" thinking of Christians in Asia and elsewhere. They look for contradictions and fail to resolve them:

Many of us in the ecumenical movement tend to see the commitment to human rights as somehow inconsistent with the commitment to engage in evangelism. . . . to cast the question as an issue between commitment to human rights and social justice over against commitment to evangelism and church growth would be a serious distortion of reality as Korean Christians see it. With this perspective, no one is served. Neither the cause of human rights there, nor the sharing of the evangelism concerns and insights of Korean churches with the rest of the world (pp. 1, 2).

During the 1970s I thought that the tensions related to evangelism and social concerns were decreasing and the wounds from rifts between various Christian groups were healing (Moberg, 1977b). However, the heavy involvement of Christians in politics during and since the 1980 and 1984 presidential elections in the USA has reflected much misunderstanding of both biblical values and the realities of political and social structures.

Groups like the Evangelical Women's Caucus and Evangelicals for Social Action were spin-offs from the 1973 Chicago Declaration of Evangelical Social Concern (see Sider, 1974). Their activities have produced a reaction among persons and groups that cling to the principle of separating "spiritual" concerns for personal evangelism from the "worldly" issues of society. As David Winter, president of Westmont College, has said,

> The antagonism that exists among Christian people [is] appalling. . . .
> And it seems to be increasing as more and more churches and
> Christian leaders proclaim "the Christian position" on social and
> moral issues. . . . We seem to allow important but secondary issues to
> prevent us from enjoying a fellowship and relationship that should
> result from our unity in Jesus Christ ("'Christian Position,'" 1982).

These controversies center around three major subjects on which Christians tend to divide into opposing camps. Some build their efforts around individual sinfulness and others around social evils. This naturally leads to efforts to cope with human problems that focus upon personal evangelism, on the one hand, or social action on the other. A corresponding emphasis upon either personal piety or social compassion usually accompanies them. The following sections examine these three dualisms.

INDIVIDUAL SIN VERSUS SOCIAL EVIL

"Sin" has become a "dirty word" in modern society. Much of the behavior once labeled as sinful has been redefined as optional aspects of one's personal lifestyle. Alcoholism and drug addiction have become "diseases" or "substance abuses." As we noted in chapter 4, the word "sin" is avoided in the therapeutic and helping professions such as medicine, psychology, and psychiatry, even as it is generally avoided in the social and behavioral sciences.

The nonjudgmental attitude that we ought not to put other people down is part of the reason for the near elimination of "sin" from our vocabularies. In addition, it represents the attempt to avoid "sectarian" concepts in a religiously and culturally pluralistic society. The applications and definitions of the word vary widely. What one group considers sinful, another believes to be neutral, and still another views as positive and desirable. (This is particularly evident in regard to certain forms of sexual behavior, such as premarital experimentation and cohabitation.) Elimination of the concept of sin has been furthered by efforts related to human rights and civil liberties to be permissive and nonjudgmental of the conduct of others as long as no immediately observable harm occurs.

Those who use the word "sin" have a tendency to apply it to the behavior of other people, using concepts like mistake, flaw, or righteous anger for their own equivalent actions. Yet Menninger, (1973), the well-known psychiatrist, believes that much good can result from reinstating the concept of sin. It is clearly a major biblical term, so Christians cannot evade it, much as some of them try.

> Sin and evil are not phantoms or mirages. They express themselves as actions—actions of individuals, groups, and nations. They permeate the structure of life. They control lives. They determine destinies.
> All of man's wickedness is seen in his cultural unfolding. Sin becomes something more than personal—it expresses itself in the spirit of the age (Webber, 1979:181).

Yet when Christians refer to sin, they tend to emphasize either its personal aspects or else its manifestations in social institutions, practices, and structures.

The conventional view of sin among fundamentalists and evangelicals interprets it as residing within individual persons. The Bible repeatedly emphasizes that all have sinned (Psa. 53:2-3; Isa. 53:6; 64:6-7; Rom. 3:23; Gal. 3:22; 1 John 1:8; etc.). The sin problem is at the root of all other human problems. Its resolution occurs by the repentance of individuals who accept forgiveness offered by God's grace through Jesus Christ.

These Christians usually hold that, since individuals create society, it can be redeemed only by winning persons one by one to faith in Jesus Christ. All groups, institutions, and political structures consist of people: dealing with their component parts (persons) will resolve the issues that pertain to the whole. This perspective has been a powerful impetus behind evangelism. It has at times produced significant changes in society as well as in individuals.

A contrasting view believes individuals are the products of society. They are born into a social system and reared in a process of socialization that gives them its values, outlook on life, and behavior patterns. Therefore the root source of sin lies in society and its institutions. We will eliminate personal sins by correcting collective evils. Theological liberals associated with the social gospel movement have been the most prominent proponents of this perspective.

The long history of the "seven deadly sins" helps us to recognize how important personal sinfulness has been in the course of human events. Pride, lust, envy, anger, covetousness, gluttony, and sloth have spread their evil influence throughout history and are very much in evidence today (Lyman, 1978). What is less obvious, however, is that their spiritually deadening and socially blighting influence is woven deeply into the core of many institutional and societal practices and structures that we respect and honor as if they were God-given. Wallis (1981: xiii), for example, has pointed out how "most advertising appeals directly to one or more of the seven deadly sins." Television programs sandwiched between those ads are not very different.

Reinhold Niebuhr (1932) made it very clear that a moral man who is fulfilling life's responsibilities faithfully, honestly, diligently, morally, and even pietistically can contribute to evil because he is enmeshed in a social system that is evil. Each business, government agency, church, school, and every other institution is embedded within still larger social systems. The locus of responsibility for both good and sinful actions is so impersonal that it is difficult to attribute them to any person. As Mott (1982:12) has indicated, "Some of our greatest evils are characterized by this absence of conscious individual decisions on the critical issues." He gives many examples: absence by a man whose work demands travel away from his family, the institution of slavery collectively sustained in ante bellum America, administrative officers easily replaced in a bureaucracy in which decisions are made anonymously and ultimately independently of individuals, and racism perpetuated by white churches.

Scanzoni (1972: 127-128) in like vein points to the individual sins of arson, looting, sniping, and similar crimes in city riots. Sociologists point to underlying causes such as exorbitant rents for substandard housing, white businessmen who exploit minorities by high prices and high credit charges while refusing them jobs, and citizens who oppose the tax increases that would provide educational innovations to help free ghetto youth from the endless cycle of poverty. These, too, are sins (Amos 2, 5, and 8; James 2 and 5), yet most affluent, middle-class churches are not apt to emphasize such applications of biblical teachings.

Some Christian students exposed to a picture of life different from that shared by their parents and home churches have become disillusioned or cynical when they have seen how middle-class Christianity is bound up with evil and self-serving cultural patterns. "In fact, many who 'lost their faith' in college do so through this chronological sequence and not by questioning key doctrines" (Scanzoni, 1972: 128). On the other hand, "if a Christian student keeps his wits about him, the sum of this exposure and similar experiences can be tremendously exhilarating and expansive, serving to emphasize the true comprehensiveness of Christianity" (p. 128).

In its extreme form the emphasis upon social evil rather than individual sin is linked with efforts to eliminate the concept of "sin" altogether. Even though "our sociology, all too often, is an examination of the effects of sin on society" (Lyon, 1976: 65), there is a reluctance in the discipline even to mention the concept. Evil is attributed solely to societal and institutional variables. Sins such as sexual immorality are defined as normal, consequently right, because a majority of the population indulge in them once or more in their lifetimes. In contrast, however, Christians in sociology assume that people are sinful. They recognize that conflicts, deviance, and even certain social institutions may exist as a result of sin (Lyon, 1976: 65-66).

The "powers" or world order against which Christians are warned in many New Testament passages constitute a social structuring of evil that is at the very core of the social system (see Mott, 1982: 3-21, and Walter, 1980: 192-198). Society is a vehicle for the rebellion of humanity against its Maker, and social institutions are responses to, if not manifestations of, the fallenness of the human race. That is why the biblical sins include both those that pertain to personal action and relationships and those that involve economic exploitation, oppression of the poor, hoarding of wealth, and other social injustices.

Awareness of the reality of social evil does not remove individual responsibility. Quite the contrary. The worldly powers continue to rule because individuals acquiese, perpetuate, and even strengthen their influence. They conform themselves to system-serving rather than system-critical behavior. "One way to increase individual responsibility is to increase awareness of social evil" (Mott, 1982: 14).

An overemphasis upon the social nature of sin denies the individual autonomy commonly known as "free will." It implies a high degree of social determinism. Yet people with similar backgrounds who are exposed to identical opportunities do not all react the same way. Inner motivations, values, predispositions, and commitments often lead to significantly different choices among the alternatives. Some people respond by indulging in righteous and others in sinful behavior. This reflects the coexistence of individual and collective or social sin. Each contributes to the other and to some degree results from it.

We cannot remove individual sin simply by changing the system; only the redemption offered by Jesus Christ can accomplish that. Nevertheless, simply attributing all evil to individual persons is also in error.

A more realistic Christian view might be that sinful human beings build sinful human institutions and social systems, which are capable of greater evil than individuals alone ever could be. A few of the more obvious examples here are the horrors of slavery, Hitler's Third Reich, Stalinist purges in Russia, and nuclear war, a foretaste of which was given by the U. S. to the world at Hiroshima and Nagasaki (Yoder, 1980: 233).

The biblical call to repentance applies to both persons and groups, small or large, including institutions, nations, social classes, and the like. Furthermore,

Evil comes about through many small, diverse, and often imperceptible movements and events. Misuse of the growth of knowledge, pollution problems, racial prejudice and the collective selfishness of nations all largely have their source in peccadilloes rather than in great crimes. It is the cumulative impact that is so devastating (Houston, 1980: 16).

To ignore either the personal or the collective dimensions of sin represents a serious distortion of the biblical message. It also reflects a warped misunderstanding of the problems of humanity.

Wholistic Christians will recognize and deal with both individual sin and social evil. They will not reduce either one to the other. They will note how personal and social sins are intricately interrelated in demonic, self-perpetuating, vicious circles (see Moberg, 1977b: 120-159, and Kerans, 1974). Their struggle against the presence of evil

. . . must correspond to the geography of evil. In combatting evil in the heart through evangelism and Christian nurture we deal with a crucial aspect of evil, but only one aspect. Dealing with the evil of the social order and the worldly powers involves social action, action in the world (Mott. 1982: 16).

EVANGELISM VERSUS SOCIAL CONCERN

Growing out of attitudes toward personal sin and social evil is another prominent dualism. A significant group of Christians focus their efforts upon personal evangelism to convert people to Jesus Christ.

They believe that is the primary, if not the only, goal of the church. An opposing group believes explicit social action to reform society is the primary task of the church. There were foreshadowings of this cleavage in earlier Christian sects, but probably the most significant social movement occurred in the "Great Reversal" of the early twentieth century.

Evangelicals in the eighteenth and nineteenth century were among the leading advocates of major social changes in England and the USA, including the abolition of slavery, prison reform, education of the masses, and improvement of working condition's (Cairns, 1960; Dayton, 1976; T. Smith, 1980).

Revivalists like John Wesley, George Whitefield, and Charles G. Finney were personally active in social reforms and stimulated many others to work for them. In his *Lectures on Revivals of Religion* Finney claimed that "revivals are hindered when ministers and churches take wrong ground in regard to any question involving human rights" (Dayton, 1976: 18, italics removed). He backed up his words with action.

"Evangelicalism in its best form is no stranger to social concern; such concern is, in fact, close to the center of what evangelical Christianity is all about" (Webber, 1979: 174). In its worst form it found rationalizations to support slavery and other evils that were part of the status quo. It never has been a solidified movement with unanimity about political, social, and economic issues.

Under the impact of the "Great Reversal," evangelical Christians retreated from their earlier social reform interests into an emphasis upon personal evangelism and only those social ministries that help the victims of problems. Weber (1979: 183) and Webber (1979: 175) believe that the rise of dispensational premillennialism was one of the major causes for this change. The rapid urbanization and industrialization of society after the Civil War, reaction to excesses of the Social Gospel, diversion to other activities and issues, population changes, and many other things contributed to it (Moberg, 1977b: 30-38).

Under the "Great Reversal" around the turn of this century most Protestant Christians divided themselves into two camps. The "fundamentalists" focused upon revivalistic conversion as their major ministry, and the "modernists" were advocates of the Social Gospel that aimed to reform society (Moberg, 1977b). Their differences were obviously linked with divergent perspectives on personal sin and social evil, as well as a host of contrasting theological assumptions and disagreeing interpretations of the realities of society and the teachings of the Bible. Much of the history of twentieth-century Protestantism revolves around this destructive dualism.

Members of the evangelistic school did not lack social concern. It was evident mainly in their "works of mercy" such as orphanages, rescue missions, retirement homes, and social services to the members and friends of local churches that were offered through deacons and deaconesses. They assumed that converting persons individually was the highest form of social involvement. They were sure that conversion to Jesus Christ would rather automatically result in the guidance and inspiration of the Holy Spirit to

> . . . make a dishonest man become honest; a criminal, law-abiding; a sexual pervert, upright; an improvident man, provident; a mentally ill person, well; a corrupt politician, clean; a lazy worker, ambitious; a rapacious businessman, kind; a greedy self-seeker, generous; a self-centered introvert other-oriented. . . . solving personal problems through converting souls to Jesus Christ will resolve all the problems of the world. Soul-winning is thus seen as the very highest form of social concern (Moberg, 1977b: 22).

Advocates of the Social Gospel retorted that such a position represents an excuse for inaction. It leaves Christian citizenship responsibilities up to God's direct intervention instead of stepping into the political and social arena to cope with injustice and suffering, so it violates biblical admonitions to demonstrate God's love by doing good to all people. Social gospelites pointed out how deeply sin is entrenched in social systems; society is so permeated with social evils that only radical reform could overcome them. Inequities and injustices in the social order twist the lives of individuals and violate their dignity as creatures made in the image of God. They must therefore be attacked directly.

Each camp had its favorite Scripture passages and claimed the other, in effect, cut away major biblical truths. Each claimed the other was hypocritical and heretical. Each pointed to its own successes and publicized the faults and failures of the other. Denominations and congregations were split over these issues. The controversies contributed to the formation of the Federal Council of Churches and its successor, the National Council of the Churches of Christ in the U.S.A., as well as the National Association of Evangelicals. Informal local and regional coalitions for cooperative evangelism or for social action efforts within and among denominations crystallized around the respective camps.

By the middle of this century many evangelicals began to realize that ignoring the need for direct social action violated their acceptance of the Bible as an authoritative, God-inspired guide to all areas of faith and conduct. They were stimulated by Carl Henry's work on *The Uneasy Conscience of Modern Fundamentalism* (1947), which called for a "new reformation" to clarify the implications of personal regeneration for social as well as individual problems. An ever-increasing flow of publications, sermons, resolutions, and action coalitions dealing with social issues from an evangelical perspective has subsequently done much to "reverse the Great Reversal" (Moberg, 1977b: 150-221).

Meanwhile, many churches in mainline denominations that stressed social action experienced declining financial and membership support, and some of their reform efforts failed. As a result, many participants in the Social Gospel camp have begun to recognize the importance of stimulating personal faith as well as trying to change society and its institutions.

In spite of great progress for more than two decades, the rupture between the evangelistic and the socially oriented Christians has not been fully healed. For example, Krass (1980) reviewed several books published by Friendship Press, the publishing arm of the National Council of Churches, which professed to deal with the wholistic mission of the church. He found that all but one focused on working for social justice as if that is opposed to emphasizing personal Christian faith. They treated the personal and social aspects of the gospel as an either-or proposition, as if anyone pursuing social justice had transcended "mere" personal faith. The only exception was the work of Esther and Mortimer Arias, *The Cry of My People: Out of Captivity in Latin America*. They maintained the fundamental New Testament balance:

> They speak not only of liberation from oppression but also of liberation from sin. . . . (The liberation from sin, they say, is "the radical liberation, because sin is the root of all oppressions.") (p. 44).

Black churches have always seen social responsibility as a part of the gospel, but they too were often caught up in the Great Reversal. Black Evangelist Tom Skinner (1980) has argued that black churches, in reaction to the oppression they experienced from white evangelicals, shied away from evangelism into a lop-sided concern with the social needs of their people. They saw how people who preached the word of God refused to defend the right of blacks to vote; they put up "For Sale" signs and moved out of their neighborhoods if black people moved in. Blacks observed one group of white Christians saying that they must clothe and feed people and give them places to stay, while another group said, "We've got to preach the Word and get people saved." Both went to opposite extremes,

> . . . one wanting to feed my belly and another wanting to save my soul. Neither one addressed my totality as a person. . . . The liberals shied away from the gospel because they saw the conservative guys not

being socially involved, and the evangelicals shied away from the gospel because they felt it smacked too much of social involvement. And neither one preached the gospel (Skinner, 1980: 12).

Ethically-oriented Christians need to realize how important basic motivations, commitments, and values are for the accomplishment of their goals. These best flow from the complete commitment to Jesus Christ that is initiated by the conversion experience and followed by solid biblical instruction to enhance spiritual growth. "Without evangelism most efforts to restructure society will fail" (Moberg, 1977b: 147).

Evangelistically-oriented Christians need to recognize and apply the totality of Scripture. It is concerned for all dimensions of human well-being, not just conversion of a narrowly conceived "soul." To omit social concern from the stewardship responsibilities of living the Christian life is just as much a process of selectively cutting out portions of the Bible as is the omission of evangelistic concern for the conversion of individuals. This was expressed well by Robert C. Campbell (1980), general secretary of the American Baptist Churches in the U.S.A.:

> The church is the Lord's. We should do the right thing or the Lord's will (identical ideas) whether we like it or not. I would like to see the social activists more concerned about genuine conversion and spiritual nurture, and the "born-again" types more concerned about applying their faith in the social and institutional areas of modern life.

PERSONAL PIETY VERSUS SOCIAL COMPASSION

When they see others who differ from themselves, people tend to indulge in namecalling. Christians are no exception. They attach stereotyped labels to other Christians. This simplifies their communcations with each other, establishes the range of thought and action that is considered correct and incorrect, sets boundaries of separation and inclusion among various categories of people, and has other social functions. It also contributes to misunderstandings, controversies between persons and groups, and unfair discrimination.

The process and the labels vary in time and place. For example, Christians who are strongly committed to social action tend to be suspicious of people who have a deep faith commitment that is expressed through personal prayer, devotional praise, Bible reading, meditation, and cultivation of the inner "spiritual" life. They think the "pietists" are "so heavenly minded that they are no earthly good." Devotionally oriented Christians look askance, in turn, at social activists who are trying to improve society through political and other channels. They think the "social gospelers" are "unspiritual" people who are caught up in fruitless attempts to reform a social system that is rotten to the core and who hence are diverted away from the most important aspects of the Christian life. Between these extremes are many other versions of labeling by which those in the one camp deprecate Christians in the other. Individuals often are wounded in the crossfire of allegations and accusations.

Historically, personal piety and social compassion have been closely linked in Christendom (T. Smith, 1980; Cairns, 1973). Only within the last century have they been separated through the Great Reversal (Moberg, 1977b) that severed evangelistic fervor from social concern. Among the early American Puritans, for example, "ethics, piety and faith were inseparably bound together. That was the bedrock on which the American experience was founded" (Paul, 1978: 36-37). The early leaders of the Pietist movement, August Francke (1663-1727) and Philip Jacob Spener (1635-1705), insisted that concern for social amelioration was an indispensable fruit of personal conversion and the life of faith. Their successors have continued to link inward liberation and spiritual devotion with attempts to establish a just society (Bloesch, 1973: 101, 122-129).

Theologically and biblically, the welfare activities of social ministry—giving to the poor, aiding those in need, feeding widows and the fatherless, clothing the naked, supporting the infirm, and other acts of mercy—have been tightly linked with the warfare of social action—struggling to reform and resist the evils found among the rulers, authorities, and power structures of society. They are based upon guidance from the written Word of God, Jesus Christ the Living Word, and the Holy Spirit. They flow from a love without which the act of giving is unprofitable to the giver (1 Cor. 13:3), even though it may still greatly help the recipient. They have a devotional orientation that sees all service to others as ministry done in the name of Jesus Christ. They are supported by a Christian community of faith and the empowerment that comes through prayer (see Moberg, 1965; Mott, 1982: 134-135).

God does not change; those who pay great attention to pietistic rites but cheat the poor and oppress the needy when they ought to help them are under God's judgment now just as much as they were in the days of Amos, the other Old Testament prophets, John the Baptist, Jesus, and the New Testament Apostles and writers of Scripture (see, e.g., Willis, 1979; Thompson, 1979). The biblical ideal links personal piety with social compassion.

> Spiritual and moral life are inextricably intertwined in all major religious traditions. . . . We all need disciplines of spiritual attentiveness . . . to help us ground our social concern concretely in practical spiritual disciplines and attitudes (Edwards, 1984: 1).

This may be one of the reasons for the research finding that there is a positive correlation between giving to churches and religious bodies and giving to secular associations. Even if it is part of a general activity pattern, other giving increases along with church giving (D. Smith, 1980: Chapter 17).

Gallup Poll data (Princeton, 1982: 76, 176-177) have shown that many more church members (37 percent) than nonmembers (22 percent) are involved in charitable and social service activities, such as helping the poor, the sick, or the elderly. Those who are evangelicals are more likely (42 percent) than others (30 percent) to be involved in such activities. Evangelicals are also more involved in personal devotions such as praying regularly, seeking God's will through prayer, and reading the Bible. They say, too, that religion is very important in their personal lives, and they choose "salvation—closeness to God" as the most important of eight personal needs. We can therefore conclude that people who are personally pious are more likely to be socially compassionate than those whose religious orientation is more conventional. Data from the Gallup Poll conducted for *Christianity Today* strongly support this conclusion (Moberg, 1980).

Similar evidence comes from a representative nationwide survey of 8,549 parishioners from 150 congregations of the United Church of Christ, a theologically liberal denomination (Campbell and Fukuyama, 1970). The authors acknowledge, "Like other liberal Protestants we too were fearful of devotionalism becoming 'escapism'" (p. 224). (Among the liberals "piety" is often a pejorative concept. It is identified with an otherworldliness alien to facing the realities of social forces and to working for necessary social change.) To their surprise, they found through a three-question Index of Devotional Orientation that the devotionally oriented people were *more*, not less, likely than others to favor action in the area of civil justice (p. 223). People of lower educational levels and social status generally were more likely to score low on civil rights and on social acceptance of blacks, but those from the same low socioeconomic levels who ranked high on devotionalism also ranked high on civil rights and social acceptance.

Devotionalism was the only type of church participation examined that reversed the results of social conditioning. A devotional orientation turned parishioners toward social concern for others in spite of their own personal social problems (p. 214).

Puzzled by this finding, Campbell and Fukuyama (1970: 214) suggested that the devotional orientation "is in some way related to a person's self-transcendence." It seems to "imply some assumption about a reality transcendent to ordinary experience" that is not necessarily implied by mere religious knowledge and organizational participation in the church.

> If the Christian is to be in the world, then he needs some basis on which he maintains perspective so that he is not of it. Perhaps the devotional man is the one who knows the "source" of his courage to be in the world, . . . and his sense of the transcendent gives him the "vision" so that he is not fully of the world (p. 223).

Jim Wallis of Sojourners Community has similarly become ever more convinced of the importance of prayer in the struggle against injustice and especially against the dangers associated with the nuclear threat hanging over the entire word. As Christians are moved to pray, they will pray for some things and against others. Following the biblical example,

> . . . prayer is not the passive, general, and abstract sort of ritual common in many of our churches. Biblical prayer is more active, concrete, historically specific, and politically informed (Wallis, 1981: 94).

Prayer is a weapon in spiritual warfare against principalities and powers (Eph. 6:18-20). It is an act of reclaiming identity with the children of God. It declares who we are and to whom we belong. It destroys false identities, "unhooking" us from the harness of the world's securities to affirm that our security is in God. It changes those who pray, modifying motivations and raising questions of complicity with evil. It humiliates us, calling us to confession and repentance. It moves us to affirm our identity with God and celebrate his authority and ultimate victory. Prayer and its results are "the most revolutionary of acts. The powers and principalities of this world are aware of this; that is why they consider those who pray in this way to be a threat" (Wallis, 1981: 96).

Prayer changes our frame of reference. It breaks down distinctions between us and our "enemies," making them into friends to protect. It thus removes hatred and undermines hostility; it humanizes them so that we begin to understand things from the perspective of others' joys and fears, feelings and struggles, pains and hopes (Wallis, 1981: 94-97).

Far from opposing social compassion, the devotional life contributes to it. To view personal piety and social compassion as antithetical to each other is to set up a false dichotomy. In a properly balanced and biblically oriented Christian life they do not compete with each other; each complements, stimulates, and nourishes the other. Any attempt to have either one without the other represents a heresy that denies the Christian gospel and contributes to its ill repute.

GETTING THE ACT TOGETHER

To some extent the tensions related to emphasis upon the personal versus the social dimensions of the gospel may parallel a cyclical pattern of Western society. Since the Industrial Revolution there has been an oscillation between a passionate collective involvement in public issues and a preoccupation with private concerns (Hirschman, 1982). Yet Christians have not blindly followed the cultural pattern. Out of firm convictions many have gone against the general trend in society to staunchly commit themselves to one emphasis rather than the other.

We have seen that Christians tend to slip into diverse patterns of dealing with the social ills and problems of humanity. One group interprets the gospel very narrowly as if it has to do only with conversion. This initial personal commitment to Christ then, they believe, will change all aspects of personal conduct. They view institutions and society itself as no more than the sum of its parts. Redeeming the parts will redeem the whole.

Christians with this perspective focus upon personalized approaches much in tune with the flaws of worldly individualism. They believe that all social evil, as well as personal sin, resides exclusively in individual persons. They therefore emphasize the need for personal piety and for proclamation of the gospel with the goal of winning converts to Jesus Christ. They assume that changed individuals will change society. Many are "evangelical monastics who appear to be afraid that even a polling booth will contaminate them" (Rees, 1982: 10). Such Christians "shout the gospel from the distance" instead of involving themselves deeply in the lives of people, feeling with them in their pains and sorrows, suffering with them in their deprivations, and identifying with them in the demeaning experiences of community life. They emphasize telling the gospel more than applying it—and all too often they are telling it only to each other.

It is not difficult for those Christians to become involved in social ministries that serve the needs of persons and families they know who are in trouble and thus to become part of a second orientation. These tend to pick up the pieces of broken persons without giving attention to the social conditions that have helped to crush them. They are far too ready to assume that all problems are caused by the sins of the victims, not realizing that often the sins of other people, sometimes including Christians, have caused or contributed to the distress.

Some of the Christians in this second group view their acts of kindness as bait to entice people to hear the message of salvation. They make social ministries a means to an end rather than an end in their own right. Dealing with symptoms rather than the roots of basic problems, they focus upon consequences rather than causes, upon the casualties rather than the inflicters of human misery, upon rescuing people from fires rather than putting out the flames.

A third group of Christians say, in effect, "What you are speaks so loudly that other people cannot hear the words you say." They believe that the most effective way to spread the gospel is to demonstrate it by deeds that put its ethical teachings into practice. To avoid the possibility of making "rice Christians," they sometimes slip into the error of having no verbal proclamation at all. Recipients of services then fail to see any linkage of their deeds with the gospel and are given no invitation to repent and turn to Jesus Christ for salvation.

A fourth pattern of Christian social concern grows out of the recognition that social systems themselves need reform. It attempts to correct the structural flaws found in the political, educational, industrial, business, mass communications, social welfare, and other institutions of society. It assumes that individual character and personal problems are consequences of social forces and conditioning. Changing society hence will change individuals.

In its most extreme form, this viewpoint merges into a reductionistic determinism that sees all individual ills labeled as "sin" as products of social evil. Eliminating the source, they believe, will eliminate both the personal and social effects, so social reform is the basic task of Christians.

Tensions between these four camps of Christians are often acute. They are related to many sets of paradoxical alternatives—orthodoxy versus the collective view of sin, personal evangelism versus social concern, devotional piety versus social compassion, conversion versus social reform, comfort versus challenge, proclamation versus demonstration, love versus justice, separation from versus identification with the world, and the like. While the opposing either-or combinations are not always fully consistent, they tend to form two major clusters:

> The basic division among Protestants today is over certain specific theological beliefs, which define two parties at either end of the theological spectrum. The two parties make different choices of church priorities for external action, though they agree on the need for programs to serve church members and their families inside the congregation. . . . The differences in preference among the two definable parties are over what type of mission outreach is preferred—evangelism or social action (Hoge, 1976: 90).

In effect, this is the old fundamentalist-modernist division in a modified form of traditionalism versus adaptation. The division cuts through all the mainline Protestant denominations. Its equivalent is found, with appropriate modifications, in Catholicism and Eastern Orthodoxy as well. It separates congregations within a religious body from each other, and it is the source of contending camps of members within them. Parachurch organizations and interchurch associations also tend to fall into one of these camps or the other.

Yet careful study of the Bible indicates that most of the action goals and ideological values of the opposing camps are valid. It is the reductionistic emphasis by members from each party that is in error. Evangelism to win souls to Christ, social action to promote justice in society, and social ministries to aid the victims of sin and structural evil are all important aspects of God's will for the Christian family.

Recognition of this balanced approach is spreading among the leadership of all camps. Many of them, of course, have always had a balanced, wholistic perspective, but individuals are always parts of social systems; organizational loyalties and commitments often bend conduct away from personal beliefs. As Krass (1973: 11) expressed it, partly out of his United Church of Christ experience,

> The church during the sixties lost . . . its wholeness. Just as it had been in many ways a partial institution before the move for social involvement, so it remained a partial institution in its new commitment to social action. . . . I think in this coming period we may be in a position . . . to find a new synthesis, a new unity of evangelism and social action, of piety and involvement, of biblical faith and relevancy. . . . The either-or church is a myth, but a very dangerous one.

Commenting on the glib statement, "It is not the mission of the church to reform society but to preach the gospel," Paul Rees (1983: 11), a World Vision board member and worldwide counselor in pastors' conferences, asked why this should be seen as an either-or option:

> Are social reforms that are ameliorative and uplifting so unimportant that they must be excluded from evangelistic concern? John Wesley held that "the people called Methodists" were raised up "to spread scriptural holiness and reform the nation." . . . For him it was *and*, not *but*.
>
> Furthermore, while preaching the gospel is indispensable to the church's mission, this is not quite the same as saying that it is *the* mission of the church. . . . If we, the body of Christ, are sent into the world after the fashion of our Lord's mission, then it is inescapable that we should serve our fellow creatures in the totality of *who* they are and *where* they are.

The renowned evangelical Bible teacher and conference preacher from England, John R. W. Stott (1978: 68-69), has come to a similar conclusion:

Our evangelical neglect of social concern until recent years, and the whole argument about evangelism and social action, has been as unseemly as it has been unnecessary. Of course evangelical Christians have quite rightly rejected the so-called "social gospel" (which replaces the good news of salvation with a message of social amelioration), but it is incredible that we should ever have set evangelistic and social work over against each other as alternatives. Both should be authentic expressions of neighbour-love. . . . I cannot claim to love my neighbour if I'm really concerned for only one aspect of him, whether his soul or his body or his community.

William Dyrness (1983), president of New College, Berkeley, has indicated that Christians must overcome the errors of separating matter from spirit, the individual from community, telling from showing the gospel, faith from works, and mission from development. He points out how idolatries easily intrude when we leave institutions to care for themselves and quotes Carl E. Braaten (Dyrness, 1983: 189):

If economic, political, social and cultural dimensions of human life are not incorporated integrally and holistically into the essence of evangelism and the substance of salvation, they become the playing field of other powers, other gods and idols, other ideologies and world views.

Canon John V. Taylor (1970: 104), general secretary of the Church Missionary Society of the Anglican Church, has discussed the question of whether to serve or to proclaim is a valid choice. The answer he gives is that both are important. Both are aspects of the primary aim of mission and the primary task of any missionary church. The aim and task is to spread from person to person a statement of who Jesus Christ is, a belief in his saving power and relevance, and a practice of his way of life.

Whether in any given situation this "spreading from person to person" can best be advanced by spoken proclamation, or by silent example of a few Christians living in deeply honest and loving community, or by compassionate service of men in different varieties of need, or by undogmatic discourse and friendship with men of other faiths, or by participation in the struggle for a more just and human society, is an entirely secondary question. . . . all these things are necessary, as facets or ingredients of the whole, and . . . the Holy Spirit provides the Christian community with a diversity of these gifts for the sake of the one Mission.

It would be easy to pile up quotation upon quotation in support of the same basic perspective. Both evangelism and social action are important. Christians of all denominations are moving verbally toward that position. Many of them also are moving that way in their actions.

In their followup study of the churches in Gaston County, North Carolina, for example, Earle, Knudsen, and Shriver (1976) found that both those who want the church to be attentive to social issues and the proponents of "nonpolitical" religion

> . . . agree that mindless, unreflective participation in social change is as empty and frustrating as utopian dreaming unexpressed in the world of everyday life. At stake . . . is not the choice between a religion of action and a religion of fundamental convictions—but the relation of the one to the other in a time of social-cultural change (p. 345, italics removed).

Many congregations in every region of our nation are effectively blending the two major emphases and their various subcomponents. The LaSalle Street Church in Chicago, for example, has an effective evangelistic outreach precisely because of its support for social ministries. Among them are camping, tutoring, and other programs for minority youth in the notorious Cabrini Green housing project; legal aid services for minorities and the poor (Claerbaut, 1978); a bookstore-coffeehouse ministry; senior citizen ministries; a racially and socioeconomically integrated housing project; Bible study groups; creative arts projects; and counseling services, to mention only some of its diverse ministries that cut across the evangelism-social concern spectrum (see Hefley, 1976). Its pastor, Bill Leslie, has played a significant role in the development of SCUPE, the Seminary Consortium for Urban Pastoral Education, and the church has provided internship positions for many theological students.

Another example of blending together the two emphases is the Church of the Saviour in Washington, D.C. and its daughter congregations. It emphasizes the need to blend the "inward journey" of a devotional life with the "outward journey" of service to others (O'Connor, 1963, 1968). Members are required to engage in individual and group devotional activities of Bible study, prayer, meditation, and spiritual growth. Each is accountable to another member as well as involved in a mission group that serves other people. Significant ministries of housing renovation, services to children, neighborhood renewal, assistance to the elderly, retreats to help people meet personal needs, wholistic health services, and much more have made a significant dent in many of the hard-shelled problems of our nation's capital. They provide an example that has been emulated in several other communities.

Mount Carmel Baptist Church in the Bedford-Stuyvesant community of Brooklyn in New York City has similarly put together ministries of spiritual healing and social outreach under the leadership of Dr. V. Simpson Turner, its pastor. It has compiled a directory of all social welfare agencies that serve the neighborhood and has trained its members to be skillful in dealing with people's spiritual needs through developing their biblical knowledge and skills for relationships. This congregation hence is of immediate help to neighbors who have physical, material, or spiritual needs (Dagley, 1980). Similar instances of "reversing the Great Reversal" may be found in every major community and region of our nation (for some, see Moberg, 1977b:150-217).

The Sojourners community in Washington, D.C., the publishers of *Sojourners* magazine, has spent a decade and a half of effective ministry to arouse the social concern of other Christians while engaging in many projects of its own. It is now launching a preaching ministry to "proclaim the gospel clearly in our historical context." This will call for conversion and spiritual revival.

> Calls for social change without the call to faith will only lead to discouragement and despair. . . . A revival of genuine biblical faith . . . is the one thing that could most undermine the injustice and violence that have become endemic in the American system. Social justice and peace will only come as the fruits of spiritual transformation. . . . We hope that out of revival many will turn to Christ and, as a result, a whole new level of public activity for the sake of the poor, for peace, for racial justice and reconciliation would emerge (Wallis, 1984: 5).

Just as the Wesleyan revivals in eighteenth century England and the evangelical awakening of the nineteenth century in the United States brought significant social reforms, the Sojourners hope to make a significant impact upon people individually and the nation collectively.

A CONTINUING NEED

Despite significant movement toward wholistic ministries, questions can still be asked about the imbalanced practice of many Christian groups. Review of a major denomination's national assembly, for example, revealed much "more concern over secular issues than with the great commission of Jesus Christ to propagate the Gospel and to speak out with authority on the great moral issues of society. . . . one wonders if we are a social/political action lobby instead of a church" (Campbell, 1982).

Sider's evaluation of evangelical social concern (1978) continues to be valid. He found that much of it "is still of the Band-Aid variety. Evangelicals tend to prefer programs that nurse the bloodied victims of destructive social structures over programs of structural change that correct systemic causes." A major part of the problem is that

Evangelicals lack the sophisticated analysis of social problems that is provided by highly-trained, brilliant economists and social and political scientists. There [are] simply not enough evangelical economists, political scientists, and sociologists committed to the biblical demand for justice for the oppressed. . . .

Evangelicals need a more biblical theology. Their theology has neglected the biblical teaching about God's special concern for the poor and the fact that sin is both personal and structural. . . . Only when evangelical preachers dare to preach about oppression, justice, and economics as frequently as does Scripture, is there any hope that those people in the pews will accept a life of costly identification with the poor and oppressed (Sider, 1978).

There is no rigid blueprint to clearly depict the precise combinations and methods of evangelism and social concern that ought to be adopted by any Christian person or church. However, the overall teachings of Scripture, as well as the example of Jesus Christ, clearly indicate that we should combine both avenues of ministry (see Webber, 1979: 169-201). As sociologist Stellway (1982: 261) expressed it, "comfort and challenge are two integral components of Christianity and . . . the emphasis on either to the neglect of the other results in a gross perversion of the Christian religion."

Working for structural changes in society and ministering to people's social, material, physical, and economic needs ideally are interrelated with helping to meet their spiritual need to be regenerated by God's grace. Giving Christians an appreciation of that balance and a vision of how the pieces fit together is a significant task for every generation. It is especially important now when Christians are so prone to slip into one or another rut of narrowly conceived, lopsided, and unbalanced interpretations of their mission in the contemporary world.

8

DILEMMAS OF RELIGIOUS INSTITUTIONS

Christian organizations face many difficulties. They are confronted by all the problems of other social institutions, but because they are centered around a set of explicit beliefs, they also carry a heavy burden of ideological responsibility (see Moberg, 1984). They are usually the setting in which conflicts occur among Christians over polarities, paradoxes, and dilemmas of the kinds discussed throughout this book.

This chapter examines four polarities that relate particularly to churches and other religious institutions. The tensions between personal faith and institutional needs, the competition between quality and size and between homogeneity and heterogeneity, especially as expressed in the church growth movement, and the issue of relevance in contrast to transcendence in social ethics are all related to five dilemmas of institutionalization that are associated with the growth and development of religious bodies.

INDIVIDUAL VERSUS INSTITUTIONAL RELIGION

Some Christian churches center all their activities upon what they believe to be the "purely individual" needs of people. They minister to "souls" as if they are isolated persons. Their subjective orientation stresses the internal spiritual needs of individuals.

Other churches give primary attention to the needs of the church as an organization or institution. They imply that its success is the goal or end of all Christian activity. They are more objectively oriented toward externals. Many of them emphasize the importance of sacraments administered by the clergy. Designed to be outward visible signs setting forth and pledging a spiritual blessing, the sacraments are believed to convey divine grace upon the recipients. The sacramental approach tends to identify the institutional church with the Church Eternal, the Body of Christ.

Many young Christian assemblies and fellowships are first established as a reaction against religious bureaucracies. They emphasize

117

ministries to persons and attempt to serve people without any institutional structure. Ironically, they soon develop a structure of their own. Typically they have a central leader, and other persons gradually emerge as special helpers. As the group grows in size, it adds more and more positions, both for paid workers and unpaid volunteers. The relationships among them need clarification and coordination, so rules and regulations develop. New boards and committees are created. Before long, the group gains institutional trappings similar to those against which many of the members initially were rebelling when they left their earlier church. The longer and larger the new group grows, the more complex its structure is likely to become (see Moberg, 1984a: 118-126). We cannot get along without religious institutions any more than we can without educational, industrial, governmental, financial, or other types. Social structures are essential tools in every society.

When I was young, we were often admonished to "serve the church." The organization seemed to be placed in a primary position, above serving people or even serving God. Rational analysis, of course, made it clear that serving the church was assumed to be the best way to serve God and people, so these were not antithetical goals. Tensions arise, however, for every institution and all of its local, regional, national, or other branches must exercise a degree of social control over its component parts and personnel. This helps both to distinguish it from other similar associations and to protect its basic values.

Social controls operate formally through "official" sanctions of rewards and punishments. They also are informally enforced through such means as gossip, rumors, humor, interpersonal friendships and aloofness, praise, gifts, and expressions of thanks. Individuals may feel that their freedom or autonomy is threatened by the controls. One of the most extreme of these is excommunication or exclusion from membership. Frequently the persons who are close to experiencing it withdraw "voluntarily" as a consequence of being counseled to do so or of feeling ill at ease in the group.

This problem is particularly evident in groups like the covenant community that Poloma (1980) studied, Mana Community. Members rejoice in the freedom they have received from Jesus Christ. Yet their individualism cannot run rampant, for then the community itself would be destroyed. Even as overstructuring and overregulation have been evident in the rigidity of many Roman Catholic religious orders, especially before the Second Vatican Council, the need for order and hence for authority threatens to bring an oversocialization that disowns individual freedom. Mana Community has dealt with this dilemma by stressing the need for personal prayer, by encouraging members to be open to the power of the Holy Spirit in their personal lives, by discussing decisions with others, and ultimately by requiring approval of the community for major decisions.

Mana Community has also had to cope with the problem of the tendency to formalize or institutionalize religious experience. Christians who have experienced charismatic renewal develop both a theology and accompanying social structures based upon their experience. Instructional programs were established in Mana to integrate interested persons into the structure and, presumably, the charismatic experience. When practices associated with such action are routinized, it is easy to lose sight of the power of the Holy Spirit. Mere progression through programs results in graduation to new "spiritual" levels. The community, rather than Jesus Christ, can then become the center of life. Its practices become ends in themselves. Balancing these and other dilemmas will permit personal growth and development in the community. "If it is able to live with dilemma situations (rather than attempting to eliminate them), Mana will come closer to its own goal of being truly a living organism" (Poloma, 1980: 627).

Various rites and ceremonies develop within every religious group, whether they are labeled as such or not. Liturgies evolve into such hardened patterns that any deviation from them is viewed by many participants as a betrayal of the proper expression of their faith. Even nonliturgical churches that claim to follow no liturgy usually develop an "order of worship" that is difficult to change. Certain customs evolve into "traditions" that must be kept at the appropriate seasons.

Some symbolic expressions gain such deep figurative, allegorical, metaphorical, or other meanings that they are repeated over and over. In time, however, these may become relatively empty of meaning for most participants. They then turn into a pattern to be perpetuated for its own sake or merely to maintain a denominational tradition. The symbol is readily at command; it is simple to attend church, take communion, recite a creed, say memorized prayers, drop money in the offering, and the like, but the meanings of stewardship, Christian dogma, identity with Christ, and commitment to a Spirit-filled life easily erode away. As Cooley (1909: 376) reminded us long ago, the symbol may encroach and persist beyond its function

> . . . just because it is external, capable of imitation and repetition without fresh thought and life, so that all that is inert and mechanical clings to it. All dull and sensual persons, all dull and sensual moods in any person, see the form and not the substance. The spirit, the idea, the sentiment, is plainly enough the reality *when one is awake to see it*, but how easily we lose our hold upon it and come to think that the

real is the tangible. The symbol is always at command . . . ; but kindness, hope, reverence, humility, courage, have no string attached to them; they come and go as the spirit moves.

Symbols help to sustain and reaffirm religious values, contribute to the social solidarity of the group, and satisfy psychological and other needs. They have a tendency, however, to change their meaning, to survive beyond their spiritual utility, and to be transformed from means to ends. One of the major dilemmas that churches must face is the tendency of the old institutionalized symbols to become relatively empty formalites instead of remaining instruments to promote genuine faith. There is a need for fresh expressions of the faith to fit the circumstances of people in an ever-changing society, yet change tends to be resisted (Moberg, 1984a: 68-71; see also Slater, 1978: 15-46). When a church fails to resolve these dilemmas, people are apt to think that the institution is an enemy of personal spiritual development.

People also become unhappy when they see other forms of goal displacement. One of the most prominent is the bureaucratic inclination to convert into goals or ends the institutional practices and structures that initially were but means to significant ends. Structure is absolutely essential to the progress of religious groups, institutions, and programs. Usually the disintegration of structures leads to disintegration of the ministries they offer and the missions they accomplish. People in leadership positions recognize that, but they also have a vested interest in perpetuating their jobs. They are therefore doubly susceptible to the tendency to focus efforts upon extending their job security and possibilities for future promotion. Perpetuating and strengthening the institution easily becomes the highest value, replacing the initial purpose for which the institution was established. The local church, denomination, or other Christian program or structure is so strongly identified with the kingdom of God that it is pushed as if it were itself the ultimate kingdom.

A common form of idolatry among church members is "worshiping" a church building, its beautiful stained-glass windows, a particular version of the Bible, a venerated creed, a lovely liturgy, a pastor with charismatic leadership qualities, or some other object besides God. Idolatry also occurs when the goal of church programs is to strengthen the organization for its own sake instead of for service to God and humanity. Even those laity who are "church pillars" are not necessarily the best members of the Body of Christ. If they have lost sight of the church's basic mission and are concerned only with sustaining and strengthening the organization as such, they too have become victims of goal displacement.

In his comments on research findings about dropouts from the Presbyterian Church in the United States, Bullock (1971: 46-47) stated that antiinstitutionalism is the first, and perhaps the most important, reason for dropping out:

> Institutions are more and more suspect, especially on the part of the young who discern the glaring discrepancies between stated goals and actual performance of institutions. . . . So long as institutionalism rather than community is the chief concern of the church, there will continue to be a widespread rejection of the church's witness and ministry.

Similarly, the Gallup Poll (Princeton, 1978) found that unchurched Americans had several major criticisms of the churches. They felt that the churches had lost "the real spiritual part of religion," were "too concerned with organizational as opposed to the theological or spiritual issues," and had an "excessive concern for money." It is difficult to distinguish between the "real reasons" and the mere rationalizations that people give for such conduct as dropping out, but substantial proportions of churched people also agreed on those and similar criticisms of the institutional church. Most realize that being connected to a church and being "connected to God" do not necessarily go hand in hand.

Leaders of religious organizations sometimes infuriate members by actions designed to protect them as well as their institutions. As mainline denominations have declined, conservative and sectarian bodies have been growing (for data and interpretations, see Hoge and Roozen, 1979). In addition, the rise of the "electronic church" and parachurch ministries and groups like the Moral Majority caught many by surprise. Viewing their appeals for support as directly competitive with the church, pastors and denominational leaders are tempted to oppose such ministries directly and strongly. This angers people who feel they personally are served by the parachurch groups. It makes them think that the only concern of conventional religious leaders is with meeting "the needs of the church," not meeting the needs of people. Some mass media preachers capitalize upon that, reacting with countercriticisms that reinforce the antichurch attitudes of their audiences. Added to the tensions that arise from choosing sides on other dualisms and dilemmas, this backlash helps to push some members out of conventional churches.

Cohesion of a religious group is a prerequisite for its survival and relevance, but it can be structured around corrupted activities and goals.

> It is only when cohesion is seen as a result of faith on the one hand, or as a means of fortifying the faith on the other hand that its

function is maximized in the total context of a Christian strategy (Mol, 1969: 29).

In summary, the needs of both individuals and the religious institutions that serve them must be kept in a wholesome, dialectic balance. If either is neglected, the Body of Christ suffers. When individuals drift away in order to gratify their real or felt needs, the institution declines and becomes less capable of serving people. Then, as a result of the membership loss, it may serve others still less effectively. They, too, are hence all the more likely to drift away. Once a vicious circle of this kind begins, it tends to perpetuate itself until the institution dies or a miracle of renewal reverses the trend.

QUANTITY VERSUS QUALITY

Closely related is the issue of what constitutes institutional success. Is it better to have fifty members with high levels of commitment in a congregation than to have two hundred and fifty or a thousand of average or low levels? During the early 1970s when many mainline churches were declining in size, some of their pastors rationalized that the loss in numbers represented a gain in quality. Members who disagreed with their policies or doctrines allegedly were the ones who departed. These ministers claimed to be happy with the declining numerical strength of their congregations. They assumed that smaller size meant deeper commitment and healthier levels of spirituality.

Some religious leaders evaluate success almost exclusively in terms of numbers. Membership, attendance, receipts from offerings, and similar measurements are used as if nothing else is important. Pulpit committees seeking ministerial candidates typically look at trends in such criteria, as do reporters from the mass media. Denominational records similarly focus upon such data. Social scientists are attracted to them because of their adaptability to statistical manipulation that provides "objectivity" in research. The "bigger is better" criterion of American society has strongly influenced almost all aspects of church life.

In contrast to crassly materialistic perspectives, there has been a growing emphasis upon quality in many areas of contemporary life. For individuals the goal increasingly is to add life to the years, not just years to life. As David Neiswanger (1982), president of the Menninger Foundation from 1941 to 1958, put it,

> If each of us can be helped by science to live a hundred years, what will it profit us if our hates and fears, our loneliness and remorse will

not permit us to enjoy them? What use is an extra year or two to the man who "kills" what time he has?

A primary goal of Christian churches is to improve the quality of people's lives, helping them to find spiritual well-being, the "abundant life," or "life to the full" that Jesus Christ offers (John 10: 10). Merely getting more people into a church program or building does not in itself guarantee that the quality of their lives will be improved spiritually or in other ways. Furthermore, every voluntary act of joining a church represents attraction to some quality. Qualities are not equal. Some are dishonorable or sinful. Yet, other things being equal, the chances of spiritual growth usually are greater if people become involved in church than if they shun it.

Low quantity does not guarantee high quality. Indeed, when the quantity goes down to its lowest level of zero, the quality is zero as well. Churches must gain new members to replace those dropping out by mobility and death. If they don't evangelize, they'll evaporate (Campbell, 1983).

Unfortunately, controversies over the church growth movement all too often are reduced to an argument over quantity versus quality. Its opponents claim that the only goal of growth advocates is to get more people into the church without giving any attention whatever to the matter of how, from whence, and to what they are recruited.

In fact, however, many church growth proponents have clearly indicated that growth in numbers is closely related to quality and is, at best, a consequence of it. There may be some differences about the criteria or definition of "quality," but, as Wagner (1981: 64) says, "No church growth advocates that I am aware of would deny the need for high-quality churches." Examination of the literature produced and distributed by church growth agencies like the Institute for American Church Growth headed by Win Arn and the Charles E. Fuller Institute of Evangelism and Church Growth supports his conclusion. So do the experiences of many churches.

Emanuel Lutheran Church of Hartford, Connecticut, was a declining congregation until it was renewed through adopting principles of the church growth movement. Its pastor commented on the basis of his experiences,

> We could no longer console ourselves with thinking that if we could not grow in numbers, we might improve in quality. That is only a dream. Decline in numbers must lead invariably to decline in quality. Declining congregations consume more and more of their available energy and resources in maintenance functions. Dying congregations

tend to exhaust people and do not lead to personal growth (Stadt-lander, 1980).

Quantity and quality are not enemies. Each enhances the other when they are kept in proper balance. Undoubtedly some churches are too large or too small for effective ministries, at least as currently administered, but even that varies with the context. There are advantages and disadvantages in both small and large congregations, but the ideal or optimum size depends partly upon what members and others in the community expect from the church (see Moberg, 1984a: 219-220). A richly diversified program demands a large membership; a tightly knit "church family" atmosphere can hardly prevail if the membership is as high as a hundred.

Wagner's (1976) plan for blending together the benefits of both large and small size represents one attempt to reconcile complications pertinent to both size and quality. He advocates having three components in the infrastructure of a single church. The "celebration" would bring together all the members for worship. "Congregations" would serve as smaller and more homogeneous units. They in turn would consist of many "cells," small spiritual fellowship groups.

Wagner's pattern appears to work in metropolitan areas where large megachurches are possible, but it may be difficult to develop fully in small and rural communities. Even in them, however, there are subcongregations—cliques, fellowships, circles, organizations, classes, and task forces that appeal to varying individuals. Increasing the size, number, and variety of these contributes to church growth and probably to quality as well (Schaller, 1979: 348). The increased number of groups often results from dividing present ones.

Paradoxically, church size is multiplied by dividing. Under wise leadership, increased quantity is accompanied by improved quality. The two characteristics are complementary, not contradictory.

HOMOGENEITY VERSUS HETEROGENEITY

During the 1950s a strong movement developed in many major denominations to combine congregations that were separated mainly by race. Many mergers of two or more parishes occurred, often under the pressure of denominational help or decree. At the time I personally agreed with the ultimate objectives, but along sociological grounds I raised questions about feasibility and practicality. Social class distinctions often have been a greater barrier between people than skin color. White Protestants generally have been unable to integrate the white working class with clerical, managerial, and professional people. How can they expect to add the prejudicial barriers of race to those of social class and expect to succeed (Moberg, 1958)? Subsequent experience has shown that successful racial integration in religious bodies occurs within, not across, class boundaries.

Scripturally, all Christians are one in Christ (see, e.g., Gal. 3:26-29). Yet pragmatically the daily activities, needs, tastes, interests, worship styles, and expectations from the church are so different that it is well nigh impossible to unite people from widely diverse socioeconomic levels into single congregations. Every denomination has its predominantly white-collar and blue-collar churches. To try to merge black blue-collar congregations with white white-collar ones involves crossing two "natural barriers" and generally has not been successful.

Seldom was the move proposed for integration to be by a few whites into a predominantly black church; usually the blacks were expected to give up much of their culturally unique modes of worship. Hence even the "integrationist" thrust was in fact a largely one-sided and discriminatory push toward assimilation of the minority into the majority group. Most blacks resisted the loss of their distinctive worship patterns and their control over congregational life.

Conflict over the ideal composition of the church congregation has flared in connection with the "homogeneous unit principle" advocated in the church growth movement (for example, see Nees, 1980). It draws upon sociological, anthropological, and theological insights and holds that "Disciples are more readily made by people within their own homogeneous unit, and congregations develop into healthy communities when they concentrate on only one kind of people" (Wagner, 1979: 4). In essence, it is both a statement of fact and a principle of effective evangelism that people do not like to cross racial, linguistic, or class barriers in order to become Christians. As an evangelistic principle it therefore holds that working within rather than across specific "people groups" is the most effective way to reach unbelievers with the gospel.

Homogeneous unit perspectives are widely diffused throughout the church growth movement and strongly attacked by many outside it. Ironically, the attacks are frequently grounded on its failure to attain ideals in regard to the unity of believers that the attackers themselves do not model. By indirection their own congregations are usually homogeneous; they consist of people with similar social characteristics.

The assumption of growth advocates is that once people have become disciples of Jesus Christ, they should be taught that all of God's people are one in Christ. Appropriate church structures will enable them to experience that oneness. Each "congregation" consists of a distinctive ethnic, racial, socioeconomic, or other type of homogeneous unit, but the "celebration" is made up of several diverse congregations.

"Festivals" of large conventions, crusades, camp meetings, and convocations bring together even more of the heterogeneous groups of Christians and model how all are one in Christ (Wagner, 1981: 166-183). Those who advocate the integration of heterogeneous people and groups within Christian congregations in effect argue for an assimilationist policy. This would compel minorities to reject their ethnic, racial, language, and cultural identities in order to become a part of the Christian group. Such ethnocide or "cultural circumcision" confuses the gospel with cultural values. It constitutes "religious cultural chauvinism," whether it occurs on a remote mission field or at home in America (Wagner, 1979: 81-83). It seems to fly in the face of the worldwide revival of ethnic identities (Smith, 1981).

To insist that Christians the world over conform to but a single pattern of rituals, activity programs, institutional structures, worship forms, and the like is clearly a form of arrogant cultural imperialism. Is it not the same when it is done within the confines of a single community?

On the basis of bitter experiences our nation has decided that the old melting pot ideology, by which all ethnic groups were expected to blend into a single new "American" one, is demeaning and undesirable. Instead a cultural pluralism that allows, or even encourages, ethnic and religious differences is more beneficial to the nation and its people. Christians similarly ought to recognize that there is a place for distinctive subgroups within their larger fellowships. Their most effective outreach will occur as subcultural differences are permitted within local churches, communities, and denominations.

The natural solidarities of people can be linked effectively with the Christian solidarity of all believers. The prejudicial barriers between groups will weaken as people learn the ethics that spring from their faith and across group boundaries. All groups will, of course, be open to everyone who wishes to participate in them. No one will insist that, in order to become Christians, people must deny their social, racial and cultural identities. A voluntary self-selection process will reflect and respect individual choices as each seeks and finds a congregation into which she or he fits.

There are, to be sure, many dangers to overcome. It is easy to distort the Scriptures to fit the predilections of each homogeneous group. An ethnocentric pride can develop that eventually disowns or violates the rights and privileges of people who are not its members. This feeling of pride-filled superiority may prevail within each group. Yet on the whole, this policy of encouraging both homogeneity within each group and heterogeneity among them seems to have fewer flaws than the utopian ideal that attempts to fuse all Christians together.

Lyle Schaller (1979) is perhaps the best known church consultant of our generation. He has concluded on the basis of wide observation and study that "The congregation that claims it is trying to reach everyone in its efforts to grow is engaged in a venture guaranteed to produce frustration, disappointment, and unfulfilled goals" (pp. 346-347). Specialized ministries for targeted audiences are much more likely to prove effective both for church growth and for meeting personal needs.

RELEVANCE VERSUS TRANSCENDENCE

A common criticism aimed at theologically conservative Christians is that they are "so heavenly minded that they are no earthly good." This world is not their home; they're "just a-passing through." One would expect them to give the world little concern beyond meeting their subsistence needs. Yet they often inconsistently accumulate earthly comfort and treasures. Their main orientation to outsiders, however, is to try to get them to join the heavenward pilgrimage. The orientation of their faith toward transcendent goals leads to an emphasis upon evangelism to try to win converts to Christ.

Many theologically liberal Christians react against such a stance. They claim that it represents a denial of love for their fellow humans, rejection of the stewardship responsibility for all earthly resources, and a renunciation of citizenship responsibilities. They argue that the church should be relevant to the immediate needs of people by trying to correct the problems of society and improve conditions in the world. The ethical orientation of their faith leads them into efforts to reform society.

The tensions related to these polar positions have contributed to the alternative types of solutions for the "Christ and culture" problem that Niebuhr (1951) so aptly described. They have led to criticisms and recriminations against each camp by the other along the lines of some of the dilemmas discussed elsewhere in this book. Each has a tendency to imply, and sometimes openly to state, that the other is not fully "Christian."

Otherworldly believers emphasize the supernatural work of God, while thisworldly Christians stress people's natural circumstances and social conditions. Both appeal to the love of God, but in somewhat different ways. The one polar type views it as delivering souls from the wages of sin to the gift of eternal life through Jesus Christ, the other as the motive for rescuing lives from earthly suffering. What is relevant for the former is oriented to an eternity beyond the grave; for the latter it is based upon the conditions under which people live here and now. This tension between an emphasis upon the here and now or upon a glorious future is related to the biblical juxtapositions of judgment and acceptance, justice and love, punishment and mercy. It also relates to the constant experience of receiving various negative and positive evaluations from society. This contributes to the prevailing tendency in many churches to emphasize the one side of God's love alone, showing "a remarkable aptitude for absorbing twentieth century consumer attitudes" (Mol, 1969: 108). Their use of the concept of "relevance" is usually oriented toward the immediate circumstances of people in contemporary society. Thisworldly Christians use that word much more than theological conservatives who try to live above or apart from "the world."

The plea for relevance often takes the secular standards of intellectual society that are currently in vogue as the basis for the Christian agenda. It easily becomes a "trap of cultural seduction." This is a form of idolatry that lifts worldly values to a position above and prior to biblical criteria. "To argue about the essence of Christianity using the ethnocentric concepts of a particular culture (relevance) is not the most fruitful way to interpret Christ's message!" (Redekop, 1970: 119).

Invariably social relevance means 'relevance in terms of the expectations of society at large.' The potentially sophisticated relevance of being oneself in an age where nothing seems secure is either implicitly denied or not consciously defended (Mol, 1969: 108).

The issues that are interpreted as "the most relevant" for Christian action tend to shift rather frequently. The target of attention may move from infant formulas in developing countries to the complicity of multinational corporations in the apartheid system of South Africa to exposures of injustice in Central America.

Perhaps it is feasible to work on only one issue at a time, for it is impossible to keep up with all the details and permutations of even one major set of events. Yet even when victory is won on one issue, it may be forfeited on a dozen others that were ignored but are equally significant. Sometimes the focus upon one or two major relevant issues encompasses numerous specific side issues that deserve long-term attention for strategic action. However, people tend to become impatient and disenchanted if goals are not reached within a year or two, so it is difficult to sustain long-range interest and support.

Concentrating work upon the relevant issues runs the risk also of leading into single-issue politics. In a pluralistic society this may indirectly lend support to sinful positions on other issues because of the complex intermingling of many positions on the part of each political party and each representative.

Selective emphasis upon one or a few relevant issues can divert attention away from the theological and ethical development of basic principles for Christian social ethics. As a result, Christians may be thoroughly prepared and mobilized for action on one set of conditions while lacking the foundation to deal with others as they arise.

There is also a problem with timing. Major efforts can be made to deal with one specific issue only after people recognize the problem or need, take time to analyze it, and identify one or more potential solutions. By the time all this is done, events may have rushed past to a different combination of the puzzling, ever-fluid set of problematic circumstances. A focus upon "relevance" is therefore likely to cause Christians to be behind the times, working on the problems of yesterday rather than those of tomorrow.

Many seekers after relevance try to be radical in their appraisal of current conditions and accompanying reform efforts. Walter (1980) shows, however, that they actually are bowing before the "sacred cows" of modern society. Hence they end up being as conventional as possible. A classic example, he says, is Harvey Cox's (1965) *The Secular City*. It advocates a traditional culture religion that accepts society as it is and provides a theological legitimation for it. "Cox perfectly fulfills Marx's view of religion as an opiate. . . . Cox is therefore both politically and theologically one of the most traditional thinkers on the market" (Walter, 1980: 166). (In all fairness, we must indicate that this has been partly corrected in Cox's 1984 followup study.)

When Christians feel out of touch with the modern world, they typically try to become relevant by

. . . taking modern modes of thought, especially the scientific and rational modes, as the starting point from which to interpret Christianity. Thus the Bible, church practice and dogma are all filtered through the sieve of rationality, efficiency and science . . . . This view that the thought forms of the modern world are the only valid ones is incredibly presumptuous and arrogant, not to mention ethnocentric (Walter, 1980: 165).

"Relevance" therefore is a highly relativistic concept. Judgments are made on the basis of limited knowledge and in relationship to selected values and specialized areas of interest. One person's relevance is another's irrelevance.

Asserting for ourselves the unqualified right to decide what is relevant and assuming that there can be no argument about it indicates a failure in imagination. And it indicates an even greater failure in imaginative sympathy. For it is to deny to others the right to live within the same universe with us unless they think precisely as we do.

. . . The fact that we are urged to seek relevance rather than truth makes conformity a virtue. . . . Man has achieved nearly every advance in his knowledge . . . by showing the irrelevant to be relevant (Hamilton, 1973: 71, 70).

To break loose from the shackles of cultural entrapment and pride that define what is relevant for Christian action requires an unwavering orientation toward the One who is Absolute. Keeping imminently in tune with our transcendent God helps Christians to attain a relatively high level of evaluative detachment. This helps us to view our own cultural scene as if we were outside of it so we will not wrongly accommodate ourselves to either the status quo or to misguided methods or goals for changing it.

In his critique of my Finch Lectures Charles Kraft suggested that a new occupational specialty may be needed in Christian circles. Ethnotherapists or sociotherapists can lead churches in coping realistically and consistently with these and such other issues as the form-usage-meaning distinctions, the appropriate scale of action, and the dynamic equivalence issues of applying biblical principles in modern society.

The Christian Scriptures provide evaluative criteria of what is relevant, for they transcend every culture, standing in judgment over them all. They comprise a "transcultural Archimedean point" (Mol, 1969: 108-109) that spawns both a secular and a heavenly vision. They provide leverage to be "the fall of chauvinism, parochialism, bigotry, absolutism, cultural imperialism, negative individualism, and vulgar snobbery" (Higgins, 1974: 19).

Biblical values can correct the tendency to accept rigid concretizations. They provide the universal foundation of principles that transcend every immediate historical and social situation. They enable Christians to draw upon eternal truths and guidelines for action without waiting for a few leaders or experts to determine what is "relevant" for current Christian action.

Emphasizing biblical values that transcend every society has radical implications for behavior under every set of circumstances. By such action Christians can be permanently and genuinely relevant in every set of circumstances in the midst of our ever-changing world. Distancing ourselves in mind and heart from the values of our culture

helps to overcome the danger of blind, uncritical compliance with the status quo. It exercises a self-correcting influence upon those who consciously cling to its ethical-theological system of values. . . . Both cultural imperialism and cultural entrapment can be overcome only if we make a conscious commitment to values which transcend every culture and every individual (Moberg, 1978: 15).

DILEMMAS OF INSTITUTIONALIZATION

Churches and other Christian organizations face many more dilemmas than those posed by the alternatives mentioned in this chapter. (All of the issues discussed elsewhere in this book impinge directly or indirectly upon them and their leadership.) As they pass through their life cycle from first emergence to maturity and eventually to possible disintegration and death, they are typically confronted with a series of five major dilemmas that have been neatly summarized by O'Dea (O'Dea and Aviad, 1983: 56-64).

The early members of a new religious group usually have highly focused, single-minded motivations for their participation in it. As their descendents succeed them and new members enter, these motives become more diverse. Their clergy and professional leaders seem to become more "worldly" than the first ones were, and most of the lay members tend to be passive or lukewarm in their commitment. This is the *dilemma of mixed motivations*.

As indicated earlier, there is a tendency for worship rituals to become objectified and routine. Religious symbols gradually tend to lose their original meaning. The perception of sacredness in ritual is lost through rote repetition. Resonance between the rites and the feelings and attitudes of the members dissipates. Yet the spiritual must be embodied in those profane vehicles, so there is a loss of the sense of ultimacy. This *symbolic dilemma* contributes to the loss of members. It sometimes leads to the formation of new sectarian protest movements and splinter groups.

The *dilemma of administrative order* occurs as the original leaders who are believed to have supernatural gifts (charisma) are replaced by appointed or elected bureaucratic officers. The structures and procedures that were developed under the early conditions of the group prove inadequate for its larger size and changed circumstances. Those who hold positions gain a vested interest in keeping the basic structure unchanged, as well as in making certain that their positions will continue. They may become alienated from rank-and-file members, as in the anticlericalism that is evident in much of the history of Roman Catholicism.

Over time the message of the group must be protected against heresies and interpretations that conflict with its central doctrines. It originated in a specific social context and was relevant to the daily activities and concerns of early followers. To remain relevant, it must be adapted to changing conditions in society and the new members. It is therefore necessary to redefine the dogma and to adapt the rituals and symbols so that they do not become quasi-magical substitutes for genuine worship. Paradoxically, this *dilemma of delimitation* relativizes the religious and ethical message at the same time as it concretizes it. It poses the risk of translating ethical insights into rigid rules that are inconsistent with the spirit originally behind them.

The *dilemma of power* comes to those religious groups that gain a dominant position in society. Compromise with cultural values occurs, and the religious views of the church seem self-evident. Church leaders may begin to rely upon the general social consensus or even upon legal authority to compel or convince people to join. Nonbelievers and defectors seem to threaten society as well as the church, so intolerance and even persecution tend to emerge. The apparent strength of the religion often conceals private cynicism and growing unbelief among the citizens.

These dilemmas suggest that church growth is not an unmixed blessing. Like everything else, it has many effects. When it reaches the extreme form of dominance by one religious group over an entire region, nation, or culture group, it can harm the cause of Christ. Many then will assume that all who reside in the territory are automatically "Christian." False gods will be relied upon for salvation, and even unethical deeds of the power structure may wrongly be seen as "Christian" by outsiders.

Wholistic Christianity recognizes the importance of both personal faith and religious institutions. It seeks qualitative spiritual growth of persons and groups along with growth in size. It is relevant to the totality of human concerns, not just to a few issues selected under the political and intellectual pressures of the day. It recognizes the temptations and hypocrisies that easily flow out of the dilemmas accompanying church growth and historical development, and it takes steps to control them. All of its actions are under the Lordship of Christ, loyalty to whom transcends all institutional commitments.

9

CHALLENGES FROM SOCIAL CHANGE

When sociologists describe contemporary society, they often say, "The only thing permanent is change." Change is occurring so rapidly that each generation is reared during a different historic era. Kenneth Boulding (as quoted by Toffler, 1971:13) has said,

> The world of today . . . is as different from the world in which I was born as that world was from Julius Caesar's. I was born in the middle of human history, to date, roughly. Almost as much has happened since I was born as happened before.

In the midst of rapid and often radical change, disciples of the changeless Christ are often perplexed. Their attitudes toward change are confused. They are puzzled about the kind of action to take. They often reach conclusions that are directly opposite to those of others who have the same faith commitment. Instead of working together, Christians fight each other over issues related to change, cancelling out their potential influence on society.

In this chapter we shall first examine the nature, scope, and implications of contemporary changes, then some general lessons that we can glean from the past. We'll follow that by reviewing what is negatively taught through mistakes that Christians have made, and, finally, summarize some principles to guide Christian action in a changing world.

THE OMNIPRESENCE OF CHANGE

There have been many periods of war, conquest, natural disaster, revolution, and other social upheavals in the history of humanity, so change is not new. Today, however, change is so general and widespread that the entire world is changing more rapidly than ever before. Even this swift rate of change seems to be accelerating. Its consequences reverberate around the globe; "virtually no feature of life is exempt from the expectation or normality of change" (Moore, 1963:2).

133

Technically, cultural change can be distinguished from societal change. Changes in the culture pertain to the content and patterns of values, ideas, norms, and other aspects of the cognitive systems that shape the behavior of people. Societal changes are transformations in the social organizations and systems of relationship that govern the interaction between individuals and groups (Burwell, 1982:386). Rather than attempt to differentiate these from one another, we will treat them as interacting aspects of "social change," as in Yinger's (1982:293) definition: "Social change . . . is the process of movement from one relatively stable structural-cultural-characterological system toward another."

New forces may enter the social system so rapidly that realignment cannot proceed fast enough to attain equilibrium. Societies therefore do not necessarily move from a situation of relative balance through periods of disruption into new situations of balance.

> A situation where structural, cultural, and characterological elements are continuously out of phase with each other may now be endemic. . . . Nor should we assume that change must begin with one part of the system. . . . Whichever part of the social change process occurs first, its impact will be strongly influenced by the extent and direction of changes in the other parts (Yinger, 1982:294).

There are many types of social change. Changes motivated internally (within a person, group, institution, or society) can be distinguished from those that are motivated by outside influences or social controls. Changes in organizational structures are usually distinct from those in behavior, technology, or assumptions and values (Schaller, 1972:34-39). Many significant changes, especially in religion and philosophy of life, involve transformations of thought. They shift the emphasis within an established tradition rather than discard the tradition (Slater, 1978:91).

To those who ask whether changes will ever stop, whether there is anything constant that we can count on in this world,

> . . . the answer is no: change is the only thing that is permanent. This law was decreed by an astute observer of the universe after years of study and consideration. His name was Heraclitus, and he lived in the 6th century B.C.
>
> There is a tendency these days to assume that constant change is a phenomenon peculiar to modern Western society. In fact, all recorded history is a story of change flowing in a never-ending stream . . . ("The Pressure of Change," 1982:1).

Today we are exposed to numerous mass media trying to be the first to report news and developments in science, technology, society, and industry, so we are more conscious of change than our forebears were. There are many more of us to produce changes—nearly five billion, compared to one billion in 1850, two billion in 1930, and three billion in 1960. The base of information and technology upon which to build is vastly greater today than in the days of our grandparents.

Tensions from inequality and class struggles, environmental challenges, social disorder, and political ideologies all contribute to change. These may be no greater today than in the past, but the isolation of societies from each other has significantly diminished. Contacts between the members of different societies greatly facilitate change by borrowing culture traits, including values and social arrangements as well as technology. We not only know more about current changes, but we are more aware of them, and they indeed are occurring at a more rapid rate than ever before.

Despite all this, some Bible-believing Christians deride the idea that social change is significant. They quote Koheleth, the ancient Preacher:

> What has been will be again,
>   what has been done will be done again;
>   there is nothing new under the sun.
> Is there anything of which one can say,
>   "Look! This is something new?"
> It was here already, long ago;
>   it was here before our time (Ecclesiastes 1:9-10 NIV).

Psychologists, pastoral counselors, social workers, psychiatrists, and others in the "helping professions" who focus upon individual personality needs tend to agree. There are new diagnostic labels, measuring tests and tools, and therapeutic techniques, but people basically remain much the same from generation to generation even when the world around them changes.

> To the best of our knowledge, in all periods of time, all cultural settings, and all ethnic groups people need to love and to be loved, to give and to receive, and to have a variety of other needs fulfilled— needs that are psychological and emotional, physical and material, sociological and political, intellectual and cognitive, spiritual and religious. In that respect, people remain the same, regardless of the circumstances around them (Moberg, 1977a:4-5).

The paradox of seeing more change than the world has ever known before, yet finding in Scripture the argument that there is nothing new under the sun, is easily resolved. The world is indeed filled with changes in technology, institutions, and customs, yet basic human nature remains relatively constant. The ancient Book of Books known as the Bible contains all the eternally abiding wisdom necessary to guide faith and conduct, even though the world is in flux.

CONTEMPORARY SOCIAL CHANGES

Significant changes are occurring in every domain of human activity, many of them so "naturally" and silently that we hardly notice them. For example, the US labor force has shifted from one in which blue-collar laborers were dominant to one in which professional and white-collar employees greatly outnumber the unskilled, semiskilled, and skilled workers. Hospitals have replaced homes as the most common place in which to be born and to die. For many television has replaced family conversation as the chief medium for passing the cultural heritage along to the next generation. Other institutions have replaced the family as the chief place to care for the retarded, mentally ill, dependent elderly, and disabled persons.

The divorce rate in the US has more than doubled since 1960. Nonmarital cohabitation has increased dramatically. Premarital and extramarital sexual liaisons are so common that the mass media give the impression that something must be wrong with any adolescent or adult who practices the "old-fashioned" virtue of limiting sexual intercourse to marriage. There are almost as many induced abortions as live births in a typical year. Companionship of the spouses, not child bearing and rearing, is by far the most prized objective in marriage. (Specific statistics are available in Duncan et al., 1973; Caplow et al., 1982; and most college textbooks on social change, social problems, and the family.)

These and other characteristics make the contemporary family considerably different from that of a century ago. Whether the changes represent deterioration or improvement of the quality of life depends upon one's values. Some argue that it has never been stronger, for dissident spouses now are free to depart instead of being held in pseudoslavery to a marriage because of vows that are difficult to break. Others attribute juvenile delinquency, drug abuse, cult inductions, and most other problems of society to family flaws.

Families reproduce their culture, not only the human species. The dead parent or grandparent once lived on through the survival of his or her culture and values.

In periods of rapid social change, however, this may not be possible, and it can be distressing for older people to realise that their values and culture, as well as their body, may not be immortal (Walter, 1980:66).

Loss of the family's role in giving children civic socialization has resulted from the increase in common law families, "the erotic sexual revolution that has drenched everything in sex, and the rise of feminism which has brought with it the decline of the family," according to Edward Shorter of the University of Toronto ("Decline . . . ," 1982:17). He believes that high rates of adolescent crime, vandalism, broken families, "an emotional iron curtain between adolescents and their parents," alcoholism, and indifference to the morals of others are among the consequences of the new "permanently unstable" family. "If things continue the way they are today, I can see the time when we might have to have armies to control the cities." Others take a more moderate view of current trends, but they recognize that changes continue to occur in the family (see, e. g., Bernard, 1982).

Change continuously occurs in human populations. Babies are born, people die, health deteriorates with advanced age, and changes of residence occur. The life cycle of individuals is reflected in similar life cycles of communities and social institutions, including the church (Moberg, 1984a:118-124). While growth is still evident in the population of the United States, it now occurs at a slower rate than during any previous period since the 1930s. One segment, however, is increasing much more rapidly than the rest—those past age 65 and, within it, especially those past 80. This is an important part of the explanation for the large number of older people in many churches.

As life expectancy at birth continues to climb slowly upward, the number and proportion of widows will continue to grow, for the differences in longevity between men and women are still increasing. (Women now live about eight years longer on the average.) If birth rates do not unexpectedly climb, the percentage of elderly people will continue to increase. Of course, every community is different; one must not assume that national characteristics describe a local situation (Moberg, 1983).

Changes in the size and composition of the population affect numerous other areas of life, including types and amounts of clothing and other manufactured goods, social services, recreational facilities, church programs, educational institutions, medical services, pharmaceutical products, and housing arrangements. Population growth has been accompanied by sprawling cities and the conversion of millions of acres of agricultural land to urban uses. Inner city areas have become blighted, partly as a result of the outward movement of middle-class people, which reinforces urban deterioration. Only recently has gentrification (the rehabilitation of slums for middle-class people) begun to reverse the trend, but it also introduces housing problems for those poor people who are displaced. The revitalization of cities, protection of the agricultural resources necessary for food production, and the health, safety, and welfare of people are thus intricately interrelated. To be effective, any policy developed must produce partnerships among public, private, and civic agencies (American Assembly, 1980).

Meanwhile, many social forces continue to compartmentalize the population. "One of the most important and far-reaching trends of the twentieth century is the division of the population along lines that reflect religion, age, education, marital status, income, wealth, race, culture, ethnic background, language, and social position, *and the increasing geographical separation of these groupings*" (Schaller, 1969:160). Problems of communication and understanding between ethnic and racial groups, generations, social classes, and other subcultures are intensified as a result (pp. 160-167).

Tensions between our central cities and their suburbs flow to a considerable extent out of these springs. Social problems are augmented and their solutions hindered when Christians fall into the temptation to conclude that their neighborly responsibilities apply only to the immediate vicinity of their residences, their occupational groups, or the membership of their church congregations.

SOCIAL REVOLUTIONS

Some developments are so significant that they have been labeled as "revolutions"—changes that occur so swiftly and with such great and far-reaching impact on social structures and people's lives that they have revolutionized society. *The organizational revolution* has made many people into serfs bowing before corporation masters in big business, big professional associations, big multinational corporations, and even big governmental agencies, educational institutions, health and welfare establishments, and labor unions. *The property revolution* has increased public controls over the private domain and removed many distinctions between the public and private sphere. It has produced numerous repercussions, not the least of which is the question of who actually owns the billions of dollars invested in private pension funds. *The financial revolution* has made it extremely easy for people to pile up debts beyond their ability to repay. It also has shifted the patterns of investment and distribution of monetary resources throughout the world.

An occupational revolution has reduced the total years of active full-time employment, brought women into labor force areas from which they were once excluded, squeezed persons of marginal capabilities onto welfare rolls, made it necessary for the average worker to change careers several times during a working life, created problems for churches and other agencies that depend upon volunteers and discretionary time programming, and compounded the burdens of unemployment compensation and social security programs. *The sexual revolution* has brought profound changes in sexual morality, including the disastrous effects of "the new morality" (see Moberg, 1978b), millions of induced abortions every year, unprecedented divorce rates, and the rapid spread of new venereal diseases. *The revolution of rising expectations* has augmented the discontent of minority groups, especially those with improving status who were led to expect full and immediate gratification of their desire for equal attainment without passing through the necessary intermediate stages.

The cybernetic revolution linking automated machines with electronic controls in vast loops of self-correcting feedback networks has displaced thousands of marginal workers with highly skilled technicians and is speedily producing robots to do assembly line work once done by people. *The computer revolution* is sweeping through all areas of production, communications, and record keeping in business, industry, government, and service enterprises. *The communications revolution* is rapidly bringing the population of the whole world within listening, viewing, and speaking distance of each other, while *the nuclear energy revolution* includes the possibility of destroying the entire human race.

Some of these revolutionary changes have attracted special labels. Toffler (1981) believes we are entering a "third wave," following the agricultural and industrial waves of all previous civilization. Coleman (1982) argues that ours is an "asymmetric society;" corporate actors dominate contemporary social life, with considerably different concepts of rights, risks, and responsibilities from those that prevailed when natural actors were in control. Naisbitt (1982:249) says that we live in "the time of the parenthesis, the time between eras, . . . clinging to the known past in fear of the unknown future." Evans (1980) thinks we are entering a "micromillennium" with microprocessors replacing human labor and providing ultraintelligent computers and robots as a new source of intellectual power.

Rukeyser (1982) calls ours a litigious society because of the proliferation of litigation as the means of resolving disputes and disagreements. It has also been called a narcissistic (Lasch, 1979), privatistic (Hadden, 1969), heretical (Berger, 1979), and therapeutic (Rieff, 1966) society, to mention but a few of the labels that have been used. It is a society of homeless people who lack the "sacred canopy" (Berger, 1967) of a framework of meaning to protect them from the fragility of human existence and shelter them from the possibility that life may fall apart, disintegrating into nightmares of despair.

The sacred values of traditional society may have been torn to shreds even more in Britain than in the United States:

> The decline of Christendom, of the institutional church and its stable view of the world, has left modern man peculiarly homeless. In Christendom, people were able to place themselves in relation to the Christian God who was conceived (among other things) as the Creator of the Universe; people thus had a place in the cosmic order of things and were at home in the universe. When God 'died', with the end of societal validation of his existence, Man became as it were a wanderer on the face of the earth, alone in the universe (Walter, 1980:17).

Revolutionary changes in society thus are accompanied by significant modifications of the self-concepts, personality orientations, interpersonal relationships, and individual behavior of its people. Many experience bewilderment, frustration, and disorientation as change piles up on change. They suffer culture shock within their own cultural setting. This causes the misinterpretation of reality, broken communication patterns, and a reduced ability to cope. They may even experience the "mass neurosis" from premature arrival of the future that Toffler (1971) has called "future shock." Whether the results are that extreme or not, every aspect of personal and social life has been affected by social change.

To be sure, the revolutions have brought numerous benefits to modern society, or at least to major segments of it, while also bringing controversy, deprivation, suffering, and other undesirable results in their wake. Fixing attention selectively upon some of the effects rather than some others contributes to conflict and policy disagreements.

Rapid and sweeping changes are transforming society and our entire way of life. Wishful thinking about an allegedly glorious past cannot restore it to us. Bemoaning the changes will not halt their rapid progression. Trying to reverse major trends may be as futile as attempting to change the direction of a single car in a speeding freight train. Seeking to promote changes in but one small area of social life without attention to the major trends of the larger society is likely to prove equally unsuccessful. As Yinger (1982:309) has said,

> . . . we are in the midst of a major civilizational transformation. The critical issue that humankind faces today is how to create a rolling adjustment to the incredibly rapid and drastic changes taking place on the planet. We're faced with the problem of rebuilding the station, relaying and changing the gauge of the tracks and accommodating vastly more passengers, while still keeping the trains running.

Yinger (1982) shows that countercultures—each of which consists of "a set of norms and values of a group that sharply contradict the dominant norms and values of the society of which that group is a part" (p. 3)—"highlight, dramatize, and anticipate drastic problems" (p. 310). They may be viewed as early warning signals, voices crying in the wilderness, or symptoms of major disorders. In either case they have much to offer society as it continually weaves new threads into the social fabric of civilization and occasionally but unwittingly sets up a new warp as well.

Evangelical Christians are one part of the counterculture, a part that is gaining an increasingly respectful hearing from leaders in many areas of society. If they respond wisely to the challenges of current and emerging social changes, they will become a significant counterbalance to many forces of evil that threaten the well-being of all people on the face of the earth. If they fail to do so, they will hypocritically deny the gospel that they verbally proclaim and become connivers in the infectious spread of evil throughout the world.

CONSEQUENCES OF CHANGE

Historians and social scientists have found that the impact of many past events is so complex, diffused, and comprehensive that there can be no end to research into causes and effects. Changes related to the Reformation, the Renaissance, the Industrial Revolution, Marxism, Freudianism, Darwinian evolution, individualism, pluralism, secularism, and other trends and conditions profoundly affect our lives far beyond our awareness of their influence.

Even a single technological development can have a tremendous impact. The invention and widespread adoption of the contraceptive pill, for example, increased the rational control of family size and child spacing, but it also contributed to many unplanned consequences. Among these are the increased flux of mothers into the labor force, the modification of cultural norms about sexual morality, and increased pre- and extramarital sexual intercourse. These in turn contributed to increased divorce rates, the decline of daytime women's programs in churches, and the weakening of those church and community programs that depend on female volunteers.

The pill has contributed to battles over social policies pertinent to sex education, to controversies about the dissemination of contraceptive information and supplies in public welfare programs, and to pressures to modify income tax and inheritance regulations for unmarried cohabiting couples. The decline of US birth rates since 1959 can be traced in large part to the pill. Its effects spill over into every area of economic, political, and social life, including, paradoxically, the high rates of adolescent pregnancies and abortions.

It took longer for the automobile to become widely diffused in US society. This was due in part to its higher cost, but mainly because its efficient use depended upon such other changes as the need for wider roads with improved surfaces and smoother curves, facilities for the storage and sale of gasoline, repair shops, parts distributors, and other supporting activities.

Motor vehicles have had an enormous influence upon all social institutions. They greatly modified the marketing of farm produce, facilitated the location of factories away from railroads, increased the centralization of merchandising in rural communities, led to the consolidation of rural schools, contributed to the death of many country churches, enabled the rapid development of suburbs and decentralized shopping centers in metropolitan areas, changed the vacationing patterns of many people, and significantly affected patterns of dating, courtship, and mate selection. They raised many problems of relationships between local, state, and federal governments regarding such issues as taxation, licensing, police powers, and the building and maintenance of highways, roads, and streets. More people have been killed in motor vehicle accidents in the USA than in all the wars of the nation's history.

Changes were predicted soon after the coming of the first automobiles. An article in *Scientific American* in 1899, for instance, anticipated that life would be greatly changed:

> The improvement in city conditions by the general adoption of the motor car can hardly be overestimated. Streets clean, dustless and odorless, with light, rubber tired vehicles moving swiftly and noiselessly over their smooth expanse, would eliminate a greater part of the nervousness, distraction and strain of modern metropolitan life ("Crystal Ball," 1972).

The dust from horse-drawn vehicles on unpaved streets, the odors of previously omnipresent horse manure, and the populations of horseflies and English sparrows all declined as motor vehicles replaced horses as the main source of local traffic. Instead we now have serious problems of air pollution, huge expanses of agricultural land replaced by streets and parking lots, parking problems, and vastly more accidental deaths and maiming of people. Drivers no longer are brought faithfully home by "Old Nell" when they are sleepy or after they have been drinking, and the response speed needed for emergencies in traffic has greatly increased. It can hardly be said that "the nervousness, distraction and strain of modern metropolitan life" have been substantially reduced by the flowering of the automotive age!

The coexistence of changes does not prove that one caused the other. When two phenomena are causally connected, variation in one will produce changes in the other, but simultaneous or successive changes may occur because both are the effects of the same set of causes, or each may have shifted fortuitously by chance alone. Thus the fact that European communities with high birthrates had more storks and more cabbages does not prove the old folktales that storks or cabbages are the source of human babies. (The explanatory variable actually was that rural communities had more storks, cabbages, and babies.) Much alleged "evidence" used to support various proposed reforms is no more solidly based. Statistics are easily abused. Individual examples or cases do not prove a general relationship.

Changes are interrelated. All parts of a society are interwoven into a complex social network. A change in any one part affects other closely related parts, and they in turn influence still others. For instance, research by Richard M. McKenzie of Clemson University (Kenney, 1982) has shown that each one percent increase in the national unemployment rate is associated with 37,000 more deaths, 920 more suicides, 650 more homicides, 4,000 more admissions to state mental hospitals, and 3,300 more state prison admissions than under previous conditions. The decline in the self-esteem and morale of those put out of work and the increase in marital and family problems are harder to quantify. Communities with plant closings experience reduced property tax income, increased social welfare expenditures, and fewer people earning incomes (Kenney, 1982). The impact of economic recession thus spills out into every area of personal and social life.

What is more, "change and social progress will continue to produce a demand for additional changes, a reordering of priorities, and a redefinition of the goals" (Schaller, 1969:205). The effects of social changes are more complex than the patterns from concentric ripples flowing out and crossing each other when a thousand pebbles are thrown into a calm pond. Change begets still more change.

Changes that are highly desirable therefore usually have both desirable and undesirable results. Many social problems result from normal human behavior that seeks to attain wholesome goals without any malicious intent.

> That social problems are caused by bad people is probably the most widespread fallacy of all. . . . social problems are as often caused by good people who are minding their own business as by bad people who are being bad. . . . Social problems persist because nice people tolerate and support the conditions that produce them (Horton and Leslie, 1981:10).

The search for personal, organizational, or institutional scapegoats on which to place the blame for social problems has often distorted our interpretations and hampered effective action.

The consequences of change are unevenly distributed. Many people earn a living through the misery of others. What would happen to the medical profession if there were no illness, to dentistry if there were no caries, gum disease, or broken and misplaced teeth, to clinical psychologists and psychiatrists if there were no mental illness, to auto mechanics if there were no auto breakdowns and accidents, to police if there were no crime and other problems of social control, to attorneys and judges if there were no torts, crimes, and legal misunderstandings, and to social workers if there were no poverty, maladjusted people, broken families, and other welfare needs? Where there is a free market, employers benefit by having unemployed people available to take up the slack for irregular work needs. The protective disposal of industrial wastes may reduce the dividends of corporation stockholders and eventually increase the consumer price of a product. Landlords benefit but tenants suffer from a shortage of rental properties. High rates of interest benefit investors but deprive lenders of money. Most often, the wealthy benefit from both the status quo and planned political changes, while the poor suffer, and the middle class is caught wavering among many dilemmas and paradoxes.

Changeovers in a society are never complete. Even when revolutionary goals are attained, they never completely overturn all the elements of the social order. Old idolatries hang on in modified forms even after major reform movements seem to have eliminated them (Walter, 1980: 181-183). Indeed, most of the customs and practices that pertain to daily life remain largely unchanged or change only slowly under the impact of even such major transitions as military coups and political revolutions.

All changes spring from the seeds of past conditions, values, and ideologies. Rarely, if ever, are all areas of life radically changed by major reforms. Failure to recognize this fact brought derision upon Christian reformers whose simplistic solutions for social problems failed. Evangelist Billy Sunday, for example, believed that prohibition of the sale and use of alcoholic beverages would solve all the other problems of society. When the Eighteenth Amendment to the Constitution was passed, he declared,

> The reign of tears is over. The slums will soon be only a memory.
> We will turn our prisons into factories and our jails into storehouses
> and corncribs. Men will walk upright now, women will smile, and the

children will laugh. Hell will be forever for rent (quoted by Sinclair, 1964:248).

The advocates of single-issue politics—those who believe that one specific reform will bring about all needed changes in society—usually destroy their own case because of this fact. Their perceptions of society are distorted by their simplifications. Invalid assumptions contribute to myths like racism, ageism, and sexism that increase the difficulty of seeing the truth in a social situation (see Heddendorf, 1980).

The complexity of social change and the intermixtures of beneficial and detrimental consequences that flow from it accentuate the diverse attitudes toward it in Christian circles. Conflicts emerge about every aspect of causes, effects, and especially appropriate responses.

LIMITATIONS OF PLANNING

Whenever attempts are made to plan for the future, numerous problems arise. Values about the desirability of present and anticipated changes conflict with each other. Much of the tension over such issues as racial balance and integration in schools reflects disagreements about both the ends and the means of proposed policies. This is a long-standing problem. For example,

When the British Admiralty built a string of lighthouses in the Bahamas a century ago, the Islanders were furious; this ended their plunder from the ships they lured onto the reefs with false signal lights. . . . Plenty of well paid, pleasant jobs for all would mean that the dirty, unpleasant work would simply not be done. . . . Genuine equality of opportunity would mean that successful parents could no longer pass on their advantages to their children. Should genuine peace between nations break out, the social and economic dislocations would be most painful to a great many people (Horton and Leslie, 1981:11).

All social issues can be interpreted from the perspective of conflicting values. Disagreements about central values and their interpretations provide the basis for most political and civic controversy. Internalizing discrepant values and associated applications and meanings may also be a primary source of many neuroses and psychoses. The analysis of such conflicts provides a major route toward the improved understanding of people and society.

People may not agree that a given condition constitutes a problem. Divorce, for instance, can be viewed as either a problem or a solution to the problems of marriage and the family. Many consider the temperate use of alcohol and marijuana as a means for alleviating personal distress; others see all uses as outright evil. Not a few citizens see lotteries, bingo, and other forms of gambling as appropriate forms of recreation or of collecting money for charitable and religious causes. Others view all gambling as inherently evil in its consequences. Some think a great arsenal of nuclear weapons is a means of assuring world peace, while others believe that it constitutes preparation for the eventual destruction of the human race. Induced abortion is interpreted as murder by many, while others consider it to be merely the disposal of unwanted tissue, scarcely different from an appendectomy, in order to prevent future problems. Altogether too many people feel that just passing a law about an undesirable condition resolves it, not realizing that no law can be any better than its enforcement.

"Pictures in the mind" provide people's interpretations and definitions of a situation. Whether or not they are consistent with the known facts and with the professed values of those who hold them, these mental definitions provide the basis for personal decisions and actions.

> Popular misinformation about property values and race is one of the greatest obstacles to housing integration. Popular superstitions about drug addicts, sex deviants, and mental illness are barriers to their effective treatment. The antiurban bias and the myth that local government is more honest and efficient than federal government are obstacles to the sensible handling of many problems (Horton and Leslie, 1981:607-608).

Obviously, this means that anyone who wishes to bring about social change must try to understand the mental images of the people he or she wishes to influence. Propagandists and special pleaders, both in and out of politics, attempt to arouse images of current and changed situations that are consistent with their cause. In a free and open society counterpropaganda presenting the other side sometimes confuses people more than it enlightens them. It does offer the opportunity, however, to become aware of contrasting perspectives and, hopefully, to gain a more balanced understanding of controversial issues than would otherwise prevail.

People in the USA have a tendency to take pride in being practical instead of being theoretical. An antiintellectual bias has long been a dominant characteristic of their society (see Hofstadter, 1963). Nevertheless, even those who claim to act solely on the basis of common sense, precedent, pragmatism, or "practical answers" are in fact acting on the basis of implicit theoretical understandings about the nature of humanity, society, social change, and other phenomena. As Horton and Leslie (1981:18) put it,

. . . in social policy, as in most other fields, theory and practice are inseparable. Every practical policy flows from some theory of causation, and every theory carries some implications for control or treatment. The person who tries to separate them merely reveals an ignorance of their relationship. . . . People who imagine themselves unmoved by theoretical considerations are, in fact, slaves to the theories of some dead economist or philosopher.

Whether they oppose or support proposed changes, people act on the basis of theories. These are less often stated than unstated. They lurk implicitly in the background of public policy except on occasions when Marxists tangle with capitalists, behaviorists with existentialists, cultural determinists with advocates of free will, and the like. The ability to identify the underlying theoretical orientations of the antagonists and protagonists of proposed changes is an invaluable tool for all who are a part of the struggle to improve the quality of life.

The greatest battlefield related to social change hence is in the realm of values. Attitudes in the minds of people largely determine their orientations to social issues and the proposed solutions for personal, social, political, and other problems. Their always-limited knowledge of pertinent facts, of the myths and stereotypes that bias their opinions, of the ideological commitments that provide a guiding rudder to their actions, and of other elements of their definitions of the situation center around the values they hold. These values are often modified as a result of experience, but the new learning is governed to a considerable extent by prior attitudes. Perceptions of events therefore tend to be selectively supportive of preexisting value orientations. Values that coexist may complement each other, but they may also reflect the ambivalence and dilemma that come from simultaneously holding antithetical opinions. Change advocates and opponents are trapped when discerning foes recognize that they are inconsistent or "hypocritical."

Planned change usually requires sacrifice. People who have a vested interest in the status quo are required to give up some of their income, prestige, property, or pride. It is far easier for anyone to advocate changes that demand sacrifice by others than to support those that may take away one's own privileges.

Planned change is therefore always resisted. It has many economic, social, psychic, political, and other costs, so opposition to it occurs in every society. Those who advocate change are typically opposed by other groups: minorities who do not accept the majority interpretation of circumstances, people in "the establishment" whose interests would be harmed by proposed changes, bureaucrats whose administrative domains would be reduced by new regulations, people who think their taxes would increase beyond the value of the benefits they would gain, those who believe cherished values or traditions would be compromised, and many more. The dominant thrust is generally to protect and "preserve the major values and institutions of the existing society. Whether one views this as good or bad depends upon one's own degree of radicalism or conservatism" (Horton and Leslie, 1981:7). The risks of change "help to explain why innovation normally is resisted by any organization or institution" (Schaller, 1972:54).

The actual results of planned changes are never completely as intended. The good that is expected from a reform is never fully attained; similarly, the ills predicted by opponents are seldom completely realized. This is partly because of selectivity in the processes of observing and reasoning, which tend to be biased in the direction of one's prejudices. It also reflects the resilience of the human spirit and the persistence of social institutions. They both have a self-regenerating and healing tendency similar to that of the human body. Most of all, it is a consequence of the relative ignorance that prevails about every phenomenon. The "John Wesley syndrome" sometimes comes into play: piety produces an accumulation of wealth with the glamor and power it brings; as a result, the piety itself is endangered and may fade away (Yinger, 1982:301; Niebuhr, 1957:70-72).

Knowledge about social change is very incomplete. That is true on both the theoretical level about the general processes of change and the pragmatic level of methods and principles for producing change. Knowledge continually increases, but facts alone do not solve problems. They have meaning only as they are interpreted in the context of values, which in a pluralistic society diverge widely and are themselves shifting.

Facts are important, of course. They help to provide a basis for recognizing the problematic nature of certain conditions, trends that should be enhanced or opposed, and rationalizations for or against change that may be contrary to reality. Ultimately, however, our theories are never fully tested, and our base of factual knowledge is never complete.

Research, by its very nature, is always on things past. Even when predictions are made, checking is later needed to determine whether or not they materialized. Although the base of knowledge is expanding, "the things we would *like* to know about social change will always outnumber those we think we *do* know" (Duncan et al., 1973:2). Any action to promote change, therefore, is only a proposed solution, never a certain solution. It represents an act of faith.

The solutions introduced to solve problems often produce or aggravate other problems (see Boudon, 1982, and Sieber, 1981). The improved control of infections and disease brought the world's population explosion. The high standard of living that resulted from technological progress aggravated environmental pollution. Flood control projects without control of land use made lowland areas attractive building sites, so the total impact of less frequent flooding is more destructive than ever before. "Practically every solution, even if it works, brings new problems" (Horton and Leslie, 1981:610). Iatrogenic diseases caused by the treatment are not limited to the medical services (see Sieber, 1981; Schneider, 1975:4-14).

Solutions intended to resolve one problem may work against those introduced to solve another. For example, many urban expressways built to relieve traffic pressures actually contributed to increased traffic congestion. They also increased urban blight while other government agencies were trying to abate it.

Piecemeal efforts to work on but one issue at a time have often produced disastrous results. Whitesburg, Kentucky, spent $180,000 for a reservoir and water system, but the reservoir was completely filled with silt from upstream strip mining operations even before the dam was finished. The lack of accompanying land-use programs made its expenditures a total waste. Solutions must be integrated with one another if they are to be effective (Horton and Leslie, 1981:610). The difficulty, however, is that everything in our society, and eventually in the entire world, is interrelated. It is impossible, even in totalitarian societies like the Soviet Union, to accomplish the efficient integration of every interacting unit.

THE NEED TO PLAN

Social change is unavoidable. It is occurring at a more rapid rate than ever before in world history. Its consequences both for better and for worse spill out into every area of society, including religion.

Even though planning to deal with change has many limitations, those who believe that everything should be brought under the dominion of Jesus Christ must do their part to accomplish the Lord's will. This means coping effectively and constructively with change and with the disagreements and conflict that flow from it within Christian circles as well as outside them. It requires effective action to cope with the paradoxes and dilemmas that intrude whenever one desires to act in accord with God's will. Such action is most likely to be fruitful when it occurs in the context of wholistic Christianity.

The final three chapters of this book give suggestions and principles for practicing wholistic Christianity. After indicating some further aspects of its basis, we'll present a series of strategic principles for confronting change and, finally, some tangible steps toward implementing wholeness.

PART V

PRACTICING WHOLISTIC CHRISTIANITY

10

THE BASIS FOR WHOLISTIC
CHRISTIANITY

The preceding chapters have emphasized the description and analysis of problems, conflicts, paradoxes, and dilemmas that face Christians in contemporary society. We are confronted by the pressures of individualism, pluralism, and freedom that have contributed to reductionism, secular humanism, and ethical, moral, and religious relativism. There is no overall value consensus to guide action on most current issues in society. Behaviors once conventionally viewed as sinful have been changed into options for personal choice as a part of people's civil liberties. Even the word "sin" is in disfavor, and liberty often seems to have tyrannical results.

Biblical paradoxes and the dilemmas of modern life contribute to tensions within Christianity between those who advocate one side of numerous theoretical and practical alternatives and those who choose the opposite. Among the domains in which the tensions cause Christians to choose sides or else to waver between two opinions are the diverse dimensions and styles of personal Christian commitment, the competition between personal ministries and those to meet collective needs, the dilemmas of religious institutions, and the challenges related to social change. In every instance we noted that a biblically defined Christianity recognizes the truth and error that are found on both sides of these issues and the validity that inheres in each of the opposing positions adopted by various Christian groups.

There are many other tensions in Christendom. Most are related to topics we have discussed. Some have led to major systems of classification of religious orientations, such as the church-sect-mysticism typology of Troeltsch (1931) and various derivatives, such as Yinger's (1957) elaboration of it into six major categories of religious bodies. Church-like groups are usually closely identified with the power structures and cultural values of society, while sect-like groups lack power and oppose established social patterns. Some sects try to avoid contact with society. Others aggressively oppose its main themes and aim at revolutionary social reforms. Still others accept most societal values and practices and deal only with the sins and failings of individuals.

An "ethic of escapism" develops when Christians try to remain detached from the secular world and uninvolved with it by keeping themselves separate from it (Cotham, 1979). In contrast, an "ethic of involvement" attempts to be in a meaningful, dialogical relationship with the world without being of it, thus trying to change it. (For other typological classifications, see Moberg, 1984a:73-99).

It is especially easy for fundamentalists and evangelicals to get impaled on the horns of various dilemmas. Believing with good biblical support that there is but one way to heaven, they are easily led to believe that there is only one truly "Christian" position on everything else. Yet the same divisive tendencies are found among "mainline Protestants" and other groups as well.

> Now, when the earlier distinctions between Catholics and Protestants have in many places been overcome, and when "neo-orthodoxy" seemed to have had the result of attenuating the either-or distinction between liberals and fundamentalists, Satan is up to a new trick. He seems to have polarized the erstwhile "liberal modernists" into two opposing camps. The one advocates evangelism; the other advocates social action. The one seeks for "piety," the other seeks for "involvement." The one looks for "orthodoxy," the other aims at "relevancy." In other words, we once again have an either-or church, but now right within that entity sometimes triumphalistically described as "mainline Protestantism" (Krass, 1973:7).

The Great Deceiver typically tricks people by distorted appeals to the good, the true, and the beautiful. Rather than coming as a horrifying creature with cloven hooves, pointed ears, and a spiked tail, "Satan . . . masquerades as an angel of light. It is not surprising, then, if his servants masquerade as servants of righteousness" (2 Cor. 11:14-15 NIV). Now as in the early years of the Christian church, Christians must take care lest they be led astray by "false apostles, deceitful workmen, masquerading as apostles of Christ" (2 Cor. 11:13 NIV).

Individuals need help to turn the conflict that arises in marriage and the family, at work, in friendships, in the church, and in their inner selves into positive and growing experiences (Krebs, 1982). Controversies and disagreements between and within Christian groups similarly can be viewed as opportunities for creativity. The paradoxes and dilemmas that tend to separate them can be turned into positive challenges to learn, to grow, and to become more effective servants of the King of kings. Demonic dualisms can become dynamic dialectics when they are confronted properly.

Some of the ways to accomplish that goal are presented in these last three chapters. Earlier sections have given suggestions on how to overcome the respective problems discussed. We will not repeat them all here, so Part V is not a summary, strictly speaking. It does, however, give an overview of wholesome perspectives and principles for action that can help us move toward a truly wholistic Christianity.

THE NEED FOR WHOLISTIC CHRISTIANITY

We have seen that when Christians become involved in social action, they tend to be reactive, focusing upon negative conditions in society, rather than proactive, presenting a positive program for improvement. Both their individual and their social ethics tend to center upon sins and problems. They protest against circumstances and trends that are deemed wrong or undesirable. Whether the protest is oriented against a proposed freeway, the armaments race, nuclear energy, using corn to fatten beef, driving after drinking, violence to children, abortions, racial discrimination, divorce, or other undesirable conditions, the main message seems to be "Stop!"

Far fewer are the attempts of Christians to step ahead of the secular world by developing positive plans for public or private policy in order to correct harmful conditions, rehabilitate victims, prevent their future recurrence, or alleviate their severity. If the Bible is a sufficient guide to conduct, why are Christians so seldom in the forefront of constructive change, identifying positive actions that flow out of their faith and stimulating Christian citizens to influence the body politic? Is it not desirable for Christians to be known for what they advocate, in the public arena, not only for what they oppose?

> One of the most difficult, yet most essential concepts to communicate . . . is the concept of being proactive rather than reactive. It seems that the inclination to respond to crisis or need is significantly more powerful than employing one's energies to create, organize or change structures and systems that affect God's creation. . . .
>
> To hold the position of reactor in society is a statement of weakness. From this position of weakness, individuals and sometimes the church too easily declare innocence when confronted with the reality of the deterioration of our cities and our world. We so often act as if we were not stewards of God's creation (Frenchak, 1983).

We also have noted the tensions related to evangelism and social concern. They pertain to the issue of getting words and deeds, preaching and practice, or proclamation and demonstration together in a constructive biblical harmony. Unfortunately, there still are people at each extreme who have no use for the biblically based teachings of the other. Some still cling to a reactionary perspective that either the present status quo or the conditions of some romanticized past represent the ideal society. Others work for revolutionary liberation from the inequities and injustices of current social, political, and economic systems. A more honest perspective will see the need for a selective modification of society, and hence will try to change some aspects of it while preserving its wholesome elements.

These polarities, in turn, relate to general orientations toward the world, change, and other Christians. Various degrees and forms of openness and closedness may be observed. Seeking flexibility, some groups allow deviations from established norms and customs. Others seek stability and order, shunning modifications and attempting to retain such a high degree of "purity" in their faith, worship, social relations, and action programs that they become rigidly authoritarian masters over their members.

The acceptance of new members or the reluctance to receive them is related to such attitudes and actions. Open groups welcome and integrate strangers more quickly than the closed ones that aim for perfection in every detail of belief and conduct. Closed groups put people on trial and under suspicion until they have passed the tests for full fellowship.

Actually, recognition of the limitations of applications and interpretations of what is right and wrong could resolve most of the conflict that tends to erupt between these groups. Their normative systems are human constructions, even when based upon biblical principles.

Christians also divide over other issues pertinent to the Christian life. Some who emphasize glossolalia (the charismatic gift of "speaking in tongues") tend to consider nonglossolalic Christians as, at best, second-rate. Those who have mystical experiences are sometimes disowned by others as eccentric. People who live in community are prone to look upon those who maintain their own private homes as self-seekers. Some believers view the inner life as sacred and central and the external one as secular and unimportant, while others take the opposite stance.

In these and numerous other issues, an orientation toward the complementarity of the contradictory aspects is needed for wholeness. Not either-or but both-and is a biblical perspective that deserves much more attention in our fragmented world. In a majority of the controversies that have resulted in dualistic polarities, there is truth on both sides of the issues. As psychologist Paul Clement said in a discussion period at the Finch Lectures that are the background of this book, life is like a rowboat in which there are two persons. Each has one oar. They must row together, but it's unclear who is in charge. We can add that if only one rows, they will move in large circles. If one rows forward and the other backward, the circles will be dizzyingly small. If they do not always row with equal strength, the course of the boat will be anything but straight.

The coordinating direction that can help the Christian "rowboat" move forward with a minimum of energy loss and a maximum of attainment is anchored in four interlocking commitments.

CORNERSTONES OF CHRISTIAN WHOLISM

The chief cornerstone and foundation of wholistic Christianity is a sincere and complete commitment to the triune God. God alone is the unchanging "I AM," the only absolute to whom all else should be oriented. Whenever anything else is treated as if it is changeless or as if it is the dominant motive, goal, drive, or end of life, we are guilty of idolatry. We are born into God's spiritual family through accepting God's grace under the influence of the Holy Spirit. Because we are then a part of the Body of Christ, we must maintain a central focus on Jesus Christ. It is he for whom we are named *Christ*ians. He is the model of mature humanity (Phil. 2:5-13), the perfect example to follow (Eph. 4:11–5:2; 1 Pet. 2:21), and the head of the church, giving direction to the body (Eph. 1:22-23; 4:15-16; 5:23-24; Col. 1:18). Titles such as Lord, Shepherd, and Master indicate that his eternal kingdom, not simply the well-being of an institutional church or the worldly advancement of its members, should be our central organizing principle and goal. As we individually and together "seek first his kingdom and his righteousness," all other needs will be met as well (Matt. 6:33).

It is easy to let other concerns take first place in our priorities. We can organize our lives and activities around important things such as the institutional church, denominational programs, social justice, service to people in need, personal or social morality, fiscal solvency, paying off a building debt, the search for life satisfaction, financial success, or other goals. Instead of "majoring in minors," we need to stress the wholistic approach that meets all the significant needs of humanity through believing in Jesus Christ, following Jesus Christ, proclaiming Jesus Christ, and living Jesus Christ.

A second cornerstone of wholistic Christianity is emphasis upon the Bible as the authoritative guide to faith and conduct. Christians are "people of the Book." We grow toward the richness of wholistic Christianity by reading and applying the teachings of Scripture. Led by the Holy Spirit into the knowledge and implementation of the truth, we will glorify Christ in our attitudes and actions (John 15:7-15). "There is only one trustworthy way for us to know what God wants from us and for us. That is for him to tell us. In the Bible he has done just that" (Hubbard, 1982:1).

The Bible will not be an adequate guide if we first reach conclusions about our conduct and then afterwards select snippets of verses taken out of context to support our prior conclusions. It will not guide us if we focus only upon its applications to specific needs and situations of the past, for our circumstances change over time. We will then always be led by events instead of our leading them.

Neither will the Bible guide us dependably if we use it only as an occasional reference text. Instead, we should hide the Word in our hearts and minds so the Holy Spirit can call it forth in every moment of need.

Too many Christians are more concerned about protecting the Bible and their interpretations of it than they are about the Bible itself. The adamant proclamation, "The Bible says," must always be interpreted correctly. Except when Christians are directly quoting it, what is really meant, whether they recognize it or not, is "*My interpretation* is that the Bible says . . . ." Furthermore, even religious people misread the Bible when they fail to recognize that Jesus Christ and the good news of his grace is its central message and "the key to understanding the whole of it" (Morgan, 1982:32).

A third cornerstone of wholistic Christianity is loving God with our minds. This means using knowledge, insights, and skills accumulated through the intellectual and scientific disciplines for God's glory. It calls for acknowledging the fact that "all truth is God's truth" (Holmes, 1977). Instead of fearing the extension of human knowledge, we should rejoice in it and benefit from it. The New Testament makes it clear

> . . . that the truth about Christ is the focal center to which all other truth about everything in creation is ultimately connected. Whatever we understand about nature is ultimately about his creative wisdom and power; whatever we do in human art and science ultimately comes from the creative and rational potential that God invested in men by making us in his own image. To understand this centrality of Jesus Christ in all knowledge gives perspective to moral and social issues, to interpersonal relations, marriage, and work, in fact to everything in all the arts and sciences of men. With a unified view like this, we can think whole (Holmes, 1977:12).

Learning about people, society, the earth, and the entire universe are aspects of this important orientation. Christ-centered living must relate wholesomely to the realities of God's creation. It cannot be isolated from the environmental setting. As Ray Bakke expressed it, we must "exegete the world" as well as exegete the Word ("The New World," 1982).

The fourth cornerstone is the body of believers commonly called "the church." Most actions of Christians occur within its context, indirectly when not directly. Coping with the dilemmas and paradoxes of the Christian life and witness usually occurs largely in the context of the local church. Even the parachurch organizations that relate to various aspects of the work of God's kingdom are best seen as supplements to the local church (Dugan, 1980). The teaching and scholarly research in theological seminaries, the training programs of Bible colleges, creative studies reported in Christian periodicals and books, the informational and inspirational programs of numerous camps and conferences, and many other resources are all oriented ultimately to helping lay and professional ministers to fulfill their stewardship responsibilities in whatever location God has placed them. Their lives and service suffer if they lack a personal relationship with other believers.

These four cornerstones are closely interrelated. They cannot be isolated from each other if one wishes to have total well-being. Yet many Christians deprive themselves and those they influence of much of the riches of the "abundant life" or "life to the full" (John 10:10) that Jesus came to give. There are several ways in which this is done. Some do so by distorted views of God:

> In fact, both within biblical revelation and subsequent Christian experience, balanced, wholesome Christian faith is centered in God the Father, God the Son, and God the Holy Spirit. An undue emphasis on God leads towards universalism, an overemphasis on Jesus Christ nudges us in the direction of humanism, and pneumatic fixation leads to charismatic excesses and sometimes into expressions of moral nihilism (Shenk, 1984:3).

Others are aware of the heresies and distortions that have resulted from an overemphasis upon human learning and reason. They hence defensively give too little credence to the direction and enlightenment of the Christian's pilgrimage through the power of the human mind. They need to love God with their entire being. This includes coordinating the observations of their senses and creatively analyzing where they stand and whence they have come in relationship to the goals and objectives set forth in the Christian Scriptures. Christian faith does not exclude the intelligence. Neither does it forbid one from digging deeply into the vast store of human knowledge. Quite the contrary!

Still others impoverish themselves and deny other people the benefits of their spiritual gifts by trying to live the Christian life all alone.

We need others to help our search for God's will, whatever our specific circumstances of life. We need others to correct our sometimes imbalanced interpretations of the Bible. We need others to give opportunities for sharing our time and resources. We need others to provide support when we experience suffering, setbacks, and temptations. We need others to control our sinful pride and greed when all is going well and when we are "successful" in terms of the world's standards. "For none of us lives to himself alone and none of us dies to himself alone" (Rom. 14:7 NIV).

One of the most difficult and perplexing of these cornerstones is the issue of properly interpreting the Bible. Controversies have arisen in part because

> . . . the variety of Scripture—history, poetry, law, visions, parables and prophecies—and the maze of theology make it easy to play down one aspect of God's revelation or take another aspect and inflate it beyond reason (Neff, 1984).

Another source of disagreement over Bible interpretations is the paradox and antinomies that are found in the written Word of God. It includes double meanings, plays on words, parallelisms, reflections of the original cultural context, lessons that are implied rather than stated, and many other structural details. These give rise to ambiguities that can actually be creative, inspirational, and instructional when rightly faced (see Davies, 1982). They help to make the Bible ever fresh. Although they enable us to see something new at every reading, they also cause conflict among those who believe they have found the only correct interpretation but disagree about what it is.

Possibly the most serious wellspring of controversy over what the Bible teaches is the inclination to take a position first, then to seek biblical justification for it. When we ally ourselves only with people similar to ourselves by occupation, social class, racial and ethnic characteristics, education, and the like, we increase the likelihood of reinforcing social prejudices and biases through our Bible study.

Unconsciously we all tend to notice, learn, and recall news events and other materials that reinforce already existing perspectives on controversial issues. Contrary views are dismissed as bias. (Ruth Wilson, 1984, reports some recent research on this by psychologists Lee Ross, Mark Lepper, and Robert Vallone at Stanford University.) As a result, "the Bible says . . . whatever we like" on such controversial issues as capital punishment (Alexander, 1982).

We unconsciously tend to assume that our own social institutions and cultural practices are biblically based and "Christian," while those that differ are not.

That the moral practices and social institutions of the day have been too easily hallowed by the church is evident in regard to war, slavery, work, sex, marriage, the status of women, and, especially in America, a capitalist economy and democratic institutions. Rather than uncritically assuming that current principles and practices are fully Christian because they were influenced along the way by Christian ideas and because they seem better than some other alternatives, we should rather keep every moral practice and social institution under the constant judgment of God's law and constantly seek better ways of implementing that law in everyday life.

In theological matters also, the history of heresy is largely the history of identification of the faith with current religious and philosophical ideas (Holmes, 1977:18-19).

We live in an era of exceptionally rich aids for using the Bible. There have been at least 159 translations of the Bible into English since 1900. Numerous concordances, commentaries, and other study helps make this a "golden age" of biblical resources (Wessel, 1984). Yet many are so concerned about "rightly dividing the word of truth" that they see only narrow, individualistic applications of it to the daily lives of Christians.

It is important to recognize the original social context in which Bible teachings were given, then to determine the ways in which and the extent to which our own social context differs from and is similar to it. It then provides a much better basis for discovering, with the inspiration and help of the Holy Spirit, what God's will is for us today. An informed understanding of the social dynamics and political realities that God used in scriptural settings helps us to apply the Bible to our contemporary settings. An analysis of the importance of status in New Testament society and in its message, for example, is a crucial key to biblical social ethics (Mott, 1984).

"Dynamic equivalence" and "contextualization" are very important principles for a proper use of the Bible. The transfer of messages and meanings from one cultural situation to a different one is not a simple matter of finding equivalent words. What is sacred is "the content expressed, not the forms in terms of which that content was originally expressed" (Kraft, 1979:319). When this is done well, we realize that the Bible is not a dead relic from a distant past but an ever fresh, living, communicating guide to faith and practice. Its supracultural norms for action transcend all cultural settings in every time period of history. It thus provides a set of objective criteria for evaluating every nation, culture, group, and person, and it supplies guidelines for confronting the bewildering paradoxes, dilemmas, and decisions that lie before us. The Bible is old, yet it is ever new.

All four of these cornerstones can be viewed analytically as dynamically interrelated aspects of a single unity. Commitment to God through Jesus Christ, commitment to others in and through the Christian community of faith, commitment to a proper use of the mind for interpreting the realities of the natural and social environment, and commitment to the Bible as the infallible Word of God are all a part of the total commitment that is at the center of wholistic Christianity. If any one is downplayed, there is a hole in the whole.

This means that both the Christian life and Christian institutions can be interpreted as open systems. Both continually face dissatisfaction, tension, strain, conflict, and imbalance because of the competing choices related to dilemmas and paradoxes. They must repeatedly adjust to changing circumstances and adapt their goals and strategies for mission. They can seldom deal with but one issue or task at a given time. Instead they "must handle them *simultaneously*. Handling the diversity of processes required for survival or mission is not an 'either-or' but a 'both-and'" (Scherer, 1980:13).

The potential for stresses and strains is always present. All institutional structures face a constant state of tentativeness. As open systems they operate under revelation, the mandate from God, yet they labor within the situational context of changing societal contingencies. They "must frequently *adapt to* environment *for the sake of* mission" (Scherer, 1980:23; italics in the original).

As Christian people and institutions maintain a constructive balance both internally and externally in relationship to other persons and organizations in society, they will be "swinging" in the best sense of that word. They will evade error as they pursue truth and implement their goals and objectives. They will exegete properly both the Word and the world as they try to understand the Scriptures in relationship to the people and environmental contexts to which they direct their wholistic ministries, as Raymond Bakke has perceptively counseled ("The New World," 1982:4).

BARRIERS TO WHOLISTIC ACTION

Try as we will to be wholistic, we often fail. All of the dilemmas, dualisms, and paradoxes discussed in earlier chapters tend to intrude. We are under pressure from our families, friends, and Christian fellowships to choose one side or the other. In every area of disagreement and controversy, information and attitudes are shared that accentuate the good of one side and the negative aspects of the other. Meanwhile opponents are doing precisely the opposite. Each camp pridefully gives too little attention to the weaknesses, disadvantages, fallacies, and errors of its own side and the strengths of the other.

It would be far better for both sides to aim at understanding the total picture, seeing it also as the opponents see it. Then they could arrive at a clearer appreciation of each other and possibly reach consensus on some modified position that integrates more benefits and fewer weaknesses than either position would have by itself.

It is very easy to postpone action because of our need for further analysis, research, and study. Resolutions, committee reports, position papers, and verbal dialogue all have a place, but they can become a substitute for making and implementing plans. More than concerned feelings is needed. Seldom, if ever, can we do enough research to have all the answers. Even with the use of all the resources and tools of all the scientific and humanistic academic disciplines, we typically answer any one question by raising three or four more. As human knowledge expands, so does our knowledge of the scope of our ignorance. Even while seeking answers, we must do our best to carry out God's will in our own lives and in the larger universe of which we are a part.

Sometimes we give so much attention to handling people's problems and giving help that we fail to equip them to help themselves. When that occurs, our ventures may actually perpetuate or increase the problems of frailty and dependency.

We need to take care also that we not promise more than we can attain. It is not wise to build up high expectations by the hyperbole of public relations programs patterned after mass media advertising. The frustrations of coworkers, the people who support us, and those we serve are likely to erupt in harmful negative reactions when the truth is discovered that there has been little or no change in fundamental conditions.

We must avoid the temptation to try to do too many things at a time. Better to do one or a few things well than to attempt many and fail at all. Various constraints and costs are associated with every action. To use the words of a British sociologist,

> Any response which attempts a simultaneous solution of all problems will eventually collapse. Only a skewed response, adopting a tactic which attacks certain fundamental issues at the expense of others can succeed. Lack of skew is as fatal as too heavy a skew or the solution of too small a range of problems. Moreover, there will always be a waste element. At least some difficulties will have to be left relatively unreduced and unsettled (Martin, 1979:155).

Cultural pressures both within and outside of Christianity tempt a departure from a wholistic perspective. A separation of the allegedly intangible "spiritual" domain from the secular is a reflection of the ancient Greek division that saw the spirit as good and the body as evil. Although it is reflected in the New Testament epistles, originally written to Christians in the Greek world, it contrasts sharply with the wholism that is evident throughout the Bible.

Current attempts to develop syncretistic blends of various Eastern religions with Christianity exhibit a similar error. In addition, they assume "that what saves is the ascetical effort at detachment and union with God, and not the efficacy of the Cross in Jesus Christ" (Danielou, 1964:152).

The assumption that people are capable of reaching God by their own efforts is also found in many other forms and religions. Despite some similarities, Christianity sharply contrasts with them by its emphasis upon the incarnation of God in Christ and his vicarious atonement for human sin through his death and resurrection.

> It is not enough . . . to say that man alienated himself by turning toward the exterior world, and that he has only to turn aside from the life of the body to discover the pure spirituality which is his very being. For Christianity, it is not the body which is the principle of sin, but the whole man, soul and body, is the captive of evil and God alone can liberate him from this captivity, through grace (Danielou, 1964:153).

Not everything that is labeled as "holistic" is necessarily so. Many in the "holistic health movement" have a very one-sided emphasis upon nutrition, exercise, self-actualizing acts, meditation, or other activities. Their imbalance suggests a closer kinship with the English word *hole* than with the Greek *holos*. That, plus its kinship with our word *whole*, is why many of us prefer the word "wholistic." We emphasize the importance of including spiritual wellness along with physical and mental health and other components in the concept of wholistic well-being.

Christianity is oriented toward the whole of life, not just some selected parts. Of course, that means it is concerned with all the parts as well. We must not be like

> . . . many fanatic "holists" [who] blithely forget the parts in their pursuit of the ineffable whole. The result is not wholism at all but yet another fragmentation. Their wholism is halfism (Toffler, 1981:303).

As we examine the respective parts, we must always be aware of the larger whole to which they belong.

When we are eager to implement the principles of wholistic Christianity, we may on occasion be tempted to use methods of physical or psychological manipulation, violence, or oppression to attain our goals. This is especially likely when we join with those who are trying to liberate racial minorities, the poor, or others deprived of human rights at home or abroad from conditions, groups, and social forces that exploit them. As William Pannell of Fuller Theological Seminary reminded us in his discussion of my Finch Lectures, Christians must be like our heavenly Father, not like the oppressors. We must avoid the tragedy of being conformed to our enemies. Martin Luther King, Jr., is a good example of exercising redemptive responsibility to one's oppressors. He in turn followed the nonviolent teachings of our Lord (Matt. 5:38-48; Luke 6:27-36).

"Those controlled by the sinful nature cannot please God" (Rom. 8:8 NIV). Even in our anger at the evil and injustice around us, we must not sin. The sin of others is no license for us to sin in opposing them. The righteous end does not justify sinful means.

Any comprehensive effort to understand the total picture of society and the human condition is very complex. In the never-ending, always-shifting processes of social life, we see complex and confusing mixtures of good and evil. We are tempted to observe selectively and generalize in terms of either optimistic improvements and beneficial changes, or else of pessimistic deterioration and undesirable trends. It takes a special effort to maintain the balanced perspective that sees the total picture fairly. Much of the training of social and behavioral scientists in research methods is oriented in the direction of that kind of "objectivity." One need not be one of them to benefit from the methods, techniques, tools, and precautions they have developed.

We easily fall prey to the "ecological fallacy" as well (Moberg, 1983). It is the mistake of generalizing from overall characteristics of a whole to each of its specific parts. A parallel error is to generalize from one or a few parts to the whole. For example, a population characteristic of the nation as a whole, such as the percentage of people who are black females aged 65 and over, is not the same for every state, city, county, or village within the nation. Knowing that a church congregation is declining in membership does not warrant the conclusion that its denomination is declining. Characteristics of the whole may suggest a possible characteristic of its part, and vice versa, but the generalization is only a hypothesis to test until solid evidence supports the conclusion.

Whenever change of any kind is proposed, there are significant resistances. Psychological defense mechanisms protect personal habits and group customs. Scriptural warnings about the ways they trick us into disobedience to God apply to us, not just to other people. "The heart is deceitful above all things and beyond cure. Who can understand it?" (Jer. 17:9 NIV). "All a man's ways seem right to him, but the Lord weighs the heart" (Prov. 21:2 NIV). That is why "he who trusts in himself is a fool" (Prov. 28:26 NIV).

Because evil thoughts and behavior come from within, Jesus emphasized the importance of purifying our hearts or, as we might say today, making certain that we have Christian commitments and value orientations. (See, for example, Matt. 12:33-37; 15:10-20; Mark 7:14-23; Luke 6:43-45.)

Ironically, try as we will, we can never be completely wholistic. We are doomed to deal with only small fragments of reality. We are too finite to grasp the totality of anything with which we deal. We can observe but a small part of the complexities of the universe. The scope of our attention is childlike, for it is difficult to concentrate on more than a few minutiae. Our span of observation is very short. Even longitudinal research that extends over several decades or generations covers only small samples and just a tiny fragment of human history.

Even when we gain a fairly comprehensive picture, we lack many details. We usually miss important aspects of the complex historical background, including previous cultural systems that impinged upon its development and other antecedents that were significant but have been tracelessly lost from our purview. Seldom can we recover the mental processes and pictures in the minds of the people whose choices produced the current situation, and a host of other significant facts are forever gone. On top of all this, our own subjective "reality"—our stereotypes, symbols, language, and mental images—brings distortions.

There is a significant difference, however, between the two approaches. Being limited and particularistic in a spirit of reductionistic determinism that makes one believe that he or she has attained a full grasp of a subject is one. The contrasting view recognizes that a wholistic orientation is an important corrective to overcome the pride that alleges one's limited culture-bound picture fully represents the totality. The one perspective represents the haughty spirit of hubris, the other a humility that imitates the spirit of Christ.

Our finiteness becomes ever more apparent as the exponential expansion of scientific knowledge increases, rather than decreases, the questions we wish to have answered. Only God knows all things, including the future that we are creating by the decisions we make in our personal lives, our churches, and our society.

. . . Where there is knowledge, it will pass away. For we know in part . . . , but when perfection comes, the imperfect disappears. . . . Now we see but a poor reflection. . . . Now I know in part . . . (I Cor. 13:8-12 NIV).

To know that we can know only in part induces humility. It prevents us from succumbing to the "nothing buttery" fallacy, the ontological reductionism that assumes that one's interpretations explain the totality of a phenomenon as if it is "nothing but" whatever our research concludes (MacKay, 1974).

In light of the need for wholistic Christian orientations, the cornerstones upon which they must rest, and the barriers to such action, we must learn to cope consistently and effectively with social change. The next chapter suggests a series of principles that we can apply in the midst of our ever-changing world.

11

STRATEGIC PRINCIPLES FOR CONFRONTING CHANGE

The pervasiveness and rapidity of social and technological change in the modern world pose many problems for Christians. Planned change has complex consequences and many limitations. As we saw in chapter 9, this presents significant challenges and many opportunities.

In this chapter are a series of principles for prudent action that can enable us to confront change as people worthy of bearing the name of Christ. The ten suggestions constitute a general outline rather than a specific blueprint. In other words, they are on the level of strategy, not tactics. They heed Mol's (1969:98) admonition:

> It is no use formulating a strategy which presumes that the churches can be relevant once they know what changes to expect, if in fact the churches are powerless to implement any policy. This means that as in a battle, a strategy is to be based on a realistic appraisal of one's own position in the field, the means at one's disposal, and trends in other social institutions and ideologies.

TEN PRINCIPLES

The strategy presented here can be applied in Christian groups and churches of any size and composition. It is relevant for Christians from all racial and ethnic groups, cultural settings, social strata, educational levels, and ages.

The principles are all interrelated. They should not be seen as successive or sequential so that one must occur before the next. Instead, all should be implemented together at the same time.

1. *Be biblical.* A solid understanding of human nature, the work of God in history, the relationship between faith and works, and Christian social ethics provides an indispensable foundation for all action to cope with personal and social change (see Wallis, 1976). This, of course, means study of the entire Bible to appropriate its overall message, not just the picking out of a few favorite proof texts to support preconceived ideas.

169

It is far too easy for Christians coping with actual or anticipated social changes to first adopt a position on the basis of occupational interests, socioeconomic status, political identification, group membership, or other self interests, and then to go to the Bible to find "biblical support" for it. Proof texts and biblical concepts taken out of context can be found for almost any imaginable position. A similar distortion occurs when "troublesome" Bible passages are interpreted so as to fit the reader's bias. Divergent groups of Christians then arrive at different pragmatic conclusions from the same Scriptures (see Alexander, 1982).

Prosperous Christians tend to spiritualize passages such as Luke 4:18-19 about the poor, prisoners, the oppressed, and other needy people, claiming they only apply to "the spiritually poor" or to those imprisoned by spiritual darkness. Modern versions of the ancient Manichaean heresy divorce spiritual from material concerns, consider hope in Christ as pertaining solely to the next world, and neglect the claims of this life on the assumption that all material things are evil. Instead of being misled by it, we must follow the biblical pattern of concern for all dimensions of human affairs in this life and the life to come. This wholistic orientation provides stabilizing ballast for our voyage through life in the shifting seas of cultural interests and values.

2. *Be Christ-centered.* Our faith is based upon Jesus Christ, and he provides us the ideal model to follow. He exemplified compassionate action for people as individuals and as multitudes. He demonstrated concern for the rich and powerful as well as for the poor and dispossessed. He associated with the majority groups of his society (male Jews and Roman soldiers), but he also extended his love to Gentiles, Samaritans, women, the poor, the powerless, and people experiencing downward social mobility (Kraybill, 1980).

If we follow his example, we will try to change the world by both radical identification with people and radical differences from the majority—differences that made many persons exasperated with Jesus because he violated conventional rules and traditions, smashed expectations, and compelled people to act (Pippert, 1979). Our deeds should be sincerely in his name, not for the sake primarily of promoting ourselves, our church, or any other agency.

In the course of their life history, social institutions, including religious bodies, often experience goal displacement. Their staffs are then so concerned for the survival of specific programs, positions, or the institution itself that all efforts are oriented around perpetuating institutional structures instead of striving for the objectives and purposes for which they were originally established. People can also get so busy doing "church work" that they forget the basic work of the church.

Such diseases of bureaucratic structures can be averted through a conscientious focus upon the basic purpose and tasks of the organization. Veneration of a building as "God's house" may result in the belief that God is confined there. Maintenance of the material forms of windows, altars, and spires then may become the basic goal of all church efforts instead of ministry with people.

Throughout history people have worshiped many false gods. Continual stress on the importance of being Christ-centered helps to overcome such idolatry.

3. *Be humble*. Our knowledge is very limited, our vision sometimes dim, and our foresight obscure, so we all make mistakes. Actions introduced with good intentions sometimes have harmful results. When we disagree with others of good will, it is possible that we are wrong and they are right. A haughty spirit that implies that we have all the answers will turn many away; humility will win respect and often friends as well.

The assumption that only devout Christians know the answers to social problems is particularly harmful. All too often non-Christians have better insights and more realistic programs for social and political action than Christians do. The alternative choices to cope with a changing society are seldom either purely right or completely wrong. They typically demand decisions between a position that is right on the basis of certain important values but wrong on the basis of others and other alternatives that similarly are partly right and partly wrong. "They are between good and better or bad and worse, not between absolute perfection on the one hand and total corruption on the other" (Moberg, 1965:93). Furthermore,

> Simply to affirm or to oppose either the new or the old is not to answer but evade the questions. We need continuous and intensive study of the various consequences of the new and old standards (Yinger, 1982;309).

We have a tendency in political, religious and other controversies to compare our ideals with the actual practice, imperfect attainments, and horrible mistakes of our opponents. Instead, to be honest and fair, we should compare their ideals with our ideals and their behavior with our behavior. We must confess our own sins and listen respectfully to others as we cope with current issues. Sometimes that involves repentance for the sins of our Christian forebears as well:

> . . . for the most part the rear guard action of religion has been dysfunctional to the realization of social and economic justice. Too often this has meant a defense of unscrupulous and unethical political and economic practices that have been used to oppress and exploit

people. Too often the church has taken a stand or position that proved to be diametrically opposite to that of the Old Testament prophets and Christ (DeSanto et al., 1980:662).

Because of past and present sins, we need to be "converted" repeatedly from the errors of our ways. This means repenting humbly and changing directions appropriately as the Holy Spirit guides our growth in understanding (see Wallis, 1981).

4. *Be thoughtful.* Loving God with our mind as well as our heart, soul, and strength (Luke 10:27) includes using all of our mental abilities. Surface appearances are often deceptive, for society is exceedingly complex. Systematic research into the social, political, economic, and other forces that have contributed to current conditions and changes provides an important background for our work. Understanding the nature of social issues, the multicausal background of social problems, and the mixed results of social action is essential to effective planning.

A thoughtful approach recognizes that continuity is often best promoted by change. Many a political regime has collapsed because it refused to make a series of minor adjustments when internal or external circumstances and events modified the lifestyle, aspirations, values, or behavior of the citizens.

Some churchmen have failed to recognize that the unchanged retention of word forms, organizational structures, church programs, and schedules that were once very functional may fail to serve people, communicate a greatly different message, and be detrimental to the gospel when the world around them has changed. Their "unchanged" posture is actually a significantly different one in relationship to the altered social and cultural environment. Much of the work of contemporary hermeneutics, social ethics, and other branches of theology involves adapting the communication and applications of the never-changing gospel of salvation to the circumstances and people in our ever-changing world.

The rates of change are not uniform. It is usually easier to change material things than it is to change the attitudes and values of people or the institutional arrangements that need adjustment to the new material developments. This phenomenon, called "cultural lag," helps to explain many maladjustments in society.

Furthermore, subgroups within a society adapt to change at different rates and in diverse ways. In a pluralistic society with numerous components, minorities who disagree with the nature, rate, direction, or lack of change sometimes have the power to wreak havoc on the whole (Toffler, 1971:476). Just a few persons taking hostages or threatening other destruction and violence can force their demands upon an entire society, at least temporarily. The balance of power in a pluralistic society often resides in relatively small groups that can shift their political support to fit special interests.

Most social problems can be traced ultimately to sin, which typically is manifested directly or indirectly in the form of the "seven deadly sins" (Lyman, 1978). In the immediate contemporary sense, however, the causes are often too complex to attribute directly to explicit sins. Victims are not necessarily worse sinners than others (Rom. 3:9-23; Luke 13:1-5; John 9:1-3).

Some social problems are a result of natural catastrophes, and some come from the innate processes of aging, the normal human conditions of frailty, genetic limitations, and the like. Others are the by-products of institutional practices that cause such undesirable conditions as unemployment, pollution, and industrial accidents while producing generally wholesome services and products (Moberg, 1965:66-69).

To interpret all social problems as the direct result of personal sins without recognizing that many of them constitute the detrimental side effects of desirable social structures and processes is very shortsighted. It leads to fruitless attempts to correct structural or systematic flaws by trying to change individual persons without also changing the social system.

It is easy to be seduced by worldly values. The primary criterion of the success of the Christian church is not its attendance, membership, or popularity. Societal criteria of "relevance" may rest upon values that are antithetical to the Scriptures. The arguments by non-Christians about what Christians "ought" to do often flow out of cultural standards rather than biblical norms. The ultimate source of values for Christians is God's will as revealed through the Bible, Christian interaction, prayer, and enlightenment by the Holy Spirit. Such values transcend and stand in judgment over the values of every human society.

Many are tempted to try to restore a golden past. There never was a "golden age" in which Christian values were fully implemented in all domains of individual and collective life. Christ's millennial kingdom is not one of the past. Even if there had once been a utopian society, conditions in the modern world are vastly different from the past, so it could not be replicated.

Some churches have a tendency to allow past precedent to become a tradition to be upheld at all costs. The words, "We've never done *that* before," or "We've always done it *this* way," indicate possible idolatry. The past, even as recent as five or ten years ago, was so different from today that it cannot offer an unimpeachable precedent for action under current conditions. As Mol (1969:102) noted in his analysis of the relevance of Christianity, "Sometimes a dangerously mistaken notion of sacredness and an idolatrous concern with the trappings of traditional behaviour hold the church back." Most Christians in Nazi Germany cooperated in Hitler's sins against humanity by their oversimplistic acceptance of the biblical admonition to submit to governing authorities (Rom. 13:1-7). Their post-World War II repentance constitutes a lesson to Christians the world over to be more discerning in their relationships with the power structures of society.

Whenever anything other than God is made an ultimate concern, we fall into the trap of idolatry. This can happen when we give absolute loyalty to our nation as if it could never do wrong, to a personal habit or hobby as our reason for living, to a theoretical orientation as if all else must be subservient to it, to a therapeutic technique as if it were the only valid approach to healing human ills, to a political party as if its platforms and candidates were always without error, to an ideology as the lord over our theories and praxis, or even to a church as if it were infallible. Nothing should become an idol that takes priority over our commitment to God (see Walter, 1980:13-16). All of our other commitments must be provisional, tentative, and subject to correction. Thoughtfulness hence includes theological awareness and care.

5. *Be perceptive.* When Jesus looked at people individually and collectively, he saw their needs and had compassion on them. We, too, ought to evaluate the needs of people in our church fellowships, neighborhoods, communities, nation, and world. Having seen their needs, we can examine the resources available to help meet those needs, identify gaps in the resources or in their delivery to those who need them, and take appropriate steps to fill those gaps. In other words, we can plan our action in relationship to the realities of the situation, always in the context of biblical values. Sometimes, of course, a frontal attack against erroneous behavior may actually amplify harmful deviance rather than control it (Yinger, 1982:245); we will then act indirectly.

We must not confuse fluency with accuracy. Gilded oratory from trusted spokespersons is not necessarily truthful. Besides, there are many levels of discourse. For example, President Reagan was reported in the news on September 16, 1982, as saying that blacks were better off now than when he took office. According to certain selected criteria, that may indeed have been true, but the vast majority of blacks strongly disagreed.

Whenever claims are made or allegiances sought, watch for underlying criteria, the definitions used, alternative interpretations of the same sets of facts and circumstances, additional information that may refute or support the generalizations, and other perspectives. Remember that "It's true because I said it" may be far removed from "I said it because it is true." Truth may be couched in poorly expressed, stumbling sentences, while error flows forth smoothly from eloquent sources.

Labels must also be watched carefully. Glittering generalities, name calling, and stereotyping are prominent propaganda techniques that confound the truth, whether used by people of goodwill or by self-seeking charlatans. A prominent current example is the popularity of "holistic" health programs; many are very limited, based on occult world views, outside of traditional treatments, and anything but truly wholistic (see Fish, 1979).

6. *Be innovative.* To assume that we can cope with change only through the "tried and true" methods of the past is counterproductive, for current conditions have never prevailed in the past. Instead of cutting off the inspiration for new action that comes from the Holy Spirit, task forces of Christians should cope earnestly and realistically with the question of what to do and the means and methods for doing it in their specific context. Flexibility and openness are obviously important traits for this reason.

7. *Be cooperative.* One of the fascinating lessons of the Bible is that God often works through nonbelievers, even outright wicked people, to accomplish his purposes. When Christian objectives coincide with those of secular persons and groups, formal or informal coalitions will often accomplish what none could do alone.

Cooperation is essential to attaining planned change. In a pluralistic society every subgroup is a minority. The majority rule of a democracy can be achieved only through coalitions of minorities. Such a society protects us from becoming victims of tyrannical authoritarian persons and groups. It likewise prevents us from oppressing those who disagree with our values or deviate from the policies we desire. It makes sharing our viewpoints a respectable means of informing others where we stand and why, as we try to convince them to accept our perspectives and cooperate with us in changing the body politic. How to gain full advantage of the pluralistic, democratic situation without succumbing to its potential harm is a lesson that most Christians have only partly learned.

A high degree of specialization characterizes modern society. Cooperation among the numerous disciplines, occupations, and professions that relate to social issues is absolutely essential to the discovery, testing, implementation, and evaluation of effective changes. Even as no one is an island living only to himself or herself, no group can be an isolated enclave living as if there were no others in the contemporary world. They all need the others.

Christians also need to support one another. Congregations can share the specialized forms of social service that are needed in a community or neighborhood, for example, through interfaith coalitions. Each can sponsor a different ministry instead of indulging in the outmoded kinds of competitive action by which each tries to outdo the other by duplicating programs that try to serve the same people in the same way.

Within congregations a similar division of labor is needed. Some members can engage in background research on issues related to change, others in strategic planning, and still others in the many activities required to implement the plans. Too often there is a tendency in church congregations

> . . . to overwork the overworked and ignore the idle. This is consistent with the normal institutional pressures that place the highest priority on getting the job done and a much lower priority on making sure it is a rewarding experience for the person who is given the responsibility (Schaller, 1969:39).

Instead, it is wise to spread the work out to a larger number of people through acknowledging a broader scope of potential responsibilities. By motivating and enabling everyone to find an appropriate role, church members will become partners in ministry instead of merely objects for ministry. They will then be using their spiritual gifts effectively (1 Cor. 12:1-31).

8. *Be persistent.* Instead of giving up at early signs of resistance, reluctance, or opposition to planned innovations, we must work wisely and steadily toward the goal. This may involve many adaptations, to be sure, in the midst of the ever-changing social context. It may demand an occasional respite to take care of intervening problems that intrude. "Let us not become weary in doing good, for at the proper time we will reap a harvest if we do not give up" (Gal. 6:9 NIV).

We should not expect quick results on major changes. Current conditions are part of a sequence of events that goes back over decades or centuries of development. Just as long-engraved personal habits are not easily reversed, the customs of a society or a church tend to endure beyond the biological generations of its members. Changes that take a generation of education, motivation, and stimulation are still very quick against the panoply of historical time. Even minor modifications in human conditions and gradual changes in behavior should be viewed thankfully. Furthermore, the ultimate reward of the Christian will come only after we have left this life. We live in hope.

Because of the complexities of the changing world in which we live, it is likely that we will never see complete success in regard to many of the projects on which we work. It is easy to get discouraged and simply give up. Keeping realistic goals, having a clear sense of our mission, understanding our limitations, building support groups, and recognizing the early symptoms of burnout are all a part of the process of coping.

> But even the most dynamic Christian . . . is in danger of burning out if he lacks what is perhaps the most crucial element of all in coping with burnout: balance. . . . Most certainly it will mean balancing the ideal and the real, vision and actuality.
> . . . Once we spot the symptoms, we must apply the antidotes: self-awareness, acceptance, reassessment, proper motivation, diversion and daily renewal, praise, closeness, pacing, and balance. . . . The flame in our spiritual lamps must burn the oil in the wick, not the wick itself . . . (Kehl, 1981:1577).

In his principles for leading churches through change Walrath (1979: 123) points out that persistence is required in order to establish any innovation:

> A new structure or a new set of procedures or a new program seems to be an imposition to a congregation, in much the same manner as a new routine feels awkward to an individual. Only with the passing of time does any innovation become natural. It usually takes years to penetrate deeply enough into church members' experience to be routine.

9. *Be prayerful.* We must always plan and act in faith, for the outcomes of our efforts are largely unpredictable. Hence we need the wisdom that only God can give. As we struggle against the forces of evil, putting on the full armor of God, we are told to "pray in the Spirit on all occasions with all kinds of prayers and requests" (Eph. 6:18 NIV). Numerous other biblical admonitions and instructions remind us of the importance of prayer in Christian service.

> Through prayer we can move past arrogance to an earnest search for truth as we oppose all ideas and philosophies which seek to undermine the gospel of our Lord Jesus Christ. Prayer also will enable us to act with love toward those who differ with us. . . . Pray for God's help to be moral and to act morally; to be fully human and to act in truly human reflection of God's image in us. Pray that the roots of our Christian faith will issue in the fruits of righteousness, good works, peace, and justice. . . . Pray that our commitment to the great values and ideals which characterize the Christian faith may not be minimized and trivialized by secular standards ("Some Suggestions," 1982:16).

10. *Be wholistic.* It is easy to succumb to the temptation to emphasize but one aspect of the Christian life and witness, thus having a

lopsided ministry that produces unbalanced and lopsided Christians. The imbalance often comes from stressing one or another side of the numerous paradoxes, dilemmas, and opportunities that confront us in our modern, rapidly changing world. Too many Christians slip into the pattern of confronting change with only rhetoric or only social action, for example, instead of combining both in a wholesome blend of demonstration plus proclamation of the gospel of Jesus Christ.

God calls us to help people become whole even when we and they are living in the midst of broken people in a broken world. We can help them to become whole by implementing these principles, by our individual and collective examples, and by biblically balanced ministries to serve their needs in the name of our Lord Jesus Christ.

HOPE IN THE MIDST OF DESPAIR

Rapid social change is an outstanding characteristic of modern society. We live in the midst of revolutionary changes that may bring even greater differences in the next generation than those that have characterized our own. Confronted by these circumstances, it would be easy to drift, complacently letting social forces push one individually, as a Christian group, or as a church. To do so, however, is to allow "the world" to set our agenda.

Christians who are alive to God will not let the authorities and powers of this dark world and the "spiritual forces of evil in the heavenly realms" (Eph. 6:12) push them around, but rather will "be strong in the Lord and his mighty power" (Eph. 6:10). They will actively struggle against evil and for God. They will love him with their minds, using their intellects for systematic study and planning. They will be proactive (advocating positive changes), not merely negative and reactive (known only for what they oppose). The best way to overcome evil is to do good (Rom. 12:14-21).

Alert Christians will also recognize that there is no such thing as neutrality in a democratic society. Whenever people claim to be neutral, they are actually giving implicit support to those who win in the political process. Usually this is an indirect form of approving of the actions of those who are powerful or wealthy, as if they were always morally right on controversial issues. It implicitly proclaims that the Christian message is irrelevant to the practical problems of current affairs. It is equivalent to denying the direct, literal statements of hundreds of passages in the Bible that indicate that Christians must be actively concerned about the human needs we call social problems (Moberg, 1965:14-16).

It is true that political action typically involves compromises, but it is better to move toward the attainment of ideals than to ignore them completely by giving up and pretending to stay out of politics. Sometimes becoming involved leads to the error of single-issue politics. There is a great deal more at stake in modern society than the issues implicated in either abortion, evolution, homosexuality, prayer in public schools, anti-Communism, pornography, nuclear disarmament, or any one other problem. It is often advisable to join coalitions with groups that are working on single issues. Yet as we do so, we must not think either that the resolution of one issue will resolve all others or that the one alone comprises the totality of our responsibility as Christian citizens.

We must also try to be friendly toward even those who disagree with us on certain issues (Rom. 12:18-21). They may become collaborators on another issue as we form the ever-shifting coalitions essential to producing effective change in our pluralistic society. This applies above all to fellow Christians who do not agree with us on specific positions. We should avoid being led astray by those who create divisions and cause dissension within the church (Rom. 16:17-18; 1 Cor. 1:10-13; 3:3-9; Jude 16-19). Be particularly cautious about getting into foolish controversies and contention about moot points of Christian faith and conduct (Tit. 3:9-11).

Change will never resolve all social issues. With but rare exceptions, such as the conquest of certain specific diseases, the problems are deeply rooted in the total fabric of the structures, values, and practices of society. They are strongly interrelated with each other. Our actions have many limitations. Therefore we can at best move toward the amelioration of the worst effects of social problems but never expect to eliminate all of them completely (see Heddendorf, 1980:122-124).

Past history has shown partial success in the treatment of such social problems as migrant labor, poverty, the population explosion, environmental degradation, racial and sexual discrimination, and many illnesses, but failure outweighs success in regard to problems such as crime, alienation from work, urban blight, and energy resources (Horton and Leslie, 1981:603-607). This may tempt us to adopt an unwise attitude of indifference, fatalistic resignation, cynicism, romanticizing about some idealized past, or dreaming of a utopian future (Horton and Leslie, 1981:13-17).

Many Christians are tempted to give up all attempts at directing social change. This may stem from a realistic appraisal of the limitations of social action, from failure to impose their will on the entire body politic, from the problems associated with burnout, or from an eschatology that sees this world as getting ever worse until Christ establishes the millennial kingdom. "To the confirmed cynic, all talk about social problems is a waste of time; the unfortunate aren't worth getting excited over, and the do-gooders are a bunch of hypocrites secretly grinding their own axes" (Horton and Leslie, 1981:14). Such attitudes are not compatible with the faith, hope, and love that flow from Christian faith.

"Christian hope can contribute to an explicitly purposive sociology of change" (Lyon, 1980:685). We have the Lord's assurance, "Every knee will bow before me; every tongue will confess to God" (Rom. 14:11 NIV). Jesus Christ is the source of our vision and hope. His transforming power energizes Christian work in the world and helps us overcome the poisonous temptations to ignorance and cynicism (Gladwin, 1980). We need not remain helpless and unresponsive before the pressing social issues of our day.

> If we cannot always know the proper instrument to use in dealing with social problems, we can at least cooperate with God by working with those constructive forces that seek for solutions. If we cannot solve problems, we can at least contribute to their amelioration. . . . The need is for a balanced and integrated application of both sociological and spiritual understanding. Anything less would present a distorted and, at best, limited comprehension of society and its problems (Heddendorf, 1980:123,124).

Change is foreboding to those who are fearful about the immediate future because of their weakness or their premonitions of portending cataclysm or doom. It can be costly to persons whose vested interests are threatened or whose utopian dreams are shattered (Walrath, 1979: 122-123).

But there is no need for the Christian to fear change. "God is at work in human history today, just as he has been in the past and will be tomorrow" (Schaller, 1972:13; see Burton, 1982). Now as in the midst of even darker days than ours, God makes all things work together for good (Rom. 8:28). The Bible is filled with promises about his watchcare over all his children through faith in Jesus Christ. They have a glorious future. The reassuring message is clear: "Peace I leave with you; my peace I give you. . . . Do not let your hearts be troubled and do not be afraid" (John 14:27 NIV).

Confronting change as Christians demands a biblical, Christo-centric approach that focuses upon the need of all people for wholistic well-being. Stability is offered to us in the midst of our changing world by Jesus Christ. He "is the same yesterday and today and forever" (Heb.

13:8 NIV), but this does not mean that we must adopt rigid and static approaches to the world. Quite the contrary.

The Lord does not change even though we may turn away from his decrees (Mal. 3:6-7). Yet "he changes times and seasons; he sets up kings and deposes them" (Dan. 2:21 NIV). As those who belong to the body of Jesus Christ, we must thoughtfully fit into his plans. This means that we will meet the needs of each unique situation with humility, perception, innovation, cooperation, persistence, and prayer, maintaining a wholistic perspective in all that we do. We shall then be confronting social change as Christians in deed and in truth, not by empty words alone.

12

STEPS TOWARD WHOLENESS

All action to promote wholistic Christianity must be based upon the four cornerstones summarized in chapter 10. Commitment to the triune God with a central focus upon Jesus Christ, use of the Bible as the authoritative guide to both faith and conduct, loving God with all our minds, and working in the context of all believers who constitute the church provide the foundation for constructive action. The strategic principles for coping with change that we examined in chapter 11 also provide a part of the frame of reference for effective action.

This chapter summarizes some steps that can be taken by Christians who wish to move toward wholistic Christianity. Each of them represents constructive action that can be taken to deal with the tensions, conflicts, dualisms, dilemmas, paradoxes, lopsidedness, and other problems that repeatedly emerge in the course of Christian activity. They are relevant to individual action and to collective behavior in and through church parishes or congregations, parachurch organizations, denominations, and other institutions.

GUIDELINES FOR ACTION

Obviously the steps presented here are not by any means an exhaustive list. Furthermore, every local situation is different. The application of these guidelines therefore will not result in a single pattern to be rigidly imposed in any and every setting. It will lead to diverse patterns of action as Christians seek the guidance of the Holy Spirit for their unique obligations and opportunities in their different social and environmental contexts.

1. *Examine dilemmas constructively.* If we view dilemmas negatively, as only sinful or demonic, we will lose the spiritual dynamism that can flow from recognizing that a degree of well-grounded truth is usually found on each side of paradoxical positions. Even "heresies" may

represent cultural adaptations more than theological aberrations. They often call attention to what ought to be done more than to what ought to be feared (Kraft, 1979:296).

Life at every level involves creative tensions. For example, the muscles in many parts of our bodies pull against each other, each losing or gaining strength when another does. So, too, the dialectical tensions from opposing but justifiable alternatives can increase our vigor as parts of the Body of Christ. Actively recognizing, using, and applying the strengths, virtues, and truths of each alternative position without disowning those of its counterparts will similarly improve both individuals and congregations.

To be sure, this will not occur without difficulty. A person or group that is "in the middle" trying to reconcile extremists appears to have fuzzy attitudes in contrast to the sharp "clarity" of the radical positions.

Moderates may seem to compromise important values. They as much as others are subject to the vice of smugness or haughty pride, for each group believes it holds the superior perspective. As buffers between the extremes, they may slip into the false "neutrality" of trying to be uninvolved, disinterested, middle-of-the-road independents. Such persons may believe that they are the sustaining majority or pillars of their church when in fact they impede its work and progress. "For change comes from those who care, who propose and agitate, modified by those who care differently and oppose; the rest is inertia" (Griffith, 1974:19).

The "golden mean" is not automatically nor necessarily the ideal position. Yet the careful analysis of most dilemmas and paradoxes usually reveals that they are false dichotomies. It is not necessary to be impaled on the horns of a dilemma.

Constructive analysis of the paradoxes and dilemmas that confront us includes study of the potential advantages and disadvantages of feasible alternatives from which we can choose. Careful research can help us predict which one is likely to provide the greatest net benefit and the least foreseeable harm. Of course, the good results that are anticipated do not vindicate the use of immoral or evil means and methods (Rom. 3:8). The end does not justify the means. Hence the processes and procedures to be used in moving toward the objectives must also be evaluated.

2. *Begin where you are.* Whenever we look upon the multitudes, we become aware of the complexity and the vastness of human needs at home and abroad. It is easy to become confused and discouraged. We tend to feel that we are powerless and can do nothing about the problems of the millions of suffering people.

The example of Jesus may help us to deal with this problem. He worked intensively with only twelve disciples in a restricted area of a small country occupied by an exploitive empire. He helped many individuals, but there undoubtedly were thousands of others in need who lived in Galilee and Judea but failed to catch his attention. Yet what he taught by word and deed has rippled out to the ends of the earth.

We, too, can begin small. Most of our ventures will remain small. Yet effective service in our own community may ripple outward as others are inspired to follow our example.

Beginning where we are includes learning how to use existing institutions, even though they are imperfect. If we first try to change them and wait to act until they are closer to what they ought to be, we may never act at all. Just as good structural forms may be used for evil purposes, bad structures can be used to accomplish good. Thus oppressive bureaucracies can sometimes become tools to attain constructive goals.

Usually it is easier to rechannel the work of existing organizations than it is to create completely new ones. The outward forms may then remain the same while the content and the relatively hidden meanings change. Even citizens who see the flaws in our political and economic systems can work in them to influence action through the democratic political process, using agencies like Evangelicals for Social Action and Bread for the World.

3. *Make spiritual well-being a primary goal.* Many human service programs that claim to meet all the needs of their clients are less than wholistic. Most often it is the spiritual rather than other needs that are slighted or omitted.

In the USA only the religious institutions have spiritual goals as a central responsibility. If churches are diverted into other important but secondary areas of service, the spiritual domain inevitably suffers. When that happens, meeting spiritual needs is transferred by default to parachurch agencies, cults, pseudoreligious human potential programs, and reductionistic teachers, counselors, and therapists. Many of these reduce the spiritual to limited aspects of mental or emotional health, material welfare, education, meditation, diet, exercise, or other specialties.

The goal of awakening, strengthening, and maturing people's spiritual well-being ought to be at the center of all the other expressions and dimensions of personal religion and at the core of all Christian ministries. This is not necessarily a frontal thrust that replaces other goals, but it is an underlying motivation and objective that infuses all of the other objectives. As Clinebell (1981:2) expressed it in his working principles for counseling and therapy, "A church's mission is to become a spiritual wholeness center—a place of holistic health centered in spiritual wholeness—an 'abundant life' center."

Spiritual wholeness must not be limited to direct service to individual persons. It can be an objective cutting across every ministry and outreach of the church, including action related to public policy and social issues. Okiyama's summary of Finch's perspective expresses it this way:

> Man is composed of body, mind and spirit. Spirit is the dimension which brings harmony between the dimensions of body and mind. When there is disharmony between the two, inauthenticity, then anxiety begins to speak, and it is the spirit dimension which must transcend and bring the two back into reconciliation (Finch, 1982:xxiv).

Trueblood (1975:x) observed in the preface of his reprinted 1936 classic, *The Essence of Spiritual Religion,* that "the supreme paradox of our time" is the coexistence of "obvious spiritual need with the failure to provide reasonable answers." Part of the tragedy is that, just when the world is becoming more aware of that need, the church is becoming less sure of its mission, "often moving off into bizarre and marginal developments."

The spiritual vacuum in the lives of many people cannot be maintained; it will be filled in one way or another. The widespread popular interest in astrology and the occult is but one of the evidences of that truth. When people do not satisfy their spiritual need through Christian faith and church ministries, they turn elsewhere to gain the *feeling* that their need is met. The feeling, however, may be but an empty shell used by the Great Deceiver to distract them from the search to satisfy their hunger.

Genuine spiritual well-being is much more than a feeling. Ministries to nurture it must get beyond the affective level of emotions and desires. They must also go beyond simple "decisions for Christ" to include the life of complete commitment and obedience that flows from genuine faith. True spiritual well-being touches every domain of human thought and behavior.

4. *Discover people's images of reality.* In any situation we act in terms of interpretations in our minds of what the reality is. Some of these are conveyed by the words we use. Having defined it a particular way, we respond to the definition, which may or may not correspond closely with actual reality.

We must heed W. I. Thomas's sociological dictum, "If men define a situation as real, it is real in its consequences." For example, if an epileptic is believed by family members to be possessed by evil spirits, they may try to exorcise the demons instead of seeking medical help. If a person's unemployment is attributed to personal laziness, remotivation will be the solution sought, but if it is thought to result from racial discrimination by employers, efforts may be directed toward changing the attitudes of management.

Much of the controversy over such issues as abortion, homosexuality, inflation, overpopulation, world hunger, and similar problems stems from different images of "the facts" and of their causes and consequences. Different experiences, residential neighborhoods, occupations, income levels, racial and ethnic backgrounds, religious perspectives, theological interpretations, and many other variables help to account for variations in the mental images.

Even experiences shared by everyone in a cultural setting may modify human reactions. When people realize that they are under the threatening horror of a nuclear holocaust, they become much more likely than before to join the movement to ban all nuclear weapons. Since their advent, nonbelievers are less likely to scoff at Peter's prophecy that "the elements will be destroyed by fire, and the earth and everything in it will be laid bare" (2 Pet. 3:10 NIV). What once seemed a preposterous apocalyptic statement is now within the realm of possibility. People who have grown up in the nuclear age have different values and perspectives from those of the prenuclear era.

Because of the variations in sensory perceptions, interpretations of cause and effect, and verbalizations about reality, there is no such thing as a completely objective description. It is important to discover ideas and attitudes that differ from our own, especially among members of our own groups. We can learn about these perspectives through listening to people, sharing their experiences, unobtrusively studying their viewpoints, reading widely, and debating the issues. Such action is similar to that by the Christian who listens to an atheist tell what kind of god he does not believe in. Often the response must be, "I don't believe in that kind of god either."

As we learn other people's images of reality, not just the conclusions that flow out of them, we may discover that our own images are incomplete, inaccurate, or misleading. Honesty is a requirement of the search for truth by those who follow the One who is the Truth. It will often compel us to redirect our own perspectives and behavior.

People's images of reality are often conveyed in the language they use. Language reflects world views. It often serves to distort, like sunglasses through which we filter perceptions of reality. Military buildups may be justified under the label of "security" and military aggression as "defense." Oppressive governments are "totalitarian" if perceived as enemies but only "strong" if they are friends. One side in a battle reports an event as a "military retreat" and the other as "withdrawal to regroup for a counterattack." A minor problem may be reported as a "crisis," a social change as a "revolution," and an entertaining performer as a "superstar."

> Words mean different things to different people at different times. . . . Meaning is in people, not words. . . . In recent years society at large has been suffering from verbal inflation . . . . The reckless spending of some words has subtracted from their value ("Watch What You're Saying!," 1983:2, 4).

Perceptions of a church, mission project, or minister may also differ widely. Some may label a pastor as a "crackpot" while others see the same person as a progressive, innovating, and farsighted leader (see Krass, 1984). Even views of God and the church vary.

> The African evangelical does not recognize as Savior the prophetic Christ of the Qu'ran, the hidden Christ of Hinduism, the silent Christ of African tradition, the revolutionary Christ of liberation theology, or the middle-class Christ of Western culture. Only the biblical Christ is the object of saving faith (Simbiri, 1984).

5. *Advocate Christian humanism.* Attacks upon atheistic or agnostic versions of "secular humanism" are strong in many circles. All forms of humanism are lumped together and treated as antithetical to Christianity. Jesus Christ, however, was a humanist in the best sense of that word. He loved and cared for people, healing their illnesses and satisfying their hunger. He taught them that they possessed inherent worth as individuals. He placed human welfare above the interests of institutionalized structures and practices. He never viewed people as mere pawns in the hands of political, religious, or other leaders. As we proclaim and demonstrate his love, we too are humanists—humanists because of our faith, not in spite of it.

When Christians attack all "humanism" as if it is only of one kind, they give ammunition to enemies of the faith who claim Christianity lacks concern for the well-being of people. The erroneous conclusion is easily reached that faith in Jesus Christ is privatistic, oriented only toward getting self-gratification and peace of mind for oneself, lacking all interest in feeding the hungry, clothing those who have only rags, sheltering the ill-housed, finding jobs for the unemployed, and correcting evil conditions in society that cause human misery.

In fact, however, those who claim the label of "humanist" but refuse to be concerned with the total welfare of people, which includes their spiritual needs, may not be true humanists at all. T. B. Maston has said, "The fruit of a secular humanism, which theoretically exalts man apart from God, is to debase him or at best to depersonalize him" ("Some Suggestions," 1982:8). "Christian humanism, in contrast to such atheism, affirms human worth and dignity through the Christian faith" (Moberg, 1982:13).

It is easy for middle-class and affluent American Christians to overlook the problems of the poor and, most of all, those who live under conditions of exploitation and oppression in developing countries. They cannot escape their depressed condition, for even if there were some haven to which to flee, they lack the resources necessary for such a move.

Despite such social, political, and economic entrapment, even they have an area of freedom, narrow though it be. Like those with limitations of mental and physical illness or handicap in our own nation, they have some options, however few, from which to choose in the course of life's daily, seasonal, and annual cycles. Making those options clearer and then respecting their autonomy and freedom of choice are aspects of Christian humanism.

Because of diverse exposures to the problems of humanity, we have different perspectives on them. It is easy for those who live out their lives within the confines of a relatively prosperous American community to believe that anyone who wants work can have it. It is easy for those who live in small communities where everyone knows everyone else and many are related to each other by ties of blood or marriage to believe that everybody who needs food, clothing, shelter, and medical care will be helped through kinship and friendship channels to get it. It is easy for those who live in the context of a close-knit religious fellowship to believe that all welfare needs can be satisfied through church-sponsored social services. It is easy for those who attribute all human problems to personal sin to believe that the victims are to blame for their condition, that the wretchedness of the human condition is just retribution for an evil life, and that the only responsibility of the Christian is to call such people to repentance and conversion.

Our understanding must be much broader. Recognizing the grain of truth in each of those narrow perspectives, we must also recognize their limitations and be like Jesus. He saw the masses, not just individual persons. "When he saw the crowds, he had compassion on them, because they were harassed and helpless, like sheep without a shepherd" (Matt. 9:36 NIV). He was concerned for the entire metropolis of his land, including all the people in it (Matt. 23:37).

Protection of the vulnerable—the poor, widowed, prisoners, unemployed, racial and ethnic minorities, mentally retarded, physically and mentally ill, homeless, and victims of various forms of discrimination and oppression—is a biblical calling that we must not ignore. Like all others, they have spiritual needs that only the gospel can satisfy, but while we work to meet them, we must not ignore their other human needs.

6. *Remember that we are stewards.* Everything we have—including our abilities, possessions, experiences, opportunities, and time—is a gift from God to be used in a life of commitment and service. This applies to churches and parachurch organizations as well as to Christians as individuals, but it is easiest to clarify from the personal perspective. Stewardship "is the concept of responsible management that involves at least three different aspects of the believer's life," submission of one's life to the Lord, substance (especially finances), and opportunities for ministry and service (Walvoord, 1982).

There is a wide variety of spiritual gifts, but they are all given by the Holy Spirit for the common good of the entire Christian body. "All these are the work of one and the same Spirit, and he gives them to each man, just as he determines" (1 Cor. 12:11 NIV). Small (1980) gives an excellent summary of the gifts explicitly mentioned in the New Testament.

Too often we see these gifts only in terms of what occurs within the context of the church and other Christian organizations and groups. Perhaps as much as 80 percent of the volunteer service is given by 20 percent of the members. Similarly, 80 percent of the effort of staff members is likely to focus upon the 20 percent of the tasks that are considered to be of high value (see "Shop Talk," 1982). Part of the reason for this may be too narrow a definition of the scope of services needed in the Christian congregation. Creative action and insights can extend the privilege of giving, which is more happiness-producing than receiving (Acts 20:35), to many people who currently feel that they can contribute nothing but money.

Another reason for the limitation of "Christian service" is the (mis)interpretation that applies it only to the context of explicitly "Christian" ministries. Actually, if Christian lay persons

. . . don't allow the Holy Spirit to illuminate their work they are omitting from godly influence a large part of their existence. It has to do with wholeness. If Jesus Christ is Lord of our lives, he ought to be Lord of all of our lives and that ought to include the way we perform our job or profession (Pippert, 1982:29).

Pippert suggests that ministers and leaders of parachurch organizations should pay more attention to this aspect of spiritual wholeness. A convenient way to begin is to identify one's occupation with a word and then trace the use of that word or concept through the Bible.

Stewardship is a concept of "responsible management" by which we first submit ourselves to the Lord and then commit our possessions and opportunities to God (Walvoord, 1982). How to use our time is one of the hardest choices. Because of our limited time, energy, and resources, every choice *for* something is also by implication a choice *against* something else that may also be valued highly.

Determining priorities is not always easy. Sometimes the pressures of trivialities that we are expected to satisfy hamper our calling to major issues. But what is major? What is trivial? To what extent are the trivialities essential features of the human condition? Which ones cannot be avoided or delegated to someone else? When are we manipulating that "someone else" to shift priorities in order to satisfy our own? Can we determine what ought to be the stewardship responsibilities of another person?

Accepting a position or task often carries with it a heavy load of responsibilities that were only dimly seen in advance of taking office. The same holds true of role changes in personal life such as marriage, parenthood, grandparenthood, and even retirement.

As stewards we make many predictions. Freedom of choice widens the horizons of our potentialities, but it also reduces the capacity to predict accurately the outcomes of decisions that are made.

> To choose, to decide, requires prediction. . . . whether we are thinking of an individual's intimate decisions about his own life or about the broadest decisions of the President of the United States, every decision maker seeks to know what, in actuality, the consequences of his choice will be. As the capacity to choose expands, the pressure to predict rises.
>
> This relationship between freedom and prediction is reinforced—and also complicated—by the dependence of any decision on other decisions (Ways, 1972:7).

As we predict the results of alternative decisions in order to be good stewards, we may be led by God to attempt what seems humanly impossible. Our horizons will be wider than those set by human knowledge. We are also likely to notice many options that fit our spiritual gifts and abilities. It is very difficult to say no to many of the invitations and requests extended to us, but we have only 168 hours each week, most of which are committed to ongoing requirements for living.

> Our unwillingness to say no may be a modern form of idolatry. We enthrone our own desires, our pride, and the lure of appearing busy. . . . In the name of Christian witness or service, we may have abdicated our responsibility to consider what opportunities are God's will for us, and what ones pull us away from higher priorities. . . . it is blasphemous to imply that our loving Father wants us to do more than He has equipped us to do (Fryling, 1984:6, 7; see also Banks, 1984).

No one local church, not even any one Christian denomination, and certainly no one person can do all of the work that is needed in wholistic Christianity. Wholism demands that labor be divided and shared. Doing that, in turn, depends heavily upon the church as a body, not simply upon individuals in isolation from each other (see Snyder, 1982). Special spiritual gifts are needed for the coordination and oversight of these collaborative ministries (see Small, 1980), but they also are important for the less recognized role of helping (1 Cor. 12:28).

The diversity of gifts matches the diversity of needs. To get caught in a trap that acknowledges only a few of those gifts impoverishes a church and hampers its ministries. It is spiritually destructive, if not deadening, to many of its members.

7. *Practice spiritual cooperation.* The stewardship of our diverse gifts demands cooperation within Christian circles but also beyond them. The pluralistic nature of contemporary society, for example, makes it essential to form coalitions that crisscross ideological religious lines in order to influence public policy on the local, state, national, and international levels. New and revived forms of ecumenism are emerging from such efforts. One is the pragmatic alliance of specialized groups working together to influence politics and legislation that Hitchcock ("Some Surprising Words," 1982) calls "true ecumenism." Another is a "spiritual ecumenism" made up of alliances of the sort that emerge when Christians with similar faith commitments work together for evangelistic outreach and Christian nurture.

The coexistence of different Christian groups with overlapping ministries in the same geographical area does not mean that they are not united in Christ. For example, churches of the respective Christian denominations may each reach somewhat different types of people. It is inconceivable, if not impossible, that as many people would be reached if all the churches were united, meeting in one place and with one style of ministry. Similarly, groups like InterVarsity Christian Fellowship, Campus Crusade for Christ, and the Navigators may all work on the same university campus. Each meets somewhat different types of student needs, rather than trying to squeeze all people into the same mold.

> God is not interested in Cookie-Cutter-Christians. Scripture teaches that the *unity* and the *diversity* of Jesus' followers must coexist not only peacefully and productively, but even joyfully. Unity and diversity are meant to exist in a balanced tension with each other. To emphasize one or the other is to lose that balance and be set up for a fall (Evans-Layng, 1981:23).

Even within the local community, no church can serve all the material and physical needs of its own people. Not even the Hutterite colonies, which are relatively isolated from the rest of society, can satisfy all their own needs; they buy machinery, salt, and other supplies, and they sell many products to the outside market. Community agencies, businesses, and other institutions serve most of the needs of Christian families.

Similarly, cooperation for most explicitly "Christian" ministries like rescue missions, prison ministries, senior citizen centers, church-related colleges, radio stations, and mass evangelism, usually must extend far beyond the confines of any one local church. For many specialized ministries there can be a division of labor among congregations, each picking up a different task. Together they can exemplify and practice wholistic Christianity to a degree that is impossible all alone. Dynamic interdependence is a Christian virtue.

Yet all too often Christians are serving in isolation from each other. At least 714 mission agencies are working out of Canada and the United States to spread the gospel, and less than half of their effort is centered in cooperative mission associations.

> The West is guilty of having diffused too much unbelievable splintering to the non-West. For example, at least 300 denominations exist in Brazil. Thousands of African independent movements are present in that continent. Deep at the heart of all theologies of missions is the notion that one God through one creative spirit is proclaiming the word of the one Christ to unite the nations in the building of His one Church. . . . it is certainly not by the design of that one [Holy] Spirit that when a review of evangelistic programs is carried on in a world-class city, participants sitting alongside one another discover for the first time what God . . . has been doing in their city ("Networking," 1983:4).

Not only in work abroad but at home as well Christians would serve much more effectively by establishing networks for relating to each other. The networking process involves sharing knowledge of needs and resources, identifying persons and groups with common concerns and interests, and coming together to discuss common problems. It need not be limited to Christian people and groups, for many others may share at least some of the same objectives.

When the work of Christian ministry is appropriately shared among churches and other agencies, as well as among both professional and lay "ministers," the clergy will not need to be "all things to all men." Instead of attempting to be second-rate community organizers, business administrators, social workers, psychiatrists, or clinical psychologists, they can specialize in their own unique role. With reference to their pastoral care ministries, they can become spiritual diagnosticians, drawing upon the very best of their spiritual resources—their commitment to Jesus Christ, knowledge of the Scriptures, and understanding of spiritual distress and its treatment (see Pruyser, 1976). They will then have a unique role. Instead of intruding upon the domain of other professions, they will complement and enrich them for the benefit of their clients and patients.

8. *Recognize Christian relativism.* A wide range of customs and institutional practices is condoned, and many that seem offensive to us are forthrightly sanctioned in the Bible (see Moberg, 1962). Jesus himself deviated from the folkways and mores of his time and people by eating and staying with Samaritans, associating with women in public, neglecting certain religious duties, violating rules about the Sabbath, and defying traditions.

Considerable variation in specific dos and don'ts is found among evangelical and fundamentalist Christians today. Some try to establish a rigid set of rules for Christian behavior, while others advocate different rules that conflict on at least some details.

Biblically we note that the Apostle Paul became "all things to all men" in order to win them to Christ (1 Cor. 9:19-23; see Acts 21:18-26). His epistle to the Galatians was written to uphold Christian liberty and warn against legalizers. Jesus taught a form of individual relativity in his emphasis upon judging ourselves before we judge others (Matt. 7:1-5) and in his insistence that responsibility varies with the person (Luke 12:35-48). What is right for one person may be wrong for another (Rom. 12:3-8; 1 Cor. 12:4–14:1).

The wide variety of what is permitted in Christian morality and conduct demonstrates the need of every person and group to be led by the Holy Spirit instead of by some rigid set of ever more detailed rules and regulations. Yet this is to be done with consideration of those who are weak (Rom. 14:1–15:6; 1 Cor. 8). The Christian need not be subject to legalistic regulations, for he or she has died to the elementary ordinances of the law and is alive with Christ, setting the mind on things that are above (Col. 2:16–3:4).

This type of biblical or relative relativism (Kraft, 1979; Mayers, 1974; Grunlan, 1982:53-55) contrasts sharply with those forms of cultural relativism that hold that all ideas of right and wrong are completely relative. Biblical relativism operates under the authority of scriptural principles and allegiance to the only true Absolute, Almighty God, whose will is revealed through the Living Word (Jesus Christ), the Written Word (the Bible), and the Holy Spirit, all in the context of the Christian community. Yet even the most devout Christians know only in part (1 Cor. 13:9-12), so we can never be absolutely sure that all our decisions and deeds are perfectly just, completely pure, or absolutely holy.

Humility is one of the distinctive characteristics of wholistic Christianity. It refuses to make any human plan, institution, nation, or system absolute as if it were God's only means for action, for that would be idolatry. It also refuses to relativize God as if God were limited in the same manner as people are. We are created in God's image, not God in ours.

When conflicts erupt over dualisms or dilemmas related to Christian conduct, it is wise to remember that application of the very same biblical principles may lead to diametrically opposite acts when the environmental setting or other circumstances differ. In some contexts not being openly with Christ is to be against him, while in others not being against him represents being for him (see Matt. 12:30; Mark 9:38-41; Luke 9:49-50). The meaning and results of actions are relative to surrounding circumstances and interpretations.

Everything on earth is relative; only God is truly transcendent. He is over all societies, institutions, groups, and persons, as well as over all human experience, knowledge, theories, and value systems. God alone is the ultimate judge of what is right and wrong. Recognition of his transcendence puts an end to haughty ideas of people who are authoritarian, chauvinistic, ethnocentric, racist, ageist, sexist, or otherwise vindictive, malevolent, or judgmental.

All human value systems and social institutions—even those that are as fully and truly Christian as possible—are imperfect. At their best they only approximate the biblical ideal. Try as we will to bring about justice and love, which often are in tension with each other in our broken world, we never fully succeed. Our "good deeds" often have latent evil consequences. We cannot see the end from the beginning of anything we do. Through Christian relativism we humble ourselves in the sight of each other, as well as in the sight of the Lord.

9. *Use the method of triangulation.* In surveying, navigation, forest fire lookouts, and similar activities, the location of a third point can be determined by relating its direction from two known points. We similarly use triangulation in the social sciences whenever we use two or more methods, theories, observers, data gathering devices, academic disciplines, population samples, or other techniques to study a particular subject. We then gain better insights and richer understanding than if we had used but one alone.

When caught up in problems of decision making, many Christians try to arrive at *the* Christian position on the subject. They assume that there can be but one right way for Christians to act, even as there is but one way of salvation. A similar conclusion may be reached when a satisfactory solution has been found for meeting some particular need. It is then easy to conclude that what worked once is the proper approach to every other instance of the problem.

"Therapy addiction" like that has plagued many religious groups. They have forgotten that, under new sets of circumstances in the ever-changing world, loyalty to the never-changing Christ does not demand rigid adherence to a particular method of ministry. God's household is made up of people of every kind of background and interest. The members are at different levels of spiritual maturity. As noted above, they have diverse images of reality and see different facets of many-sided situations.

The wisdom that is from above will direct us toward peacemaking (Neidhardt, 1980). It will help us to draw submissively but cooperatively upon the rich resources of our diversity instead of being one-sided and contentious (see James 3:13-18; Eph. 5:21; 1 Pet. 5:5; Phil. 2:3-4; 2 Tim. 2:14, 23-26).

In terms of appropriate Christian action the triangulation principle will help us to remember that what some see as "*the* Christian solution" is usually best interpreted as "*a* Christian solution." Christian pluralism then can be given its due recognition, even as building a plurality of approaches into the conduct of psychology gives it more than mere lip service (Van Leeuwen, 1982: 139-140). When various Christians share diverse perspectives on the same subject, they are each likely to have insights, knowledge, biblical understandings, and other aids for reaching valid conclusions that the others lack.

Communication and cooperation to gain as rich an understanding as feasible are therefore of utmost importance whenever we are caught between the alternatives of the dualisms that beset us. The Christian community needs to develop more channels for such sharing. "Plans fail for lack of counsel, but with many advisers they succeed" (Prov. 15:22 NIV; see Prov. 11:14; 24:6).

10. *Keep ultimate goals in clear view.* Even while we work on small, seemingly insignificant tasks, it is rewarding to realize that they contribute to larger objectives. Although human finiteness makes it impossible to be fully wholistic, we should place the total well-being of people, churches, and the kingdom of God in the position of highest priority. We must not be distracted into narrowly conceived perspectives that assume that some small portion of Christian responsibility is its whole. There is, of course, a paradox or dilemma in this suggestion. Because it is impossible to do everything with our limited abilities, time, and resources, we must choose among various alternatives. As we do so, it is important to keep a transcendent orientation toward the whole, for that will give balance and direction to all our specific actions.

Just now it is popular to claim to be wholistic. The impressions of Walter Elwell (1982:70), former deputy editor of *Christianity Today,* from over five hundred books related to spirituality or living the Christian life that crossed his desk in recent years are indicative:

> What stands out is a fundamental stress upon such ideas as wholeness, unity, and integration. There is a shift toward looking at life as a whole. In theory, body, soul, and spirit have given way to psychophysical unity. In practice, spiritual, emotional, and physical problems, considered as discreet difficulties, have given way to "personal" problems having various components. . . . Nothing is seen as independent of anything else; all is related to the whole human fact.

The development of Third World countries can be seen by Christians from the perspective of "the total development of the total man in which essential wholeness is found as a child of God created in God's own image" (Yamamori, 1982:11). This is a process that refers to quality rather than quantity:

> Development is a process in the qualitative change of life in which a person finds essential wholeness (socially, physically, economically and spiritually), as an individual and as a "person-in-community" (Yamamori, 1982:11).

The goals of psychotherapy at its best also have a wholistic orientation. For example, John Finch's lecture on "Nishkamakarma: The Highest Value" in the tenth anniversary of the Finch Symposium at Fuller Theological Seminary in January 1980 included this statement:

> The focus of my thrust is that in the Christian faith there *is* a self, and that self has to assume its responsibility for all it does and does not do,

and the only way to achieve nonattachment is by *being* a self—a whole self, a holy self, a concentrated self, a consecrated self—in truth, relentlessly (Finch, 1982:45).

REWARDS OF DYNAMIC WHOLISM

Scientific findings are lending their support to scriptural assurances of the benefits of wholistic Christianity. The evidence is growing that spiritual well-being is related to a large number of psychological and social variables (Moberg, 1979; 1984b; Paloutzian and Ellison, 1982). I have found no evidence whatever to contradict the conclusion that living in accord with God's will as revealed in the Bible contributes to wholesome conditions in society and life satisfaction for its members. (There are, of course, pathological forms and distorted expressions of Christianity that do contribute to personal ills and social problems.)

Christians who live wholistically have the satisfaction of knowing that they are doing God's will as a part of the community of faith. They are relieved of the guilt that results from seeing thousands of things that ought to be done for God's kingdom, hundreds of which they are capable of doing, but only one or two of which are genuine possibilities. They realize that others are taking responsibility for portions of the total task that they themselves lack the time and energy to do. They live in the faith that God is leading them and watching over them.

Wholistic Christians also have the excitement, invigoration, and freshness that comes from living the life of faith. They do not attempt to delay living and acting until all the facts are in, much as they respect research, study, and planning. Not seeing the future, but assured that their sovereign God is at work, their curiosity is mingled with hope. Putting no absolutes before God and knowing that all else is relative, they have the liberty to step out in faith to do God's will as it is revealed to them.

> The feeling that you don't know, or need to know, everything absolutely brings a great deal of freedom with it. . . . A sense of the relative is a sense of the possible; it gives us an opportunity to see things which we wouldn't see if we assumed that there was nothing there to look at (Depuy, 1984).

When problems arise, such Christians are secure because their faith is anchored in the Absolute. They know that God is at work to bring about change. They fear no evil, for God is with them. Even when they disagree with each other as they choose one polarity or another or waver between two opinions, they recognize that the differences are a part of the means God uses to stimulate creative growth and fruitful service. No one is squeezed into a rigid mold. Personal autonomy is enhanced, so they can rejoice in the uniqueness of every Christian. Under the guidance of the Holy Spirit they find nuggets of gold shining forth amid the irrelevant debris.

Those who practice wholistic Christianity are more concerned with giving than with receiving. Yet they find more happiness and fulfillment from such a life than from the one that constantly seeks self-actualization. "In giving, we receive; in receiving we give. It is truly a paradox" (Holland, 1982:29). Resources are limited in most areas of life. The more one gets, the less others have. Christian love, however, is the opposite; the more one gives, the more he or she receives. Love multiplies itself when it is shared.

When we engage in open dialogue in the spirit of dynamic dialectics, the rewards similarly tend to increase for everyone who is involved. Wholistic Christianity is not a zero-sum game in which there is a fixed reward that one player gains at the expense of another. Rather, it is like love; everybody who enters into its open spirit, sincerely seeking God's will, is a winner.

Wholistic Christianity converts the destructive dualisms that tend to divide Christians into warring armies into dynamic dialectics that spur all on to more effective service. The dilemmas become the *coincidentia oppositorum* that stimulate mental and spiritual growth, leading toward Christ-like attitudes and actions. The tensions under which we all live can be faced creatively (Krebs, 1982). They prod us into constructive evaluations of pertinent realities of the societal setting, of the people who are involved, of the anticipated consequences of alternative possibilities, and of the sometimes-competing sets of biblical norms.

In terms of worldly values, wholistic Christians often seem to be part of an upside-down community. Their success comes from humble service rather than imperial power. They choose to take up their cross daily, denying personal ambition, appearing to be social failures, and accepting ridicule and shame (Luke 9:23-26). Yet as they follow the example of Jesus, they are "successful failures"—failures in the eyes of the world, but successful disciples of their Lord (Kraybill, 1978:291-309).

To cope dynamically with the dialectics that emerge from the paradoxes and dilemmas of Christianity is invigorating. It gives one the satisfactions that come from alternating one's interests and needs instead of being stuck in a monotonous rut of repetitious sameness. Change is perhaps "the greatest energizer ever invented" (Arnold, 1979:86). That is especially so when change is in the balancing context of the stability that results from trust in our compassionate, omnipotent God.

Health of the spirit and health of social relationships in a Christian spills over to improved health of body and mind. Integration into a group thus contributes to one's personal integration. Both help one to face the inevitable paradoxes and dilemmas of life constructively instead of destructively.

Wholistic Christianity contributes to the "healing of the nations" as well as of individuals and institutions. Those who sincerely pursue the balanced perspectives of wholistic Christianity will find inspiring connections between various domains of life, even as people like John Wesley did. He linked the intellectual, emotional, and spiritual aspects of life, never separating what he believed from what he thought, preached, and lived. His personal holiness was demonstrated by social holiness in the "practical holiness" of "faith working through love" (McKenna, 1982:2; see also Kellermann, 1984).

Puzzles will always remain and will serve as a stimulus to further growth. Yet Christians who use the paradoxes and dilemmas of life constructively will win the satisfaction of bringing healing to both individuals and society in our troubled world. They will reap the immediate satisfactions of God's *shalom*—spiritual well-being, soundness and completeness in all areas of life, peace with God, and harmony with creation, other people, and themselves. They also will win the ultimate reward of being a part of the great multitude "from every nation, tribe, people and language, standing before the throne and in front of the Lamb," their redeemer (Rev. 7:9 NIV).

REFERENCES

Alexander, John, "Bleeding Hearts: The Bible Says . . . Whatever We Like," *The Other Side*, 19(9):8-9, Sep. 1982.

American Assembly, *The Farm and the City: Final Report of the 58th American Assembly*. New York: Columbia University, 1980.

American Scientific Affiliation, "Local Section Activities: Metropolitan New York," *Newsletter, American Scientific Affiliation–Canadian Scientific and Christian Affiliation*, 26(2):5, April/May 1984.

Armerding, Hudson T., editor, *Christianity and the World of Thought*. Chicago: Moody Press, 1968.

Arnold, Oren, *The Second Half of Your Life: How to Live and Enjoy It*. Irvine, Calif.: Harvest House Publishers, 1979.

Baker, Russell, "Locked Doors Give No Safety," *Milwaukee Journal*, part 1, p. 15, Nov. 8, 1982.

Balch, Robert W., and David Taylor, "Seekers and Saucers," pp. 43-64 in James T. Richardson, editor, *Conversion Careers*. Beverly Hills, Calif.: Sage Publications, 1978.

Banks, Robert, "On Doing Less and Becoming More," *Radix*, 15(6):5-7, May/June 1984.

Barclay, William, *The Letter to the Romans*, second edition. Philadelphia: Westminster Press, 1957.

Barnes, Harry Elmer, *The Twilight of Christianity*. New York: Vanguard Press, 1929.

Bayly, Joseph, "Out of My Mind: Who Are We to Judge?," *Eternity*, 33(11):59, 48, Nov. 1982.

Bayly, Joseph, "Halt, Christian Soldiers!," *Eternity*, 35(3):84, March 1984.

Bell, Daniel, *The Cultural Contradictions of Capitalism*. New York: Basic Books, 1976.

Bell, John Fred, "Laissez Faire," *Encyclopaedia Britannica*, Vol. 13, pp. 605-606. Chicago: Encyclopaedia Britannica, 1969.

Berger, Peter L., *The Sacred Canopy: Elements of a Sociological Theory of Religion*. Garden City, N.Y.: Doubleday, 1967.

Berger, Peter L., *The Heretical Imperative: Contemporary Possibilities of Religious Affirmation*. Garden City, N.Y.: Anchor Press, Doubleday, 1979.

Bernard, Jessie, *The Future of Marriage*, revised edition. New Haven, Conn.: Yale University Press, 1982.

Bilheimer, Robert S., editor, *Faith and Ferment*. Minneapolis: Augsburg Publishing House, 1983.

Blamires, Harry, *Where Do We Stand?: An Examination of the Christian's Position in the Modern World*. Ann Arbor, Mich.: Servant Books, 1980.

Blamires, Harry, "Fall 1980 Lecture Series," *Christian College News*, p. 8, Jan. 30, 1981.

Blasi, Anthony J., "Dialecticizing the Types," *Sociological Analysis*, 42(2): 163-172, Summer 1981.

Bloesch, Donald G., *The Evangelical Renaissance*. Grand Rapids, Mich.: Eerdmans, 1973.

Bockmuehl, Klaus, *The Challenge of Marxism: A Christian Response*. Downers Grove, Ill.: InterVarsity Press, 1980.

Bockmuehl, Klaus, "Current Religious Thought: The Raison d'Etre of Our Calling," *Christianity Today*, 24(4):274, 276, Feb. 22, 1980.

Bohlin, Ray, "Sociobiology: Cloned from the Gene Cult," *Christianity Today*, 25(2):84-87, Jan. 23, 1981.

Boorstin, Daniel J., *The Image: A Guide to Pseudo-Events in America*. New York: Atheneum, 1977.

Boudon, Raymond, *The Unintended Consequences of Social Action*. New York: St. Martin's Press, 1982.

Boyd, Forrest J., "Observations," *Decision*, 21(12):12, Dec. 1980.

Brom, Libor, "Where Is Your America?" *Imprimis*, 11(8):1-6, Aug. 1982.

Browne, Jeff, "Freshmen Even More Materialistic," *Milwaukee Journal*, Part 1, p. 16, Jan. 30, 1983.

Bube, Richard H., editor, *The Encounter Between Christianity and Science*. Grand Rapids, Mich.: Eerdmans, 1968.

Bullock, Robert H., "God's Wandering Sheep," *Austin Seminary Bulletin*, 86(6):44-54, April 1971.

Burton, C. Emory, "Humanism and Religion," *The Humanist Sociologist*, 7(2):15-16, June 1982.

Burwell, Ronald, "Social Change," pp. 385-400 in Stephen A. Grunlan and Milton Reimer, editors, *Christian Perspectives on Sociology*. Grand Rapids, Mich.: Zondervan, 1982.

Cairns, Earle E., *Saints and Society*. Chicago: Moody Press, 1960.

Cairns, Earle E., *The Christian in Society*. Chicago: Moody Press, 1973.

Callahan, Sidney, "Forum: Psychological Reasons Why People Shun Peace," *National Catholic Reporter*, 19(4):7, Nov. 12, 1982.

Campbell, J. Robert, "Are We a Church or a Social, Political Action Lobby?," *The Presbyterian Layman*, 15(6):12, Nov./Dec. 1982.

Campbell, Robert C., Church Bulletin Cover No. 80122. Valley Forge, Pa.: Judson Book Service, 1980.

"Campbell [Robert C.] Tells ABC Churches 'Evangelize or Evaporate,'" *The American Baptist*, 181(2):1, Feb. 1983.

Campbell, Thomas C., and Yoshio Fukuyama, *The Fragmented Layman: ¿ Empirical Study of Lay Attitudes*. Philadelphia: Pilgrim Press, 1970.

Caplan, Arthur L., editor, *The Sociobiology Debate: Readings on Ethical and Scientific Issues*. New York: Harper and Row, Colophon Books, 1978.

Caplow, Theodore, et al., *Middletown Families: Fifty Years of Change and Continuity*. Minneapolis: University of Minnesota Press, 1982.

Cardwell, Jerry D., *The Social Context of Religiosity*. Washington, D.C.: University Press of America, 1980.

Childress, James F., and David B. Harned, editors, *Secularization and the Protestant Prospect*. Philadelphia: Westminster Press, 1970.

Choy, Kathryn Cherie, "Society's Demons and God's Power," *The American Baptist*, 179(10):19-20, Nov. 1981.

Christian Life Commission of the Southern Baptist Convention, "Some Suggestions for Dealing with the Secular Humanism Phenomenon," *Light*, pp. 8-11, 16, May-June 1982.

"'Christian Position' Adds to 'Antagonism among Christians,'" *Christian College News*, p. 4, Jan. 29, 1982.

Claerbaut, David, *The Reluctant Defender: A Big-City Attorney Defends Desperate People*. Wheaton, Ill.: Tyndale House, 1978.

Clark, Steve, "Christian 'Initiation,'" *Pastoral Renewal*, 7(3):25-30, Oct. 1982.

Clinebell, Howard, "Working Principles of Growth Counseling," in *Proceedings of the Conference on Aging: The Graying of the Church, May 22-23, 1981*. Pasadena, Calif.: First United Methodist Church, 1981.

Coleman, James S., *The Asymmetric Society*. Syracuse, N.Y.: Syracuse University Press, 1982.

Colson, Charles, "A Society that Celebrates Sin," *Christianity Today*, 25(17):1258, Oct. 2, 1981.

Colson, Charles W., "The Most Fearsome Judgment," *Christianity Today*, 26(13):20-21, Aug. 6, 1982.

Colson, Charles, "Speaking for God," *Eternity*, 33(4):35-41, April 1984(a).

Colson, Charles W., "1984—Christ or Big Brother?," *LaPuz* (Westmont College), 7(4):6-12, Summer 1984(b).

Cook, Guillermo, "The Protestant Predicament: From Base Ecclesia Community to Established Church—A Brazilian Case Study," *International Bulletin of Missionary Research*, 8(3):98-102, July 1984.

Cooley, Charles H., *Social Organization*. New York: Charles Scribner's Sons, 1909.

Cotham, Perry C., "Introduction: The Ethic of Escapism Versus the Ethic of Involvement," pp. 9-20 in Perry C. Cotham, editor, *Christian Social Ethics*. Grand Rapids, Mich.: Baker Book House, 1979.

Cox, Harvey, *The Secular City*. New York: Macmillan, 1965.

Cox, Harvey, Religion in the Secular City: Toward a Postmodern Theology. New York: Simon and Schuster, 1984.

"Crystal Ball Was Cracked," *Milwaukee Journal* (from AP, Toronto), Green Sheet p. 1, March 1, 1972.

itt, Don, *Taking Leave of God.* New York: Crossroad Publishing Co., 1981.

gley, Robert, "Compassion for the City," *The Gordon* (Gordon College), 25(3):8-9, Nov. 1980.

Dagley, Robert, "Between Hard Places," *The Gordon* (Gordon College), 27(4):6, Nov. 1982.

Danielou, Jean, S. J., "The Transcendence of Christianity," Chap. 9, pp. 148-159 in Jean Danielou et al., *Introduction to the Great Religions.* Notre Dame, Ind.: Fides Publishers, 1964.

Davidman, Joy, "Smoke on the Mountain," pp. 22-23 in Timothy Dudley-Smith, *Someone Who Beckons.* Downers Grove, Ill.: InterVarsity Press, 1978.

Davids, Peter H., "'So What?'" *New College Berkeley Notes*, 5(2):1, Fall-Winter 1982-83.

Davies, Richard, "Creative Ambiguity," *Religious Education*, 77(6):642-656, Nov.-Dec. 1982.

Dayton, Donald W., *Discovering an Evangelical Heritage.* New York: Harper and Row, 1976.

"Decline of 'Post-Modern' Family Blamed on State's Social Roles," *Community Ontario*, 26(4):17, July/Aug. 1982.

Depuy, Norman R., "The Value of the Relative: The Bible Alive," *The American Baptist*, 182(1):14, Jan. 1984.

Dershowitz, Alan M., "U.S. Legal System: 'All Sides Want to Hide the Truth,'" a conversation conducted by Ted Gest and Alvin P. Sanoff, *U. S. News and World Report*, 93(6):62-63, Aug. 9, 1982.

DeSanto, Charles P., Calvin Redekop, and William L. Smith-Hinds, editors, *A Reader in Sociology: Christian Perspectives.* Scottdale, Pa.: Herald Press, 1980.

Dugan, Richard P., "The Para-Church Organization is Dead," *Journal of Christian Education*, 1(1):56-58, Fall 1980.

Duncan, Otis Dudley, Howard Schuman, and Beverly Duncan, *Social Change in a Metropolitan Community.* New York: Russell Sage Foundation, 1973.

Dupré, Louis, "Spiritual Life in a Secular Age," pp. 3-13 in Mary Douglas and Steven Tipton, editors, *Religion and America.* Boston: Beacon Press, 1983.

Dyrness, William A., *Let the Earth Rejoice!: A Biblical Theology of Holistic Mission.* Westchester, Ill.: Crossway Books, 1983.

Earle, John R., Dean D. Knudsen, and Donald W. Shriver Jr., *Spindles and Spires: A Re-Study of Religion and Social Change in Gastonia.* Atlanta: John Knox Press, 1976.

Editorial, "If God Held a Press Conference," *Christianity Today*, 26(10): 12-13, May 21, 1982.

Edwards, Tilden, "Spiritually Rooted Compassion," *Shalem News*, pp. 1-2, May 1984.

Elliott, Norman K., "Beyond the Impossible," Letter No. 82. St. Paul, Minn.: Release, Inc., May 1983.

Elwell, Walter A., "Current Religious Thought: We Act—Therefore We Believe?" *Christianity Today*, 26(19):70, Nov. 26, 1982.

Evans, C. Stephen, "Redeemed Man: The Vision Which Gave Rise to Marxism," *Christian Scholar's Review,* 13(2):141-150, 1984.

Evans, Christopher, *The Micro Millennium.* New York: Viking, 1980.

Evans-Layng, Michael, "Escape from Cookie-Cutter Christianity," *His,* 41(4):22-24, Jan. 1981.

Fackre, Gabriel, "The Crisis of the Congregation: A Debate," pp. 275-297 in D. B. Robertson, editor, *Voluntary Associations.* Richmond, Va.: John Knox Press, 1966.

Fackre, Gabriel, *The Religious Right and Christian Faith.* Grand Rapids, Mich.: Eerdmans, 1982.

Faulkner, Joseph E., and Gordon F. DeJong, "Religiosity in 5-D: An Empirical Analysis," *Social Forces,* 45(2):246-254, Dec. 1966.

Fenn, Richard, *Toward a Theory of Secularization.* Storrs, Conn.: Society for the Scientific Study of Religion, 1978.

Fichter, Joseph H., "Religious Values, A Sociological Perspective," pp. 136-144 in Donald N. Barrett, editor, *Values in America.* Notre Dame, Ind.: University of Notre Dame Press, 1961.

Fichter, Joseph H., "Sociological Measurement of Religiosity," *Review of Religious Research,* 10(3):169-177, Spring 1969.

Finch, John G., *Nishkamakarma.* Pasadena, Calif.: Integration Press, 1982.

Fish, Sharon, "How Do You Spell 'Wholistic'?" *Eternity,* 30(8):19, Aug. 1979.

Florman, Samuel C., *Blaming Technology: The Irrational Search for Scapegoats.* New York: St. Martin's Press, 1982.

Frenchak, David J., "Necessity, the Mother of . . . ," *The SCUPE Report,* 5(1):3, April 1983.

Friedrichs, Robert W., *A Sociology of Sociology.* New York: Free Press, 1970.

Fryling, Alice, "The Divine No," *InterVarsity,* pp. 5-7, Summer 1984.

Fung, Raymond, *A Monthly Letter on Evangelism,* No. 12. Geneva, Switzerland: Commission on World Mission and Evangelism, World Council of Churches, Dec. 1982.

Gallup Opinion Index, *Religion in America 1976.* Princeton, N.J.: American Institute of Public Opinion, Report No. 130, 1976.

Gallup Opinion Index, *Religion in America 1981.* Princeton, N.J.: The Gallup Organization and The Princeton Religion Research Center, Report No. 184, Jan. 1981.

Garvey, John, "Choice as Absolute: The Highest Morality?," *Commonwealth,* 109(1):9-10, Jan. 15, 1982.

Gladwin, John, "Editorial: The Temptations in Christian Social Involvement," *Shaft* (The Shaftesbury Project), No. 26, pp. 2-3, Winter 1980.

Glasner, Peter E., *The Sociology of Secularization: A Critique of a Concept.* Boston: Routledge and Kegan Paul, 1977.

Glock, Charles Y., "On the Study of Religious Commitment," *Religious Education,* 57(Research Supplement):S-98–S-110, July-Aug. 1962.

Goodman, Ellen, "It's Every Man for Himself, Survivalists Say," *Milwaukee Sentinel,* part 1, p. 10, Nov. 29, 1980.

Greeley, Andrew M., *Unsecular Man*. New York: Schocken Books, 1972.

Greeley, Andrew M., *Crisis in the Church*. Chicago: Thomas More Press, 1979.

Griffith, Thomas, "Time Essay: The Trouble with Being in the Middle," *Time*, 104(1):18-19, July 1, 1974.

Grunlan, Stephen A., "Biblical Authority and Cultural Relativity," pp. 47-65 in Stephen A. Grunlan and Milton Reimer, editors, *Christian Perspectives on Sociology*. Grand Rapids, Mich.: Zondervan, 1982.

Guinness, Os, *The Gravedigger File: Papers on the Subversion of the Modern Church*. Downers Grove, Ill.: InterVarsity Press, 1983.

Hadden, Jeffrey K., "The Private Generation," *Psychology Today*, 3(5):32-35, 68-69, Oct. 1969.

Halverson, Richard (interview by Barbara R. Thompson), "Evangelicals' Subtle Infection," *Christianity Today*, 26(18):46-49, Nov. 12, 1982.

Hamilton, Kenneth, *To Turn from Idols*. Grand Rapids, Mich.: Eerdmans, 1973.

Handy, Robert T., "The Voluntary Principle in Religion and Religious Freedom in America," chapter 6, pp. 129-139, in D. B. Robertson, editor, *Voluntary Associations*. Richmond, Va.: John Knox Press, 1966.

Hardin, Garrett, "The Tragedy of the Commons," *Science*, 162:1243-1248, Feb. 16, 1968.

Harper, Michael, "The Lukewarming of the Church: Humanism and Church Decline in the Western World," *Pastoral Renewal*, 5(3):19-23, 26, Sep. 1980.

Harris, Louis, and Associates, *Aging in the Eighties: America in Transition*. Washington, D.C.: National Council on the Aging, 1981.

Hawton, Hector, "Afterthoughts," pp. 115-117 in Paul Kurtz and Albert Dondeyne, editors, *A Catholic/Humanist Dialogue*. Buffalo: Prometheus Books, 1972.

Heddendorf, Russell, "Principles of a Christian Perspective in Sociology," pp. 113-124 in Charles P. DeSanto et al., editors, *A Reader in Sociology: Christian Perspectives*. Scottdale, Pa.: Herald Press, 1980.

Hefley, James and Marti, *The Church that Takes on Trouble*. Elgin, Ill.: David C. Cook Publishing Co., 1976.

Hendry, G. S., "Ecclesiastes," pp. 538-546 in F. Davidson, editor, *The New Bible Commentary*, second edition. Grand Rapids, Mich.: Eerdmans, 1954.

Henry, Carl F. H., *The Uneasy Conscience of Modern Fundamentalism*. Grand Rapids, Mich.: Eerdmans, 1947.

Higgins, Edward, *Sociology: Promise and Problems* (Inaugural Lecture). Grahamstown, South Africa: Rhodes University, 1974.

Hirschman, Albert O., *Shifting Involvements: Private Interest and Public Action*. Princeton, N.J.: Princeton University Press, 1982.

Hitchcock, James, "Squeezing Catholicism into a Secular Mold," *Pastoral Renewal*, 9(1):1-3,11-13, July/Aug. 1984.

Hofstadter, Richard, *Anti-Intellectualism in American Life*. New York: Alfred A. Knopf, 1963.

Hoge, Dean R., *Commitment on Campus: Changes in Religion and Values over Five Decades*. Philadelphia: Westminster Press, 1974.

Hoge, Dean R., *Division in the Protestant House: The Basic Reasons Behi.* *Intra-Church Conflicts.* Philadelphia: Westminster Press, 1976.

Hoge, Dean R., and David A. Roozen, editors, *Understanding Church Growth and Decline: 1950-1978.* New York: Pilgrim Press, 1979.

Holland, Betty G., "Receiving Is Blessed Too," *Ministry,* 55(11):28-29, Nov. 1982.

Holmes, Arthur F., *All Truth Is God's Truth.* Downers Grove, Ill.: InterVarsity Press, 1977.

Horton, Paul B., and Gerald R. Leslie, *The Sociology of Social Problems,* 7th edition. Englewood Cliffs, N.J.: Prentice-Hall, 1981.

Houston, James M., "The Ordinary Christian," *Regent College Bulletin,* 3(3):1, Summer 1973.

Houston, James, "The Threat of Technolatry," *Radix,* 12(2):13-16, Sep./Oct. 1980.

Hubbard, David Allan, "What Specific Help Can the Bible Give Me?," *Fuller Theological Seminary Bulletin,* 32(4):1-2, Dec. 1982.

Hunter, James Davison, *American Evangelicalism: Conservative Religion and the Quandary of Modernity.* New Brunswick, N. J.: Rutgers University Press, 1983.

Jacquet, Constant H., Jr., editor, *Yearbook of American and Canadian Churches, 1982.* Nashville: Abingdon Press, 1982.

Johnson, Pierce, *Dying into Life: A Study in Christian Life Styles.* Nashville: Abingdon Press, 1972.

Jones, George W., "Pluralism: Agenda for the 80's," *Dialogue on Campus,* 15(1):2, Fall 1979.

Kehl, D. G., "Burnout: The Risk of Reaching Too High," *Christianity Today,* 25(20):1575-1577, Nov. 20, 1981.

Kellermann, Bill, "John Wesley and the Methodist Revival Movement," *Sojourners,* 13(3):20-23, March 1984.

Kenney, Ray, "Plant Closings Traumatic," *Milwaukee Sentinel,* part 2, p. 4, March 11, 1982.

Kerans, Patrick, *Sinful Social Structures.* New York: Paulist Press, 1974.

King, Morton B., and Richard A. Hunt, "Measuring the Religious Variable: Amended Findings," *Journal for the Scientific Study of Religion,* 8(2):321-323, Fall 1969.

King, Morton B., and Richard A. Hunt, *Measuring Religious Dimensions.* Dallas: Southern Methodist University Press, 1972.

Kraft, Charles, *Christianity in Culture: A Study in Dynamic Biblical Theologizing in Cross-Cultural Perspective.* Maryknoll, NY: Orbis, 1979.

Krass, Alfred C., *Beyond the Either-Or Church.* Nashville: Tidings, 1973.

Krass, Alfred C., "Beyond Either/Or Theology," *The Other Side,* 16(12):42-44, Dec. 1980.

Krass, Alfred C., "An Allegory for Our Times," *The Other Side,* 20(5):28, May 1984.

Kraybill, Donald B., *The Upside-Down Kingdom.* Scottdale, Pa.: Herald Press, 1978.

ybill, Donald B., "Jesus and the Stigmatized: A Sociological Analysis of the Four Gospels," pp. 399-413 in Charles P. DeSanto et al., editors, *A Reader in Sociology: Christian Perspectives*. Scottdale, Pa: Herald Press, 1980.

Krebs, Richard L., *Creative Conflict*. Minneapolis: Augsburg Publishing House, 1982.

Kurtz, Paul, "A Secular Humanist Declaration," *Free Inquiry Magazine*, vol. 1, no. 1, Winter 1980.

Lamont, Corliss, *The Philosophy of Humanism*, fifth edition. New York: Frederick Ungar Publishing Co., 1965.

Lasch, Christopher, *The Culture of Narcissism*. New York: W. W. Norton, 1979.

Lifton, Robert J., "Protean Man," pp. 311-331 in R. J. Lifton, editor, *History and Human Survival*. New York: Random House, 1970.

Loewen, Jacob A., "Anthropology," pp. 135-146 in Robert W. Smith, editor, *Christ and the Modern Mind*. Downers Grove, Ill.: InterVarsity Press, 1972.

Lyman, Stanford M., *The Seven Deadly Sins: Society and Evil*. New York: St. Martin's Press, 1978.

Lyon, David, "Sociology and Secularization," pp. 9-30 in Brian Daines et al., *Christian Commitment and the Study of Sociology*. London, England: The Ilkley Study Group, 1975.

Lyon, David, *Christians and Sociology*. Downers Grove, Ill.: InterVarsity Press, 1976.

Lyon, David, "Social Change and Utopia: Evaluating Modernization, Marxism, and Post-Industrialism," pp. 665-690 in Charles P. DeSanto et al., editors, *A Reader in Sociology: Christian Perspectives*. Scottdale, Pa.: Herald Press, 1980.

Lyon, David, *Karl Marx: A Christian Assessment of His Life and Thought*. Downers Grove, Ill.: InterVarsity Press, 1981.

Lyon, David, *Sociology and the Human Image*. Downers Grove, Ill.: InterVarsity Press, 1983.

MacKay, Donald M., *The Clock Work Image: A Christian Perspective on Science*. Downers Grove, Ill.: InterVarsity Press, 1974.

Martin, David, *The Breaking of the Image: A Sociology of Christian Theory and Practice*. New York: St. Martin's Press, 1979.

Marty, Martin E., "The Denomination in America Today," *Evangelical Newsletter*, 8(16):4, Aug. 7, 1981.

Marty, Martin E., "Search for Coherence," *Context*, 16(1):5, Jan. 1, 1984.

Mayers, Marvin K., *Christianity Confronts Culture*. Grand Rapids, Mich.: Zondervan, 1974.

McGuire, Meredith B., *Religion: The Social Context*. Belmont, Calif.: Wadsworth Publishing Co., 1981.

McKenna, David L., "Our Unfinished Task," *Response* (Seattle Pacific University), 5(4):2, July 1982.

McKenna, George, "Introduction: Social Issues of the Eighties," pp. 1-9 in George McKenna and Mirella Baroni-Harris, editors, *Taking Sides: Clash-*

ing Views on Controversial Social Issues. Guilford, Conn.: The Dushkin Publishing Group, 1980.

McLean, Cynthia, "The Protestant Endeavor in Chinese Society, 1890-1950: Gleanings from the Manuscripts of M. Searle Bates," *International Bulletin of Missionary Research*, 8(3):108-112, July 1984.

Melton, J. Gordon, editor, *The Encyclopedia of American Religions.* Wilmington, N.C.: McGrath Publishing Co., Consortium Books, 1978.

Menninger, Karl, *Whatever Became of Sin?* New York: Hawthorn Books, 1973.

Mills, C. Wright, *The Sociological Imagination.* New York: Oxford University Press, 1959.

Moberg, David O., "Religion and Personal Adjustment in Old Age," Ph. D. dissertation, University of Minnesota, 1951.

Moberg, David O., "Social Class and the Churches," *Information Service* (NCCC), 27(12):6-8, June 14, 1958.

Moberg, David O., "Cultural Relativity and Christian Faith," *Journal of the American Scientific Affiliation*, 14(2):34-48, June 1962.

Moberg, David O., *Inasmuch: Christian Social Responsibility in the Twentieth Century.* Grand Rapids, Mich.: Eerdmans, 1965.

Moberg, David O., "The Encounter of Scientific and Religious Values Pertinent to Man's Spiritual Nature," *Sociological Analysis*, 28(1):22-33, Spring 1967(a).

Moberg, David O., "Science and the Spiritual Nature of Man," *Journal of the American Scientific Affiliation*, 19(1):12-17, March 1967(b).

Moberg, David O., "The Christian and Social Change," *Paraclete: Journal of the National Association of Christians in Social Work*, 4(1):3-25, Summer 1977(a).

Moberg, David O., *The Great Reversal: Evangelism and Social Concern,* revised edition. Philadelphia: J. B. Lippincott Co., 1977(b).

Moberg, David O., "Presidential Address: Virtues for the Sociology of Religion," *Sociological Analysis*, 39(1):1-18, Spring 1978(a).

Moberg, David O., "Sociocultural Values, the New Morality, and the Family," *Counseling and Values*, 22(4):251-266, July 1978(b).

Moberg, David O., editor, *Spiritual Well-Being: Sociological Perspectives.* Washington, D.C.: University Press of America, 1979.

Moberg, David O., "Do the Properly Pious Really Care?," *Christianity Today*, 24(16):1046-1048, Sep. 19, 1980.

Moberg, David O., "Humanism and Christianity: A Review Article," *Newsletter of the Christian Sociological Society*, 10(1):12-14, Oct. 15, 1982.

Moberg, David O., "The Ecological Fallacy: Concerns for Program Planners," *Generations*, 8(1):12-14, Fall 1983.

Moberg, David O., *The Church as a Social Institution*, second edition. Grand Rapids, Mich.: Baker Book House, 1984(a).

Moberg, David O., "Subjective Measures of Spiritual Well-Being," *Review of Religious Research*, 25(4):351-364, June 1984(b).

Moberg, David O., and Patricia M. Brusek, "Spiritual Well-Being: A Neglected

Subject in Quality of Life Research," *Social Indicators Research,* 5(3):303-323, Summer 1978.

Mol, Hans, *Christianity in Chains: A Sociologist's Interpretation of the Churches' Dilemma in a Secular World.* Melbourne, Australia: Thomas Nelson Ltd., 1969.

Mol, Hans, "Time and Transcendence in a Dialectical Sociology of Religion," *Sociological Analysis,* 42(4):317-324, Winter 1981.

Mollenkott, Virginia Ramey, "Toward a Biblical Basis for Pluralism," *Report from the Capital,* 37(7):4-5, July-Aug. 1982.

Moore, Wilbert E., *Social Change.* Englewood Cliffs, N.J.: Prentice-Hall, 1963.

Morgan, Richard Lyon, "The Book We Came Back To," *Christianity Today,* 26(6):32-33, March 19, 1982.

Mott, Stephen Charles, *Biblical Ethics and Social Change.* New York: Oxford University Press, 1982.

Mott, Stephen Charles, "The Use of the Bible in Social Ethics II: The Use of the New Testament: Part 1," *Transformation: An International Dialogue on Evangelical Social Ethics,* 1(2):21-26, April/June 1984.

Murphy, Mary Beth, "Priest Works to Blend 2 Styles of Christianity," *Milwaukee Sentinel,* part 1, p. 6, Aug. 7, 1982.

Myers, David G., *The Human Puzzle: Psychological Research and Christian Belief.* New York: Harper and Row, 1978.

Myers, David G., *The Inflated Self: Human Illusions and the Biblical Call to Hope.* New York: Seabury, 1980.

Myers, David G., "The Inflated Self," *Christian Century,* 99(38):1226-1230, Dec. 1, 1982.

Naisbitt, John, *Megatrends: Ten New Directions Transforming Our Lives.* New York: Warner Books, 1982.

Nees, Tom, "Evangelism Without the Gospel," *Sojourners,* 9(2):27-29, Feb. 1980.

Neff, David, "Editorial: An Open-and-Shut Case," *His,* 44(5):32, Feb. 1984.

Neidhardt, Janet W., "The Peaceful Way to Disagree," *Moody Monthly,* 80(8):67-68, April 1980.

Neiswanger, David, Business Reply Envelope. Topeka, KS: The Menninger Foundation, 1982.

"'Networking'—Fellowshipping for Effectiveness?," *MARC Newsletter,* pp. 4-5, March 1983.

"The New World of Missions: Evangelizing World Class Cities," *MARC Newsletter,* pp. 4-5, November 1982.

Niebuhr, H. Richard, *Christ and Culture.* New York: Harper and Brothers, 1951.

Niebuhr, H. Richard, *The Social Sources of Denominationalism.* Cleveland: Meridian Books, World Publishing Co., 1957.

Niebuhr, Reinhold, *Moral Man and Immoral Society.* New York: Charles Scribner's Sons, 1932.

Nisbet, Robert, *History of the Idea of Progress.* New York: Basic Books, 1979.

North, Gary, "The Rise of the Parachurch Ministries," *Tentmakers*, 5(5):1-2, Sep./Oct. 1982.

O'Connor, Elizabeth, *Call to Commitment*. New York: Harper and Row, 1963.

O'Connor, Elizabeth, *Journey Inward, Journey Outward*. New York: Harper and Row, 1968.

O'Dea, Thomas F., and Janet O'Dea Aviad, *The Sociology of Religion*, second edition. Englewood Cliffs, N. J.: Prentice-Hall, 1983.

Ollman, Bertell, and Edward Vernoff, editors, *The Left Academy: Marxist Scholarship on American Campuses*. New York: McGraw-Hill, 1982.

Olson, Mark, "The Perversity of Freedom: A Call to Evangelism," *The Other Side*, 20(2):12-13, Feb. 1984.

Outler, Albert C., "Recovery of the Sacred," *Christianity Today*, 25(2):89-93, Jan. 23, 1981.

Palms, Roger C., "Editorial: Intoxicated," *Decision*, 24(3):13, March 1983.

Paloutzian, Raymond F., *Invitation to the Psychology of Religion*. Glenview, Ill.: Scott, Foresman and Co., 1983.

Paloutzian, Raymond F., and Craig W. Ellison, "Loneliness, Spiritual Well-Being, and the Quality of Life," pp. 224-237 in L. Anne Peplau and Dan Perlman, editors, *Loneliness: A Sourcebook of Current Theory, Research and Therapy*. New York: Wiley-Interscience, 1982.

Patterson, Orlando, "By Emphasizing Ethnicity . . . Pluralist Thinkers . . . Will Prevent Communication Between Groups," pp. 143, 149-156 in George McKenna and Mirella Baroni-Harris, editors, *Taking Sides*. Guilford, Conn.: The Dushkin Publishing Group, 1980 (selected from *Ethnic Chauvinism*, Stein and Day, 1977).

Paul, Robert S., "The Accidence and the Essence of Puritan Piety," *Austin Seminary Bulletin*, 93(8):5-45, May 1978.

Peck, M. Scott, *People of the Lie: The Hope for Healing Evil*. New York: Simon and Schuster, 1983.

Petak, George A. Jr., "In My Opinion: Certain Texts Have No Place in Our Schools," *Milwaukee Journal*, part 1, p. 19, July 12, 1981.

Petersen, J. Randall, "1981: Identity Crisis," *Evangelical Newsletter*, 8(26):4-5, Dec. 25, 1981.

"Philosophy: New Humanist Declaration Hits 'Authoritarian' Religion," *Christianity Today*, 24(20):1457-1458, Nov. 21, 1980.

Pippert, Rebecca Manley, "Jesus: Delightful and Disturbing, Our Model for Changing the World," *His*, 39(8):1,4-6, May 1979.

Pippert, Wesley, "The Moral Dimension of the News," *His*, 38(5):29-31, Feb. 1978.

Pippert, Wesley, "Faith Should Rewrite Your Job Description," *Christianity Today*, 26(15):28-30, Sep. 17, 1982.

Ploch, Donald R., "Religion as an Independent Variable: A Critique of Some Major Research," pp. 275-294 in Allan W. Eister, editor, *Changing Perspectives in the Scientific Study of Religion*. New York: John Wiley & Sons, 1974.

Poloma, Margaret M., "Christian Covenant Communities: An Adaptation of the

Intentional Community for Urban Life," pp. 609-630 in Charles P. DeSanto et al., editors, *A Reader in Sociology: Christian Perspectives*. Scottdale, Pa.: Herald Press, 1980.

Poloma, Margaret M., "A Spiritual Dialectic," *Newsletter of the Christian Sociological Society*, 11(2):6-7, Feb. 15, 1984.

Poppendieck, Janet, "Hunger in America: The Definitional Process and Its Consequences," *Humanity and Society*, 7(4):373-394, Nov. 1983.

"The Pressure of Change," *The Royal Bank Letter*, 63(4)1-4, July/Aug. 1982.

Princeton Religion Research Center, *The Unchurched American*. Princeton, N.J.: The Gallup Organization, 1978.

Princeton Religion Research Center, *Religion in America, 1982*. Princeton, N.J.: Gallup International, 1982.

Pruyser, Paul W., *The Minister as Diagnostician*. Philadelphia: Westminster Press, 1976.

Redekop, Calvin, *The Free Church and Seductive Culture*. Scottdale, Pa.: Herald Press, 1970.

Rees, Paul S., "Piece of Mind: Please Don't Overgeneralize!" *World Vision*, 27(3):10-11, March 1983.

Richards, David, "The Ghosts of Liv Ullman," *Milwaukee Journal*, Accent Section, p. 2, Aug. 15, 1982.

Rieff, Philip, *The Triumph of the Therapeutic*. New York: Harper and Row, 1966.

Rifkin, Bernard, "*Ordinary People* is an Extraordinary Hoax," *Christianity Today*, 26(7):615, April 24, 1981.

Rifkin, Jeremy, with Ted Howard, *The Emerging Order: God in the Age of Scarcity*. New York: G. P. Putnam's Sons, 1979.

Robertson, Roland, "Religious and Sociological Factors in the Analysis of Secularization," pp. 41-60 in Allan W. Eister, editor, *Changing Perspectives in the Scientific Study of Religion*. New York: John Wiley & Sons, 1974.

Roof, Wade Clark, and Christopher Kirk Hadaway, "Denominational Switching in the Seventies: Going Beyond Stark and Glock," *Journal for the Scientific Study of Religion*. 18(4):363-379, Dec. 1979.

Rouster, Lorella, "Why Christians Aren't Human(ists)," *His*, 41(4): 25-27, Jan. 1981.

Rukeyser, Louis, "Column on Litigation Didn't Suit Lawyers," (McNaught Syndicate Inc.), *Milwaukee Journal*, part 2, p. 8, Sep. 28, 1982.

Russell, Richard, "Philosophy and Sociology," pp. 31-42 in Brian Daines et al., *Christian Commitment and the Study of Sociology*. London: The Ilkley Study Group, 1975.

Scanzoni, John, "Sociology," pp. 123-133 in Robert W. Smith, editor, *Christ and the Modern Mind*. Downer's Grove, Ill.: InterVarsity Press, 1972.

Schaeffer, Francis, *A Christian Manifesto*. Westchester, Ill.: Crossway Books, 1981.

Schaller, Lyle E., *The Impact of the Future*. Nashville: Abingdon Press, 1969.

Schaller, Lyle E., *The Change Agent: The Strategy of Innovative Leadership*. Nashville: Abingdon Press, 1972.

Schaller, Lyle E., "Commentary: What Are the Alternatives?," pp. 344-357 in

Dean R. Hoge and David R. Roozen, editors, *Understanding Church Growth and Decline: 1950-1978*. New York: Pilgrim Press, 1979.

Scherer, Ross P., editor, *American Denominational Organization: A Sociological View*. Pasadena, Calif.: William Carey Library, 1980.

Schneider, Louis, *The Sociological Way of Looking at the World*. New York: McGraw Hill Book Co., 1975.

Schoeck, Helmut, *Envy—A Theory of Social Behavior* (Michael Glenny and Betty Ross, translators). New York: Harcourt, Brace, and World, 1970.

Schumacher, Edwin F., *Small is Beautiful*. New York: Harper and Row, 1973.

"The 'Sectarian Spirit' Seen as the Great Danger Among Divided Christians," *Evangelical Newsletter*, 8(9):3, May 1, 1981.

Shaw, Joseph M., R. W. Franklin, Harris Kaasa, and Charles W. Busicky, editors, *Readings in Christian Humanism*. Minneapolis: Augsburg Publishing House, 1982.

Shenk, David W., "Interpreting the Bible Missiologically," *Mission Focus*, 12(1):1-5, March 1984.

Shop Talk Editor, "The 80/20 Rule," *Ministry*, 55(11):30, Nov. 1982.

Sider, Ronald J., editor, *The Chicago Declaration*. Carol Stream, Ill.: Creation House, 1974.

Sider, Ronald J., "The State of Evangelical Social Concern, 1978," *Evangelical Newsletter*, 5(13):4, June 30, 1978.

Sieber, Sam D., *Fatal Remedies: The Ironies of Social Intervention*. New York: Plenum Press, 1981.

Silver, Maury, and John Sabini, *The Moralities of Everyday Life*. New York: Oxford University Press, 1982.

Simbiri, Isaac, "What Is African Evangelical Theology?," *East Africa Journal of Evangelical Theology*, as abstracted in *Evangelical Newsletter*, 11(3):2-3, Feb. 3, 1984.

Sinclair, Andrew, *Era of Excess*. New York: Harper and Row, Colophon edition, 1964.

Sire, James W., "Excuse Me, Mr. Maharishi," *Eternity*, 31(9):109-110, Oct. 1980.

Skinner, Tom, "An Interview with Tom Skinner," *The Gordon* (Gordon College), 25(3):12, Nov. 1980.

Slaatte, Howard Alexander, *The Pertinence of the Paradox: A Study of the Dialectics of Reason-in-Existence*. Washington, D.C.: University Press of America, 1982.

Slater, Peter, *The Dynamics of Religion: Meaning and Change in Religious Traditions*. San Francisco: Harper and Row, 1978.

Small, Gerald G., "The Use of Spiritual Gifts in the Ministry of Oversight," *Journal of Christian Education*, 1(1):21-34, Fall 1980.

Smith, Anthony D., *The Ethnic Revival*. Cambridge, England: Cambridge University Press, 1981.

Smith, David Horton, et al., *Participation in Social and Political Activities*. San Francisco: Jossey-Bass, 1980.

Smith, Ronald Gregor, *The Whole Man: Studies in Christian Anthropology*. Philadelphia: Westminster Press, 1969.

Smith, Timothy Dudley, *Someone Who Beckons*. Downers Grove, Ill.: InterVarsity Press, 1978.

Smith, Timothy L., *Revivalism and Social Reform*. Baltimore: Johns Hopkins University Press, 1980.

Snyder, Howard, "Holding a Mirror to the Contemporary Church," *Christianity Today*, 26(15):20-23, Sep. 17, 1982.

Sobran, Joseph, "Some Factual News Reporting Would Help Dispel Our Bias," *Milwaukee Journal*, part 1, p. 17, Feb. 23, 1983.

Solzhenitsyn, Aleksandr, "Men Have Forgotten God," *Pastoral Renewal*, 8(9):116-117, 123-125, April 1984.

"Some Suggestions for Dealing with the Secular Humanism Phenomenon," *Light* (Christian Life Commission, Southern Baptist Convention), pp. 8-11, 16, May-June 1982.

"Some Surprising Words from a Catholic Historian," *Christianity Today*, 26(11):71, 79, June 18, 1982.

Stadtlander, John H., "Notes from the Battlefield," *Church Growth: America*, 6(5):7-9, Nov.-Dec. 1980.

Stagg, Frank, "Humanism and a Free Society," *Report from the Capital*, 37(8):4-5, Sep. 1982.

Stein, Jess, and Laurence Urdang, editors, *The Random House Dictionary of the English Language*. New York: Random House, 1967.

Stellway, Richard J., "Religion," pp. 245-263 in Stephen A. Grunlan and Milton Reimer, editors, *Christian Perspectives on Sociology*. Grand Rapids, Mich.: Zondervan, 1982.

Stent, Gunther A., *The Coming of the Golden Age*. Garden City, N. Y.: Natural History Press, 1983.

Stott, John R. W., *Balanced Christianity*. Downers Grove, Ill.: InterVarsity Press, 1975.

Stott, John R. W., "Who Is My Neighbour?," pp. 68-69 in Timothy Dudley Smith, *Someone Who Beckons*. Downers Grove, Ill.: InterVarsity Press, 1978.

Swank, Kenneth L., "Guest Editorial: The New American Baptist Doctrine," *The American Baptist*, 182(7):15, July/Aug. 1984.

Taylor, Canon John V., "To Serve or to Proclaim," *Church Growth Bulletin*, 7(2):104-106, Nov. 1970.

Thompson, James W., "The Ethics of Jesus and the Early Church," pp. 45-59 in Perry C. Cotham, editor, *Christian Social Ethics*. Grand Rapids, Mich.: Baker Book House, 1979.

Thorn, Ivan, and William K. Kilpatrick, "The Drift of Modern Psychology," *The Freeman*, 34(8):478-487, Aug. 1984.

Toffler, Alvin, *Future Shock*. New York: Bantam Books, 1971.

Toffler, Alvin, *The Third Wave*. New York: Bantam Books, 1981.

Tournier, Paul, *The Whole Person in a Broken World*. New York: Harper and Row, 1977.

Troeltsch, Ernst, *The Social Teaching of the Christian Churches*, 2 vols. (Olive Wyon, translator). London: George Allen and Unwin, 1931.

Troyer, Ronald J., and Gerald E. Markle, "Creating Deviance Rules: A Macroscopic Model," *The Sociological Quarterly*, 23(2):157-169, Spring 1982.

Trueblood, D. Elton, *The Essence of Spiritual Religion*. New York: Harper and Row, paperback edition, 1975.

Van Leeuwen, Mary Stewart, *The Sorcerer's Apprentice: A Christian Looks at the Changing Face of Psychology*. Downers Grove, Ill.: InterVarsity Press, 1982.

Vitz, Paul C., *Psychology as Religion: The Cult of Self-Worship*. Grand Rapids, Mich.: Eerdmans, 1977.

Wagner, C. Peter, *Your Church Can Grow*. Glendale, Calif.: G/L Publications, 1976.

Wagner, C. Peter, *Our Kind of People: The Ethical Dimensions of Church Growth in America*. Atlanta, Ga.: John Knox Press, 1979.

Wagner, C. Peter, *Church Growth and the Whole Gospel: A Biblical Mandate*. San Francisco: Harper and Row, 1981.

Wallis, Jim, *Agenda for Biblical People*. New York: Harper and Row, 1976.

Wallis, Jim, *The Call to Conversion*. San Francisco: Harper and Row, 1981.

Wallis, Jim, "A Hope for Revival," *Sojourners*, 13(3):3-5, March 1984.

Walrath, Douglas Alan, *Leading Churches Through Change*. Nashville: Abingdon Press, 1979.

Walter, J.A., *Sacred Cows: Exploring Contemporary Idolatry*. Grand Rapids, Mich.: Zondervan, 1980.

Walvoord, John F., "Put Yourself in My Hands," *Kindred Spirit* (Dallas Theological Seminary), 6(3):21-23, Fall 1982.

"Watch What You're Saying," *The Royal Bank Letter*, 64(2):1-4, March/April 1983.

Watts, Craig M., "Identity and Idolatry: The Problem of National Worship," *The Other Side*, 20(7):11-14, July 1984.

Ways, Max, "The Question: Can Information Technology Be Managed?," p. 7 in *Information Technology: Some Critical Implications for Decision Makers*. New York: The Conference Board, 1972.

Weaver, David, "The Will of Our Genes: Ethical Implications of Sociobiology," *Sojourners*, 9(2):31, Feb. 1980.

Webber, Robert E., *The Secular Saint: A Case for Evangelical Social Responsibility*. Grand Rapids, Mich.: Zondervan, 1979.

Weber, Timothy P., *Living in the Shadow of the Second Coming: American Premillennialism 1875-1925*. New York: Oxford University Press, 1979.

Wermuth, Paul C., "To Whom It May Concern," *Academe*, 68(5):27-28, Sep.-Oct. 1982.

Wessel, Walter W., "Our Golden Age of Biblical Resources," *Bethel Focus*, 36(2):10-11, May 1984.

West, Charles C., "Community—Christian and Secular," pp. 117-134 in James F. Childress and David B. Harned, editors, *Secularization and the Protestant Prospect*. Philadelphia: Westminster Press, 1970.

esterhof, Jack, "Campus Comment: Beware of the Hidden Curriculum," *Perspective*, 14(5):9-10, Sep.-Oct. 1980.

White, Ronald C. Jr., "Piety and Learning," *Princeton Seminary Bulletin*, 4(2):6-8, New Series 1983.

Williams, Robin M. Jr., *American Society*. New York: Knopf, 1960.

Willis, John T., "Old Testament Foundations of Social Justice," pp. 21-43 in Perry C. Cotham, editor, *Christian Social Ethics*. Grand Rapids, Mich.: Baker Book House, 1979.

Wilson, Edward O., *Sociobiology: The New Synthesis*. Cambridge, Mass.: Harvard University Press, 1975.

Wilson, Edward O., *On Human Nature*. Cambridge, Mass.: Harvard University Press, 1979.

Wilson, Marvin R., "Hebrew Thought in the Life of the Church," *From Mt. Zion* (Institute of Holy Land Studies), 3(3):2, 1983.

Wilson, Ruth, "Report to Our Readers: Taking Sides," *Milwaukee Journal*, Accent section, pp. 1, 5, Aug. 5, 1984.

Wilson, Samuel, "The Present Major Threat to Gospel Advance?," *MARC Newsletter*, pp. 4-5, May 1984.

Winter, Ralph D., "Protestant Mission Societies and the 'Other Protestant Schism,'" pp. 194-224 in Ross P. Scherer, editor, *American Denominational Organization*. Pasadena, Calif.: William Carey Library, 1980.

Woodbridge, John D., "Biblical Authority in a 'Me' Decade," *Voices*, 10(1):3-7, Fall/Winter 1983-1984.

Woodward, Kenneth L., "Pick-and-Choose Christianity," *Newsweek*, 102(12):82-82B, Sep. 19, 1983.

Wulff, Joan, "Searching for Community in an Individualistic Age," *His*, 42(6):1a-1, 4-5, March 1982.

Wuthnow, Robert, *The Consciousness Reformation*. Berkeley: University of California, 1976.

Wuthnow, Robert, "Ideas: Say Goodbye to the 'Me Decade'?" (interview with Marvin Olasky), *Context*, 9(2):22-27, 1980.

Yamamori, Tetsunao, "'Development' Defined at Ubon Meeting," *Hope* (Food for the Hungry), 1(3):11, Dec. 1982.

Yankelovich, Daniel, *New Rules: Searching for Self-Fulfillment in a World Turned Upside Down*. New York: Random House, 1981.

Yinger, J. Milton, *Religion, Society and the Individual*. New York: Macmillan Co., 1957.

Yinger, J. Milton, *Countercultures: The Promise and the Peril of a World Turned Upside Down*. New York: Free Press, 1982.

Yoder, John Howard, *The Politics of Jesus*. Grand Rapids, Mich.: Eerdmans, 1972.

Yoder, Michael L., "Coming to Terms with Karl Marx," pp. 217-238 in Charles P. DeSanto et al., editors, *A Reader in Sociology: Christian Perspectives*. Scottdale, Pa.: Herald Press, 1980.

Zerubavel, Eviatar, *Hidden Rhythms: Schedules and Calendars in Social Life*. Chicago: University of Chicago Press, 1981.

INDEX OF NAMES

217

Yoder, Michael L., 102, 216
Yogi, Maharishi Mahesh, 27

Zabriskie, Colleen, xiii
Zerubavel, Eviatar, 92, 216

INDEX OF SUBJECTS

Many closely related concepts are indexed as one unit. For example, to find Fundamentalists, look under Fundamentalism. The singular and plural forms in the text are presented together in the Index.